Strategic Communication Research in the Age of AI

Quantitative and Qualitative Methods

Young Joon Lim
University of Texas Rio Grande Valley

ROWMAN & LITTLEFIELD
Lanham • Boulder • New York • London

Acquisitions Editor: Natalie Mandziuk
Acquisitions Assistant: Yu Ozaki
Sales and Marketing Inquiries: RLtextbooks@bloomsbury.com

Credits and acknowledgments for material borrowed from other sources, and reproduced with permission, appear on the appropriate pages within the text.

Published by Rowman & Littlefield
An imprint of The Rowman & Littlefield Publishing Group, Inc.
4501 Forbes Boulevard, Suite 200, Lanham, Maryland 20706
www.rowman.com

86-90 Paul Street, London EC2A 4NE

British Library Cataloguing in Publication Information Available

Library of Congress Cataloging-in-Publication Data

Names: Lim, Young Joon, author.
Title: Strategic communication research in the age of AI : quantitative and qualitative methods / Young Joon Lim, University of Texas Rio Grande Valley.
Description: Lanham : Rowman & Littlefield Publishers, [2025] | Includes bibliographical references and index.
Identifiers: LCCN 2024028368 (print) | LCCN 2024028369 (ebook) | ISBN 9781538197868 (cloth ; alk. paper) | ISBN 9781538197875 (paperback; alk. paper) | ISBN 9781538197882 (ebook)
Subjects: LCSH: Public relations—Research—Methodology. | Advertising—Research—Methodology. | Communication—Research—Methodology.
Classification: LCC HD59 .L553 2025 (print) | LCC HD59 (ebook) | DDC 659.2072—dc23/eng/20240711
LC record available at https://lccn.loc.gov/2024028368
LC ebook record available at https://lccn.loc.gov/2024028369

Brief Contents

Contents

Chapter 1

An Introduction to Research in Strategic Communication

Chapter Learning Outcomes

- Identify what research is.
- Understand the purpose of the research.
- Apply strategic communication to academic research.
- Describe the eight steps of research.
- Explain the characteristics of scholarly research.
- Distinguish between ordinary research and academic research.
- Discover unique approaches to scientific research.
- Recognize the disciplines of strategic communication.
- Conceptualize research in strategic communication.
- Explore benefits of AI tools.

Imagine a younger sibling asking you, "What exactly is research?" Would you have a succinct answer, or would you suggest they "Google it" or "Ask ChatGPT"? The term *research* can be broken down into its linguistic components—*re-* and *search*—implying a process of repeated searching. This leads to the question, "How long should we research?" The answer is simple: until you find the information you seek.

Defining Research

Research is a journey that begins with a question and concludes with an answer. In the digital age, with social media platforms, smartphone applications, and AI-powered tools at our fingertips, the research journey often starts and ends with a digital query. For example, if you're curious about the surnames of Romeo and Juliet, a quick Google search reveals they are Montague and Capulet, respectively. By posing a question and finding an answer, you have completed a basic research process.

Research can be an enjoyable, straightforward activity that allows you to satisfy your curiosity and educate yourself. However, when we delve into research at the collegiate level, it becomes more complex, challenging, and at times frustrating. There are rules to follow, elements to study, and methodologies to apply. Research courses are a core requirement for most undergraduate and graduate students worldwide, providing them with a fundamental academic framework for knowledge building and establishing credibility as college-educated individuals.

While challenging and demanding, research courses lay the foundation for core educational knowledge, equipping students with the academic intelligence they will utilize during and after their college life. Let's delve deeper into the definition of *research*. Here are three definitions that encapsulate the general concept of research:

- A diligent and systematic inquiry or investigation into a subject to discover or revise facts, theories, applications, etc. (dictionary.com).[1]
- The collecting of information about a particular subject (merriam-webster.com).[2]
- A careful and detailed study into a specific problem, concern, or issue using the scientific method (study.com).[3]

Rather than merely searching for information online, college-level research involves a systematic investigation using the scientific method. As budding researchers, college students are trained to follow established procedures and use scientific methods when exploring a specific topic or issue.

To become proficient researchers, it is crucial to understand the concepts of scientific and systematic approaches. While research involves finding answers to questions, scholarly researchers also adhere to academic steps to conduct research in a scientific manner. Your college research course will help you understand and identify research concepts and methods, enabling you to apply research techniques and tools to your studies. Ultimately, you will develop the ability to analyze data and share your research findings with your academic peers. See figure 1.1.

The Purpose of Research

Research courses are a staple in the curriculum of colleges worldwide, cutting across all disciplines. These foundational courses equip students with vital skills such as exploration, observation, description, and explanation of various phenomena in both human society and the natural world. Consider Britney, a college junior who begins her day by checking her social media feeds. She follows celebrities who endorse beauty and fitness products on their platforms. Through this routine, Britney explores potential products

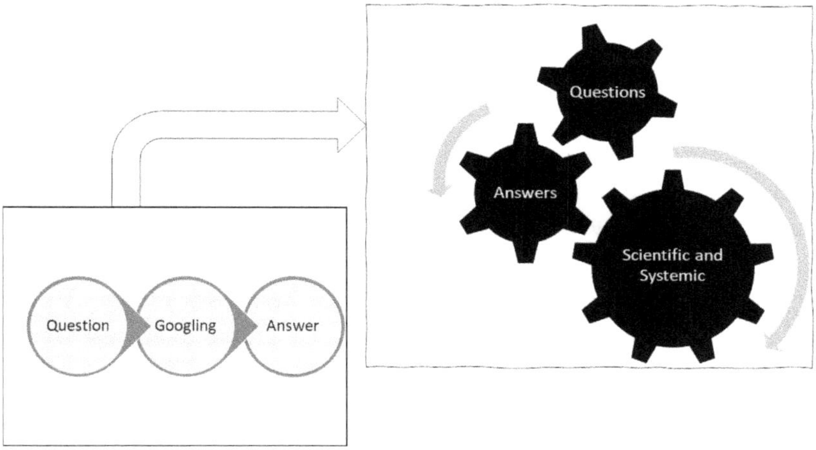

Figure 1.1 Shifting of research for college students
Source: Created by author.

to purchase, evaluates their necessity, observes how celebrities use them, and decides whether to buy them. This behavior is typical among college students who engage with social media.

However, when Britney enrolls in a research class, she is encouraged to view her daily routine from a researcher's perspective. The class prompts her to:

1. Explore: Britney's fascination with the impact of social media on political activism leads her to explore online discourse surrounding the upcoming presidential election. She is particularly interested in how social media platforms are used to amplify different voices and perspectives.
2. Observe: Britney focuses her attention on X (Twitter), observing how candidates, political commentators, and everyday citizens use the platform to share opinions, engage in debate, and mobilize support. She immerses herself in the Xsphere (Twittersphere), following trending hashtags, analyzing popular posts, and tracking the evolution of conversations.
3. Describe: Britney carefully documents the diverse ways in which political activism manifests on X. She notes the use of memes, viral videos, personal stories, and heated exchanges to shape public opinion and influence voter behavior. She describes the formation of online communities around shared political beliefs, tracking their interactions and impact.
4. Explain: Britney analyzes the X data she has collected, seeking to explain the underlying factors that drive political discourse on the platform. After she investigates the

> role of algorithms, echo chambers, and disinformation campaigns in shaping online conversations, Britney draws on theories of social movements and collective action to explain how X can both empower and polarize political activism.

This is the essence of a college research class. Students are expected to hone their ability to analyze specific human behaviors through exploration, observation, description, and explanation. They should be able to identify a specific research topic and conduct research on it. More importantly, they undertake their research with the aim of uncovering new or interesting findings and sharing them with others. A crucial aspect of college-level research is its scientific nature. It must adhere to an academically proven process to yield scientific results. The keyword here is *scientific*.

Conducting Scientific Research

Consider Tom, a 21-year-old communication student with a yen for coffee. Consuming at least two cups daily, Tom wonders about the health implications of his coffee habit. He turns to Google for answers and stumbles upon a video from the *Today Show* on NBC titled, "Study: Drinking Coffee Could Lengthen Your Life."[4] The report cites a Harvard University study that found drinking three to five cups of coffee a day could lower the risk of premature death, including a decrease in diabetes, Parkinson's, and even suicide. The study was based on a large sample of 200,000 doctors and nurses observed over 20 years.

This news validates Tom's coffee consumption, and he is further swayed by the prestige of Harvard University, the large sample size, and the extensive duration of the study. Consequently, Tom decides to increase his daily coffee intake to five cups and even encourages his green-tea-drinking parents to switch to coffee. While many might find Tom's decision reasonable and rush to their nearest Starbucks, a college research student might raise several questions about the study's results. They might question whether the positive effects of drinking coffee can be generalized to all college students, given that the study only sampled doctors and nurses. They might ask if coffee consumption has different effects on men and women, as the study did not specify gender differences. They might wonder if instant coffee and ground coffee have the same effects, or if their parents, who do not share the same work routines as doctors and nurses, would reap the same benefits. They might also question if drinking three cups of coffee daily could increase other risks such as kidney disease and heart attacks, or if being sedentary could have the same benefits compared to being physically active.

These critical inquiries demonstrate the intellectual capacity of college researchers to evaluate and analyze others' research findings. With these skills, college researchers can develop their research agenda, implement research, and present the results throughout the research class. One certainty about the Harvard coffee research is that the findings serve as valuable information to the community of doctors and nurses. This underscores that research should aim to discover something not for all people globally but for a specific group of people in a particular region or community. To ensure that your research is scientific, there are four elements to demonstrate from the very beginning of the research practice:

1. Validity: Your research should accurately measure what it intends to measure. High validity means your research produces valid results that correspond to established theories and variations in the social science world.
2. Reliability: Your research should produce the same results when repeated under the same or similar conditions. If the results are consistently achieved using the same research method under the same circumstances, the measurement is considered reliable.
3. Generalizability: Your research results can be generalized to a particular group of people. If it is found that Instagram increases the vanity of female wishes among female college students in southern France, the finding could be generalized to a group of female college students in the entire nation.
4. Accuracy: Your research must present accurate results after consolidating and analyzing the research data you collected. In the process of research, a mistake can occur, and it affects the entire research process. You as a researcher are expected to show evidence of the results to improve research accuracy.

Applying the four elements of research demonstration to research practice, we can reach the goal of conducting scientific research on a college level. In other words, we have some general ideas or concepts of scientific research by separating the typical Google search from scientific academic research. It is time to become familiar with academic procedures of research as soon-to-be professional researchers.

Scientific Research Procedures: A Scholarly Approach

Research begins with personal interests, particularly those relevant to a student's major field of study. Students learn to develop areas of interest for research and identify compelling topics. More importantly, they should consider what excites them and fuels their curiosity. For instance, students specializing in strategic communication might focus on human communication, exploring a wide range of topics such as television, radio, newspapers, magazines, online news, social media platforms, interpersonal communication, corporate communication, marketing communication, rhetoric, advertising, public relations, and communication technologies.

Unlike a simple Google search or a query to an AI-powered tool, academic research involves a systematic process. Here are the eight basic steps in the research process:

1. Identify the area of study: This should align with your college major and the subjects you generally study for your degree.
2. Develop a research topic: Brainstorm ideas that interest you. Consider an issue or problem that intrigues you and prompts you to explore it in more depth.
3. Search for background information: Use keywords associated with your research topic to search library indexes. Read news and journal articles to familiarize yourself with the research topic.
4. Formulate a hypothesis or research question: Narrow down to specific aspects of the hypothesis or research question that are focused, specific, and researchable within the constraints of your topic.
5. Gather information: Implement a particular research method, such as a survey or an in-depth interview, to gather information and answer your hypothesis or research question. This practice produces a collection of data for research.
6. Analyze data: Thoroughly examine the research data obtained from surveys, experiments, focus groups, content analysis, or in-depth interviews. Identify key points and any patterns or themes that may arise from the data.
7. Interpret data: Uncover the story that can be told from the data, focusing on your key findings. Explain what the analyzed data means to your research topic and the research community in your field of study.
8. Share research findings: After your research is complete, you may be required to present your findings in a research class. Classmates can play the role of research critics, offering questions and suggestions.

It is clear that there are significant differences between internet/social media searches and academic research. While the former is convenient, easy, and pressure free, the latter is formal, time consuming, and complex. Because academic research is more intricate than a Google search, it yields more systematic and scientific outcomes. The primary reason for such outcomes stems from a scholarly research approach to social science. See figure 1.2.

The Scientific Approach to Scholarly Research

Researchers adhering to the eight basic steps of the scholarly research process are trained to adopt a scientific approach to studying human behavior. They may choose qualitative,

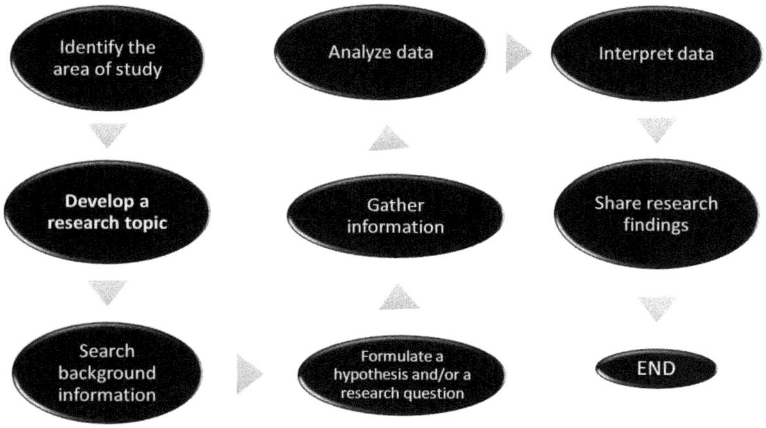

Figure 1.2 The eight academic research steps
Source: Created by author.

quantitative, or a combination of both research methods to ensure a path for scientific research. To understand the concept of scientific research, we must recognize its common characteristics, which are widely accepted by scholarly researchers. Here are the ten characteristics of scientific research in social science:

1. Systematic: The research follows an academically structured procedure in exploring topics, employing participants, and gathering and analyzing data.
2. Evidence based: The research gathers data and presents them as evidence to support scientific results.
3. Logical: The research investigates human behavior with logical research methods such as qualitative and quantitative methods.
4. Amendable: The research can be tested and retested to ensure that the same results can be achieved.
5. Replicable: The research can be repeated in the same procedure in a new environment and different settings with a new group of participants.
6. Action oriented: The research is implemented by researchers who observe and measure data to explain human behavior.
7. Minimizes scientific error: The research can produce distorted or manipulated results when researchers fail to maintain objectivity.
8. Accepts criticism: The research can have flaws in the process and in the presentation of results, as no research is perfect due to its limitations.

9. Interests the community: The research can generate useful results for specific groups of people such as college seniors, Instagram users, or car salespeople.
10. Investigates all possible explanations: The research can take an integrated multidisciplinary approach to explore multiple aspects of human behavior.

It is worth noting that scientific research in any academic discipline adopts and accepts these characteristics to ensure a scholarly research process. This leads to an attempt to find objective, unbiased information for a specific group of people to whom the researcher wishes to contribute. All the characteristics and procedures of scientific research can be consolidated into one key term, *heuristics*, which means "a way of engaging in scientific search through methods and processes aimed at discovery; a way of self-inquiry and dialogue with others aimed at finding the underlying meanings of important human behavior."[5]

THE SCHOLARLY APPROACH TO COMMUNICATION RESEARCH

Communication is a process of understanding and sharing meaning. According to the National Communication Association, communication focuses on how people use messages to generate meanings within and across various contexts.[6] Communication is a well-established academic discipline, offered as both an undergraduate and graduate course in many colleges and universities worldwide. Communication research employs social scientific methods to explore various aspects of human communication, including social, political, organizational, cultural, and media-based communication. Researchers in this field analyze messages, symbols, and meanings, assuming that communication occurs when people exchange information in a one-way or two-way process. The fundamental components of human communication are studied and analyzed to better understand this information exchange process. These components include:

- Sender: The sender is the person who imagines, creates, and sends the message.
- Message: The message is the key idea or concept created by the sender for the receiver or audience.
- Channel: The channel transmits the message between the sender and the receiver in a written or spoken medium.
- Receiver: The receiver is the person who receives the message from the sender, analyzing and interpreting the message.
- Feedback: Feedback is the responsive process of sending a verbal and/or nonverbal message back to the sender from the receiver.
- Environment: The environment is the physical and psychological aspects in which communication occurs between the sender and the receiver.

Communication research aims to understand how and why people communicate, as well as what they expect to achieve through communication. Drawing from the social science research tradition, communication research employs qualitative or quantitative methods to gain a scientific understanding of human communication. As a result, communication research investigates complex and challenging communication phenomena at corporate and political levels, as well as everyday conversations at an individual level. The focus of communication research is influenced by two foundational scholarly research developments: behaviorism and phenomenology. These two philosophical approaches have laid the groundwork for the development of communication research and continue to shape the field today.

- Behaviorism: Introduced by American psychologist John B. Watson, behaviorism is a scientific theory that explains human behavior.[7] Behaviorism posits that the analysis of behaviors and reactions is the only objective method to gain insight into human actions. Watson believed that analyzing human behavior could only be achieved through measuring observable behaviors and events. However, behaviorism also embraces the analysis of covert behavior, such as cognition and emotions, to understand human behavior from a psychological perspective.[8]
- Phenomenology: The study of "phenomena" is a philosophical exploration of the structures of experience and consciousness. Founded by Edmund Husserl, phenomenology elaborates on how internal, psychological meaning guides human behavior.[9] Phenomenology explores the appearances of things in human consciousness to distinguish from and relate to other philosophical disciplines, encompassing the structure of various types of experiences such as perception, emotion, desire, and social activity. In essence, phenomenology studies human experience in terms of consciousness.

The philosophical foundation for the emergence of communication research was established by behaviorism and phenomenology, leading to the development of three major scholarly approaches to directing research toward the demonstration of scientific outcomes: the empirical, interpretive, and critical approaches.

Empirical Approach

The empirical approach guides the researcher to search for empirical evidence. It suggests that building knowledge from concrete empirical evidence can lead to verifiable evidence. Such empirical evidence can be collected using qualitative and quantitative research methods, as the term *empirical* refers to the collection of data from a research perspective. The researcher seeks answers to research questions while collecting and analyzing the record of observations, experiments, or experiences as empirical evidence. A. D. de Groot, a Dutch psychologist and chess expert, introduced the empirical cycle, which captures

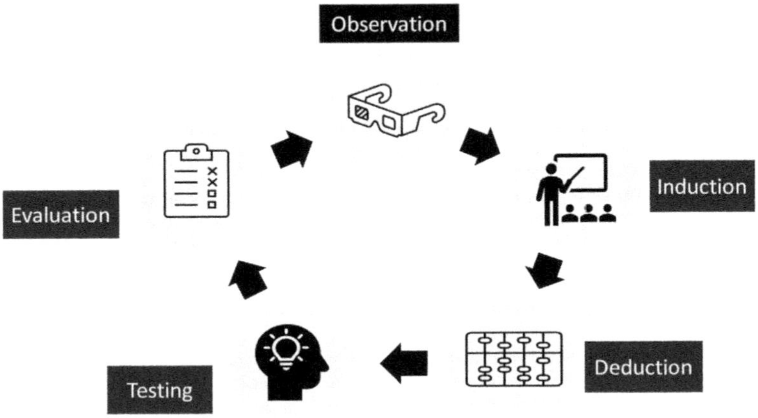

Figure 1.3 The empirical research cycle
Source: Created by author.

verifiable evidence to arrive at scientific research outcomes based on research questions and/or hypotheses.[10] In the process of empirical research, the researcher takes the five steps of the empirical cycle to conduct scientific research (also see figure 1.3):

- Observation: At this stage, the researcher collects an active acquisition of empirical data from a primary source. Observation can occur while the researcher gathers relevant empirical data using qualitative or quantitative observational methods. For example, the researcher observes a group of tenth graders during their history Zoom class session, documenting their patterns of communication behavior with the history teacher in the online class.
- Induction: Inductive reasoning is carried out to reach a general probable conclusion from the data gathered through the observation at this stage. For example, the researcher builds a general assumption that online classes via Zoom may discourage high school students from paying attention to the class in comparison with in-person class settings.
- Deduction: At this stage of deductive reasoning, the researcher formulates hypotheses by applying logic to the observation. It leads the researcher to deduce a conclusion from the observation. For example, during the online class observation, if some of the students were seen dozing off or checking their smartphones, then it can be hypothesized that Zoom classes are not as effective and educational as traditional classes.
- Testing: This stage involves the researcher testing the hypotheses after the empirical methods for collecting data are complete. The researcher now needs to make sense of his data by combining relevant analysis techniques such as statistical

tests. For example, the researcher needs to decide if the data support or reject the hypothesis of Zoom class distraction among high school students.

- Evaluation: Empirical research requires the stage of evaluation as its final step. During this stage, the researcher outlines the empirical data collected from the observation and shares the findings with other research communities, including limitations and future studies for the empirical observation process. For example, if the hypotheses were supported in favor of traditional classes for better academic achievement among high school students, the empirical research not only recommends limiting Zoom classes but also admits that a larger number of students in different Zoom classes should be observed.

Interpretive Approach

The interpretive approach refers to philosophical and methodological methods of understanding social reality. It aligns with social theories and norms associated with the view of reality as socially constructed in meaningful ways.[11] While the empirical approach emphasizes the quantitative research method, the interpretive approach values the qualitative research method that focuses on uncovering the social meanings of human behavior. It enables the researcher to acknowledge that social reality is not singular or objective but rather constructed by human interactions and social contexts. The researcher seeks to explain the complexities of socially constructed meaning as enacted in symbols, language, and human behavior. The interpretive approach is best carried out within its sociohistoric context, which continues to produce and change the meaning of contemporary human experiences. The researcher interprets meaning through a sense-making process (qualitative research) rather than a hypothesis-testing process (quantitative research). The interpretive approach adheres to a set of four principles:

1. Researcher as instrument: The researcher is regarded as part of the data collection instrument, equipped with skills of observation, credibility with the observed, and capability of data analysis.

2. Researcher as narrator: The researcher captures all verbal and nonverbal expressions of the observed, including nuances, facial expressions, and emotions, so the data can visually deliver the situation in which the research was conducted.

3. Researcher as interpreter: The researcher deciphers what the observed implied, why they behaved in a certain way, and how they acted during the observation period. The researcher interprets meaning regarding the specific behavior and thoughts of the observed.

4. Research as sense maker: The researcher embraces the ongoing process of the social construction of meaning, in which people create social narratives to exchange

human experiences. As sense making plays a pivotal role in all social activity, the researcher extracts social cues from the social context.[12]

One of the most popular interpretive approaches is ethnography. The researcher chooses a particular group of people to live with and observe their behavior in hopes of finding social meaning among the people. For instance, suppose the researcher lived with a tribe in the Amazon rain forest. During the observation process, the researcher learns and records how they communicate, hunt, and protect themselves. The researcher interprets the tribe's social interactions in the form of ethnography.

Critical Approach

The critical approach leads the researcher to view communication as a tool used to create power and wealth for the affluent. The researcher explores the critical aspect of communication to analyze the communicative impact on the powerless and the oppressed, who exist to serve the interests of powerful, wealthy individuals in a capitalistic world.[13] The critical approach also encourages the researcher to analyze the dominance of organizations with power and control because communication is exclusively consolidated for organizations in certain societal structures to promote organizational interests. Hence, the critical approach requires two levels of analyses of communication:

1. Individual level: The critical approach posits that social elites use the media to promote and secure their social power because the media advertise wealthy people's products and services, as well as propagate powerful people's ideology. Even though social media offers individual communication channels for the public to express their opinions or thoughts, the average person's impact on society via social media is not as great as that of powerful people. For instance, former president Donald Trump, who used Twitter daily, is an example of how social media can be used to promote powerful people's ideology. Similarly, celebrities such as the Kardashian sisters capitalize on their fame via Instagram, earning millions by becoming brand spokespersons on their social media platforms. Social media aids famous and powerful people in amassing more power and money. Departing from the critical approach, the researcher analyzes and criticizes how the use of communication is merely designed to boost and promote the interests of people with power and ultimately reinforce their high social status. More importantly, the critical approach assists the researcher in developing explanatory, practical, and normative analyses of what is wrong with communication.

2. Organizational level: Corporations and governmental organizations capitalize on significant imbalances of communicative power against individuals or certain social classes such as the oppressed. The key concept of this argument is communication

technology, which the researcher regards as a tool for the transmission of information, which flows from powerful organizations to the public. For example, corporations maximize the use of modern communication technologies to spread their messages, including websites, social media platforms, television, and newspaper advertising, while the public is passively exposed to corporate messages. According to a marketing survey, the average person in 2023 encountered between 6,000 and 10,000 messages every single day from traditional and social media.[14] In many ways, corporations serve as trailblazers in developing and facilitating new communication technologies, and they advance more effective communication strategies and technologies to attract the public audience's attention, especially for brand awareness. The critical approach suggests that communication exists to promote the interests of organizations with power and money.

Research in Strategic Communication and the Role of AI Technologies

The general principle of research for college students is consistent across disciplines in social science. However, this textbook is tailored for students studying communication, journalism, advertising, public relations, and integrated marketing communication. All these fields can be consolidated into the conceptual framework of strategic communication, which aims to communicate customized messages with target audiences and the general public from a research perspective. Strategic communication primarily occurs when strategies with tailored information or customized messages focus on persuading either the target audience or the public or both. Given that academic inquiry for traditional and social media, public relations, advertising, and integrated marketing communication can be considered the most popular areas of strategic communication research, we focus on exploring, observing, describing, and explaining human behavior directly related to the area of strategic communication.

In the era of digital transformation, artificial intelligence (AI) technologies have become increasingly significant in the field of strategic communication. AI can analyze large amounts of data, identify patterns, and provide insights that humans might overlook. This can be particularly useful in understanding audience behavior, segmenting audiences, personalizing messages, and measuring the effectiveness of communication strategies. This textbook will help strategic communication students in the following ways:

1. Understanding research methods: Students will achieve a clear understanding of both traditional and AI-driven research methods.
2. Applying research to projects: Students will learn how to apply the practicality of research, including AI technologies, to their research projects.

3. Familiarizing with the academic format of research: Students will become familiar with the academic format of research, including how to incorporate AI technologies in their research process.
4. Developing analytical skills: Students will develop qualitative and quantitative analytical skills, including the ability to use AI tools for data analysis, from a strategic communication perspective.
5. Understanding and applying AI technologies: Students will gain a comprehensive understanding of various AI technologies and learn how to apply them in strategic communication research.

By integrating AI technologies into strategic communication research, students will be better equipped to navigate the ever-evolving landscape of communication in the digital age. This textbook aims to bridge the gap between traditional research methods and the innovative approaches brought about by AI, preparing students for a future where AI will play an increasingly significant role in strategic communication.

Application of an AI-Powered Tool

Box 1.1
An Example of Using Google Gemini for the Research Class

Using an AI-Powered Tool (Google Gemini) to Survive the Communication Research Class

Command syntax: Elaborate on effective ways of using Google Gemini for college students required to take and pass the communication research class.

Answer: Google Gemini is a large language model, also known as a conversational AI or chatbot trained to be informative and comprehensive. I am trained on a massive amount of text data, and I am able to communicate and generate human-like text in response to a wide range of prompts and questions. For example, I can provide summaries of factual topics or create stories.

Here are some effective ways of using Google Gemini for college students required to take and pass the communication research class:

1. Develop research interests

Google Gemini can help you develop research interests by providing you with information about different topics. For example, if you are interested in studying communication, you can ask Google Gemini questions about different communication theories, research methods, and findings. This can help you to learn more about the field of communication and to identify areas that you are interested in researching.

2. Find research topics

Google Gemini can also help you to find research topics. For example, if you are interested in studying college dating patterns, you can ask Google Gemini questions about the prevalence of different dating behaviors among college students. This can help you to identify a research topic that is both interesting to you and that has the potential to make a contribution to the field of communication.

3. Advance basic writing skills for research papers

Google Gemini can also help you to advance your basic writing skills for research papers. For example, you can ask Google Gemini for help with grammar, punctuation, and style. You can also ask Google Gemini for help with organizing your thoughts and developing a clear and concise argument.

4. Design research method and sample

Google Gemini can also help you to design your research method and sample. For example, if you are interested in studying college dating patterns, you can ask Google Gemini for help with designing a survey or interview protocol. You can also ask Google Gemini for help with identifying a sample of college students who would be willing to participate in your research.

Example of TikTok and college dating patterns in research

Google Gemini can also be used to research the relationship between TikTok and college dating patterns. For example, you could ask Google Gemini to provide you with information about how college students use TikTok to date. You could also ask Google Gemini to provide you with information about the types of content that college students share on TikTok about dating. This information could be used to develop a better understanding of how TikTok is impacting college dating patterns.

Overall, Google Gemini can be a valuable tool for college students who are required to take and pass a communication research class. Google Gemini can help you to develop research interests, find research topics, advance your basic writing skills, and design your research method and sample.

Summary

- ✓ Everybody does simple research daily, using Google or Bing.
- ✓ Academic research refers to a systematic investigation into a specific subject using the scientific method.
- ✓ Typing search terms in Google (questions) is a process of research that seeks information (answers).
- ✓ Academic research requires a more complicated process than a Google search by adding scientific procedures.
- ✓ Academic research is standardized and followed by scholarly researchers.
- ✓ The outcomes of academic research are characterized by validity, reliability, generalizability, and accuracy.
- ✓ Students identify their areas of study and develop research topics in those areas.
- ✓ Scientific research can be consolidated into one key term, *heuristics*, which means a way of engaging in scientific research through methods and processes aimed at discovery.
- ✓ Conducting research aims to explore, observe, describe, and explain human behavior.
- ✓ Communication research aims to understand how people communicate, why they communicate, and what they expect as a result of communication.
- ✓ Communication researchers investigate messages, symbols, and meanings.
- ✓ The focus of communication research is influenced by two basic scholarly research developments: behaviorism and phenomenology.
- ✓ Major scholarly approaches to communication research in terms of directing a research path toward the demonstration of scientific outcomes are empirical, interpretive, and critical.
- ✓ Research in strategic communication includes such disciplines as traditional and social media, public relations, advertising, and integrated marketing communication.
- ✓ By integrating AI technologies into strategic communication research, students will be better equipped to navigate the ever-evolving landscape of communication in the digital age.

Key Terms

1. Strategic communication
2. Simple research

3. Academic research
4. Communication research
5. Empirical cycle
6. Scientific research
7. Human behavior
8. Research interest
9. Behaviorism
10. Phenomenology

Chapter 2

Foundations of Strategic Communication Research

Chapter Learning Outcomes

- Understand the purpose of research in strategic communication.
- Identify the different types of academic writing styles.
- Apply the APA style format.
- Describe induction and deduction.
- Explain how primary sources differ from secondary sources.
- Recognize the structure of the research paper.
- Describe the process of writing a literature review.
- Discover unique approaches to scientific research.
- Distinguish the different types of publications.
- Practice Boolean searches.
- Apply AI tools to a literature review.

As you embark on your journey to become a college-educated researcher, you begin with a research class. This class teaches you to conduct scholarly research independently rather than relying solely on others' findings. For instance, you might investigate the claim that drinking three to five cups of coffee daily is beneficial for health.

Requirements for Research

When initiating a research project, it is crucial to keep in mind the fundamental objectives of strategic communication research. These objectives include:

- gaining insight into why communication occurs between strategic communicators and their target audience
- identifying the communication issues of the target audience

- predicting potential outcomes for the target audience
- explaining why the target audience behaves in specific ways
- evaluating the impact of strategic communication on the target audience
- proposing practical solutions for the target audience

The goal of strategic communication research is to uncover practical insights that can assist governments, corporations, and organizations in effectively communicating their messages to their target audiences. This type of research aligns with the philosophical concepts of pragmatism and practicality. As part of a research course, college students are typically required to write a research paper and deliver an oral presentation to their classmates. While many communication students are already familiar with in-class presentations from public speaking courses, writing academic research papers in strategic communication requires learning standardized writing formats such as MLA, APA, and Chicago styles. Although some communication and journalism history researchers prefer the Chicago-style format, most strategic communication researchers use the APA-style format developed by the American Psychological Association. This textbook focuses on the APA-style format to aid students in developing their academic research papers.

To complete the strategic communication research experience, students must go through the following research phases:

1. Study fundamental elements of research, including methods of reasoning, information gathering, library searches, research paper structure, and writing style.
2. Plan research strategies, considering ethical issues, sampling, qualitative methods, quantitative methods, and resources.
3. Conduct research using a chosen method, such as interviews, surveys, focus groups, case studies, or experiments.
4. Analyze research data using analytic techniques such as descriptive statistics, inferential statistics, textual analysis, content analysis, and historical analysis.
5. Share research outcomes with your instructor and classmates through oral presentations and paper submissions.

In this chapter, we delve into the first phase, studying the fundamental elements of research in strategic communication.

Choosing a Research Topic in Strategic Communication

Without a research topic, you cannot initiate the research process. You should first consider a topic for your research paper that interests you and is feasible in terms of the time and resources you can invest. Begin by exploring several subjects of interest, including business communication, public relations, advertising, media, social media, and marketing. After this exploration, choose the subject that most interests you and break it down into smaller, related topics. Finally, narrow these broad or general topics down to a specific topic. This process can be challenging, but there are several strategies to help you choose your research topic.

As you explore and search for your research topic, consider the following pre-research questions to guide your selection:

- Who is the target population or group for your research (e.g., college students, women, Hispanics, Gen Z, advertisers, police officers, TikTokers, sorority sisters)?
- What is the discipline or focus of your research (e.g., traditional media, social media, brands, health information, corporate social responsibility)?
- Where will your research be conducted (e.g., Brazil, Kansas, a college campus, shelters, online, hospitals)?
- When does your research take place (e.g., current year, the digital age, Biden or Trump administration era, wartimes)?
- Why are you conducting this research? What is its logic and importance (e.g., relevance to the class, to the community, personal interest)?

For instance, if you are interested in exploring the impact of the post-coronavirus era on YouTube culture among female college students, you might focus your research on students at your own college. To narrow down the topic, you could examine a specific trend, such as the use of YouTube for at-home workouts during and after the pandemic. Surveying female college students on campus can provide insights into how their physical health has been affected by gym closures and reopenings. If your research shows that they have been spending a lot of time watching fitness channels and following along with coaches, you could write a research paper on their patterns of using YouTube for home workouts. Choosing a research topic and completing an academic paper in one semester can be challenging for college students. As a strategic communication student, exploring broad subjects of communication can be beneficial.

Table 2.1 contains a list of suggested research paper topics to consider.

Research Models: Deductive Reasoning and Inductive Reasoning

In research, two primary models of reasoning exist to guide researchers along an optimal research path: deductive reasoning (deduction) and inductive reasoning (induction).

Deduction

Deductive reasoning is a process that moves from the general to the specific. It involves deriving a conclusion by investigating a general set of facts and ideas. In communication

Table 2.1 Strategic Communications Research Paper Topics in Broader Subjects

branding	copyright law	good news versus bad news
corporate reputation	propaganda	social interactions across media
communication management	media bias	technology's impact on ads
effective PR campaigns	media ownership	media psychology
social media activism	political correctness	crisis communication
gender roles in advertising	portrayal of women	corporate social responsibility
marketing and social media	speech types	leadership communication
organizational images	war and crisis coverage	celebrity damage control

research, deduction involves forming a conclusion based on data collection and analysis. As a strategic communication researcher, you would begin your research journey by drawing from theories that guide you in formulating a hypothesis or research question. After determining your research questions or hypotheses, you would seek answers by collecting data, which you would then analyze and interpret to produce scientific outcomes. This process of reasoning, which begins with theory and ends with data interpretation, is called deduction or deductive reasoning.

For example, suppose you choose cultivation theory as your theoretical guidance for your research. This theory suggests that heavy viewers of television tend to be heavily influenced by what the media depict and perceive social realities based on what they repeatedly hear and watch on television. If you initiated your research from this theory, your research question (RQ) and hypothesis (H) could be formed as follows:

> *RQ*: Do individuals who watch crime TV shows experience greater fear toward gun owners compared to those who do not watch such shows?
>
> *H*: Individuals who watch crime TV shows may experience an increased sense of fear toward gun owners when compared to those who do not watch such shows.

After formulating a hypothesis and research question based on the theory of cultivation, you continue to collect data either by observing, experimenting, or surveying television viewers of crime programs. The collected data should be analyzed and interpreted for the completion of research, which follows the path of deductive reasoning.

Induction

Inductive reasoning is the process of discovering a general principle from a set of data. In logic, induction refers to an inference of a general conclusion based on data, evidence, or the researcher's discoveries. Inductive reasoning moves from specific data obtained through observations to perceptible patterns and theories. In other words, as a researcher, you begin by observing a specific group of people and detecting patterns and regularities to reach a theoretical conclusion or create a theoretical model. For example, suppose you watch *Chicago P.D.* on NBC with your college friends in a dorm room. The TV show portrays an innocent young girl caught in the crossfire and killed on the street. You witness some friends making uncomfortable facial expressions and even looking away from the scene. One of them says, "I hate guns. I won't go out if I live in Chicago." You decide to collect more data on the link between college students and police drama series on television. You continue watching more episodes of the show with more friends. After observing how your friends react to several episodes of *Chicago P.D.*, you establish a list of patterns of the viewers:

- They think gun wounds are always fatal.
- They do not want to go out for a walk alone.
- They are afraid of drive-by shootings.
- They believe so many innocent people get murdered for no reason.

After identifying the patterns, you formulate a tentative hypothetical assumption: the more people watch crime shows, the more scared they are of gun violence in reality. As a result, you can develop a theory from what you observed and identified through inductive reasoning. Induction and deduction take different routes, but they share the concepts of theory and data (see figure 2.1). Communication students need to take theory courses to have a comprehensive understanding of research in strategic communication. While

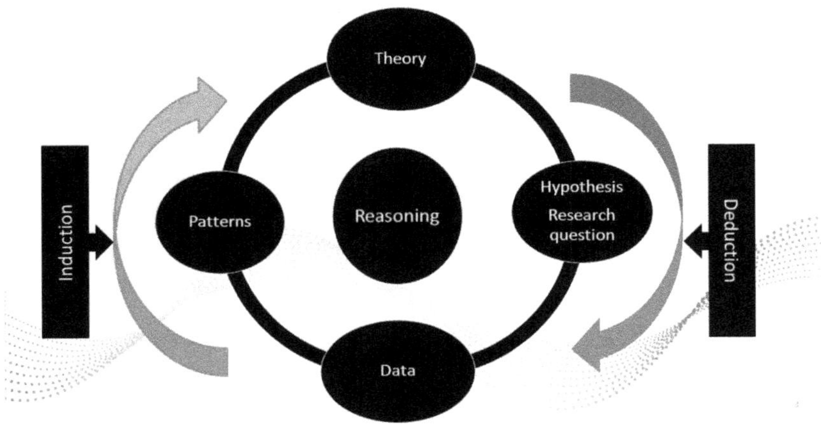

Figure 2.1 The model of deductive reasoning and inductive reasoning

Source: Created by author.

induction is exploratory at the beginning of the research, deduction requires a strict beginning from a theory. Most strategic communication researchers employ deductive reasoning to develop and practice their research projects. Therefore, as a future researcher, you need to focus on understanding and practicing deductive reasoning, viewed as the general reasoning model of research in strategic communication.

Research Paper Structure

College research classes often encourage students to conduct individual or group research and write academic research papers. For strategic communication students, the research paper should adhere to a standardized structure recommended by research scholars and professors. The first step in the communication research journey is to select a research topic. As a college student, you should consider the following:

1. Identify what interests or entertains you in the field of strategic communication.
2. Determine your specific area of interest. Are you interested in social media and marketing, sports events and advertising, movies and product placements, TV news and media effects, public relations and corporate reputation, influencers and brand, or something else?

You choose your research topic because you are the researcher for your research. After deciding on the topic, the next step is to gather scholarly journal articles related to your topic and read them. These articles will provide insights into what findings researchers have reported and how these findings pertain to a specific group of people. For example, if your research topic is to explore a possible link between the use of Facebook and depression, academic searches via the college library website will provide you with a wealth of scholarly journal articles that have already studied the topic. You can learn what has been discovered and debated from these articles and develop your specific research strategies, which will lead you to form research questions and/or hypotheses.

Why are you supposed to go through these procedures? The answer lies within the structure of a research paper. College students in a strategic communication research class are expected to write an academic research paper following a standardized structure. This structure not only provides a clear and organized presentation of your research but also ensures that your work aligns with the academic standards of strategic communication research.

It contains very specific sections, as Box 2.1 illustrates:

Box 2.1
The Structure of the Academic Research Paper

Introduction

The research topic and some background information are explained.

Literature review

The reviews of scholarly journal articles relevant to the research topic are explored.

- Research question (RQ) and/or hypothesis (H).
- Based on the literature review, RQ and/or H can be developed.

Method(s)

The process of conducting research is explained: who or what was selected for a sample, why the sample was selected, how the sample was observed and analyzed, when and where the research was conducted, and so on.

Results or findings

The researcher reveals the answers to research question and/or hypothesis after analyzing the data obtained from the sample or research participants.

Discussion/conclusion

The researcher discusses how significant the results or findings can be in comparison with what other previous studies have already investigated. Other journal articles can be mentioned to support or refute what this research finds. The section "Conclusion" can either be integrated into the section "Discussion" or can be a separate section with one or two paragraphs.

References

A list of citations must be printed in this section as additional material for a complete research paper.

The standard length of a communication research paper is typically less than 25 pages (double-spaced), plus the reference section. Given the demands of other courses, completing such a lengthy paper in a single semester can be challenging for college students. As a result, some instructors may assign it as a group project or replace it with a research design paper, a condensed version of the full paper. Among all sections in the paper structure, the literature review section requires significant effort, while the introduction section provides background information about the topic. The concept of a literature review may seem unfamiliar to many college students, as it involves discussing and exploring published information in a particular subject area relevant to the research topic. A literature review is a comprehensive summary of information found in scholarly articles, books, and other academic literature. It is held to a much higher standard than the academic research paper. The focus of a literature review is to study and synthesize the findings and ideas of other researchers.

For example, in the case of Facebook and depression, you should find and read as many scholarly journal articles about the topic as possible for the literature review section. You might find some articles claiming that (1) there is a causal link between the use of Facebook and negative effects on mental health, primarily depression and loneliness,[1] and (2) the more you use Facebook, the worse you feel.[2] On the contrary, you could also discover a news article that says Facebook makes people as happy as getting married.[3] By learning from both sides of contrasting results on the use of Facebook and its impact on mental health, you can also find another journal article that says leaving Facebook makes people happier but less informed.[4] After finding and reading such scholarly journal articles, mostly written by college professors, you can come up with more specific and narrowed research questions and/or hypotheses for your research paper.

This entire process comprehensively illustrates what we have discussed so far: deduction and research paper structure. A literature review provides college students and professors with academic guidance on a particular topic, as well as a diverse background of useful information on what is found in the field. Moreover, since the majority of research articles include theories or theoretical frameworks in the literature section, you can also learn how communication theories enrich the section.

Searching Scholarly Journal Articles

Given the importance of deduction and the literature review in strategic communication research, three crucial questions arise: (1) What are scholarly journal articles? (2) How can we find them? and (3) Why do we need to use them?

What Are Scholarly Journal Articles?

Before we delve into the nature of scholarly journal articles, it is important to recognize the three typical types of publications: popular, trade, and scholarly publications (see Table 2.2).

- Popular publications: These include newspapers and magazines that feature a variety of topics, including business, sports, lifestyle, art, fashion, etc. Articles are written by journalists working for media outlets such as the *New York Times*, *USA Today*, *People*, and *Fortune*. These articles are reviewed by the publication's editorial

Table 2.2 Characteristics of Popular/Trade/Scholarly Publications

	Popular	**Trade**	**Scholarly**
Written by	journalists	practitioners	scholars
Frequency	daily/weekly	weekly/monthly	monthly/quarterly
Articles reviewed by	editor	editor	peer review
Citations, method details	no	maybe	yes
Title	*. . . Times, . . . Post*	*. . . News*	*Journal of . . .*
Publisher	news media	trade association	academic publisher

staff, including copyediting for spelling and grammar. These articles are written in plain English for the public; no higher academic background is needed to understand them. The aim of popular publications is to supply daily and weekly news to the public for entertainment, information, and advertising.

- Trade publications: These are designed to provide practical information for professionals in a specific industry. Articles are written by industry or market experts to inform about business trends, review new products, and offer special opinions for a specific industry like automobiles and nanotechnology. Tailored for the audience that works in a particular trade or industry, these articles are commonly published either weekly or monthly. Examples of trade magazines include *U.S. Banker*, *Adweek*, *Space Technology*, *Game Industry Report*, and *Boxoffice Pro*. While trade articles often look similar to those in popular magazines, their aim is to give practical information to professionals and other interested readers about the specialized industry.
- Scholarly publications: These are what college students need to be familiar with. Scholarly articles are written by researchers or college professors in their academic fields, using specialized vocabulary, citing an extensive list of other journal articles, and are peer reviewed. The main purpose of scholarly articles is to share academic research findings with the academic community, and they are commonly published monthly or quarterly. Writing and completing a scholarly article requires significant effort due to the research process and the demanding standards academic researchers must follow. The language is highly technical, and article authors are experts in the particular topic of study. Anyone without some scholarly background might find scholarly articles hard to understand. A key difference between scholarly articles and popular or trade ones is that they include source citations and references, often footnotes or a bibliography. In particular, articles published in academic journals are called scholarly journal articles. Academic journals publish research-oriented articles, and they are also called

peer-reviewed journal articles. The process of writing a scholarly journal article is complex since the researcher has to conduct his or her research, write an academic paper, and submit it to an academic journal of the same academic field. For example, if you are a strategic communication researcher seeking an opportunity for the publication of your research paper, your possible scholarly journals can include titles such as *Journal of Communication . . .*, *Mass Communication & . . .*, *International Journal of . . .*, *Marketing Communication . . .*, *Advertising Journal . . .*, *Journal of Public Relations . . .*, or *Media Journal. . . .* More importantly, publishing a scholarly journal article requires passing the peer-review process where other scholars in the same field evaluate the content and quality of the article. Hence, scholarly journal articles tend to be held to a high standard.

How to Find Scholarly Journal Articles

After understanding the concept of scholarly journal articles, the next step is to discuss how to find them. Instead of typing search terms into Google, you should visit the library webpage of your institution. Type your search terms and find scholarly journal articles relevant to your research topic. However, there are some steps to discover more customized articles during the online library search. For example, if you wanted to research the impact of Instagram influencers and their communication strategies, first type "Instagram influencers" into the library search bar. You will see hundreds of articles from popular, trade, and scholarly publications as the search results. For your academic research, you need to focus on scholarly journal articles, so move to "Advanced Search," which the library webpage should offer with a tab or button for advanced search. When you click on it, a new online page will show the search filters, including the options of "Keyword" and "AND, OR, NOT."

These search options are called "Boolean search," which uses a combination of keywords and the three main Boolean operators (AND, OR, and NOT) to organize and narrow down your searches. Since the term "Instagram influencer" was already typed, another term, "communication strategy," can be typed with the selection of "AND." Now you should have a narrower list of articles that includes both terms, but what you need is only scholarly journal articles regarding the topic. One more step is to select "Peer-Reviewed Journals" on the menu tool. As a result, results will only show a list of scholarly journal articles with titles, author names, journal names, and brief abstracts. You can scroll down through all the articles and choose some of them that seem most relevant to your topic and read them. The library search functions also allow you to filter publication dates, meaning that if you want the articles only published from 2010 to 2024, you can set the publication date for the advanced search. You can also narrow down your search results further by using "OR" or "NOT" as well. Boolean search is a common way of conducting academic research, especially for the literature review section, which uses a series of scholarly journal articles to learn about your topic that has been studied by other scholars.

Why Do We Need to Use Scholarly Journal Articles?

As we have acknowledged the importance of conducting research and performing a literature review, it has become clear why scholarly journal articles are considered the main source for the literature review section. Academic research, unlike news or magazine articles, is focused on discovering new findings, building upon existing ones, or offering critical analysis. To achieve scientific results, research papers are written using standardized research techniques, which is a lengthy and challenging process. The ultimate goal of research is to analyze what previous researchers have uncovered and to further enhance your research to reveal something new for a specific group or community. For instance, consider the Harvard coffee study, which found that coffee had a beneficial effect on a group of medical professionals, including doctors and nurses.

Through a literature review, you will have the opportunity to examine what academic researchers have found about the topic you are interested in. In addition, you are supposed to use scholarly journal articles for the literature review section of your research paper. Another reason for using scholarly journal articles for academic research is that they are peer reviewed. When a research article has been peer reviewed, it means that the article has undergone academic scrutiny by other experts, most of whom are professors in the same field who already know the topic and approve of the credibility of the article. This rigorous process ensures the validity and reliability of the information presented in the article. Therefore, the literature review section of the research paper requires you to conduct a Boolean search in pursuit of relevant and focused scholarly journal articles. After finding a dozen articles, although your instructor may ask for more or less, you should read and learn from them. Reviewing literature demands a diverse set of skills, spanning from locating and assessing pertinent scholarly articles to seamlessly incorporating reviewed data into a cohesive reorganization. In short, the literature review section encompasses the written form of reviewing the literature.

Primary and Secondary Research Sources

When conducting research, researchers gather information or collect data from a variety of sources. These sources of information are often divided into primary and secondary, depending on their originality. Let's discuss how they differ.

Primary Sources

A primary source provides the researcher with direct or firsthand evidence about the people, events, or phenomena being studied. It is usually the main and original document for research analysis. For example, if you are researching the relationship between the coronavirus and its impact on online dating, your primary sources could be the information you collect from interviewing a specific group of people, such as college students who have used online dating apps since the onset of the pandemic. From these interviews, you gather information or data yourself, meaning that you now have your primary source of information for your research.

A primary source allows you to get as close as possible to understanding what happened during a particular event or period. However, a primary source does not have to come only from direct involvement in observation or interviews. Published materials such as news articles can be viewed as primary sources if a researcher uses them as the main object of analysis, such as in historical research that investigates past events. A primary source can be written or verbally recorded in the form of documents while representing the original thinking of participants or observers. In scientific communication research, a primary source is aimed at reporting on discoveries or sharing new outcomes. Examples of primary sources that you can gather as the main research data can include:

- interviews and surveys
- audio and video recordings
- diaries, personal letters, and correspondence
- internet communications via email and the content of social media platforms
- ads and newspaper and magazine articles written at the time
- transcripts of radio and television programs written at the time
- original documents (birth certificates, wills, trial transcripts)
- opinion polls and records of government agencies
- photographs and posters
- speeches and oral histories
- patents
- books containing first-hand accounts by the author

Secondary Sources

A secondary source is typically created by someone who did not witness or participate in the events firsthand. It is used to describe, evaluate, analyze, and summarize primary source information. A secondary source assists researchers in improving overall study quality by facilitating the exploration of what is known and unknown about the issue. In essence, academic researchers read and use secondary sources as part of their research procedures, and a literature review uses secondary sources to provide a review or critique for the literature review section in research publications. Secondary sources with citations can include scholarly journal articles for the section. Secondary research sources include the following:

- bibliographies and biographical works
- books and textbooks
- indexes and abstracts
- ads and newspaper and magazine articles written after the event

- transcripts of radio and television programs written after the event
- dictionaries and encyclopedias
- synopses and descriptions of artistic works
- commentaries and criticisms

How to Organize the Literature Review Section

A literature review can be structured in various styles, but four academic forms are commonly used: summary review, chronological review, thematic or theoretical review, and pros-and-cons review.

Summary Review

After identifying and reading scholarly journal articles, summarize the arguments, findings, and discussions related to your research topic. This summary should encompass as many studies as possible that address related or identical research findings. An exemplary summary review adheres to the high standards of academic writing in terms of clarity, rigor, and precision. For instance, if your topic is the impact of corporate sponsorship on corporate images from a public relations perspective, your literature review should provide a comprehensive summary of other research findings about (1) how corporate sponsorship operates, (2) who is sponsored by which corporations at what events, (3) the success or failure of images as a result of sponsorship, and (4) the effectiveness of sponsorship in improving images.

Chronological Review

Using the chronological method, you can describe each scholarly journal article in the order of their publication, starting with the earliest information. Typically, a chronological review explains how the findings of a research topic have evolved over time, often illustrating the emergence of the topic and concept in society. For example, if your research subject is the impact of Super Bowl ads on Generation Z, you would first discuss the history of Super Bowl ads and the concept of Generation Z, referencing specific years when other scholarly journal articles discussed these topics. Then you could chronologically discuss (a) what you learned from those articles, highlighting how Super Bowl ads influenced the television and advertising industries, (b) why Gen Z watches them, (c) how impressed Gen Z is with the ads, and (d) what Gen Z seeks from the ads.

Thematic or Theoretical Review

This approach focuses on examining theories or themes relevant to your research topic. You should organize a collection of existing literature that is crucial for investigating the connection between the topic and the theory or theme. A thematic review involves sifting through studies to extract theories or themes, guiding you toward recognizing existing theories and how they help develop new themes. For instance, if your research topic is about changes in popular communication devices, there might be separate sections discussing the production of smartphones, the dissemination of smartphone apps, an interpretation of app trends, and historical studies of communication technologies. Additionally, you can apply communication theories such as symbolic interactionist theory to analyze the phenomenon of smartphone apps among college friends.

Pros and Cons Review

This style involves describing the advantages and disadvantages of specific findings of previous research on the topic. The aim is to critically evaluate and summarize your research topic based on previous research. It highlights how some studies found something positive, while others found something negative. For example, you could list several scholarly journal articles that found the habit of binge-watching Netflix beneficial for those with stressful jobs. Conversely, you could list other articles arguing that the habit of binge-watching Netflix could increase the risk of developing health issues, including heart attacks, diabetes, and certain types of cancer. Based on such opposite outcomes on the research topic, you could develop your research question for the impact of binge-watching Netflix on college students.

How to Write a Research Paper in APA Format

The APA style, developed by the American Psychological Association, is a widely used writing format for academic work in the social sciences, including strategic communication. It is often preferred over the MLA style used in the linguistic field and the Chicago style used in the field of history. The general formatting guidelines for APA are as follows:

- Size 12, Times New Roman font
- Double-spacing throughout the paper
- Margins of 1 inch on all sides of the page
- Paragraph indentation set to one-half inch from the left side of the page[5]

For research papers, the most crucial aspect of APA style is the use of in-text citations. Researchers in strategic communication adapt to the latest version of APA style, the 7th edition, released in October 2019. As the literature review section requires a wealth of scholarly journal articles as sources, students must learn how to cite them to avoid plagiarism.

Table 2.3 presents the basic in-text citation styles.

All college students in social science need to use the APA writing style in their research papers. Table 2.4 illustrates several examples of narrative citations used for quotes and paraphrases in text.

Table 2.3 Basic APA In-Text Citation Styles

Author type	Parenthetical citation example	Narrative citation example
One author	(Sweeney, 2002)	Sweeney (2002)
Two authors	(Carey & Spears, 2010)	Carey and Spears (2010)
Two or more authors	(Lopez et al., 2013)	Lopez et al. (2013)
Group author without abbreviation	(University of Alaska, 2025)	University of Alaska (2013)
Group author with abbreviation		
First citation	(Centers for Disease Control and Prevention [CDC], 2020)	Centers for Disease Control and Prevention (CDC, 2020)
Subsequent citations	(CDC, 2020)	CDC (2020)

Note. Adapted from American Psychological Association. (2020). *Publication Manual of the American Psychological Association* (7th ed.) (p. 266, Table 8.1). https://doi.org/10.1037/0000165-000.

The structure of a research paper typically includes several fundamental sections: the literature review, method, results, and discussion/conclusion. We will discuss these further in Chapter 14. A research paper is not considered complete without a reference section at the end. The reference section lists entries in alphabetical order by the author's last name. These entries refer to all sources used for the research paper, including scholarly, popular, and trade journal articles, books, and primary and secondary sources. In-text citations correspond to entries in the reference section, which provides detailed information about the source, including the full title, volume number, issue number, pages, and web address.

The main characteristic distinguishing a reference section from a bibliography is its correspondence to in-text citations. It is important to note the difference between a reference section and a bibliography. A bibliography is a detailed list of references cited in your research paper, plus background readings or other material that you may have read but not cited. In other words, while a reference section includes only the sources used for the paper, a bibliography additionally contains "not-cited" but useful sources that you want to suggest to readers. Fortunately for students, the APA style does not require bibliographies. Therefore, you should focus on finding and reading scholarly journal articles directly relevant to your research topic and citing them in the literature review section using the APA format. Later, you can reorganize the cited sources in detail for the reference section to complete your research paper.

Leveraging AI Technologies for the Academic Literature Review

In the dynamic world of academic research, the use of AI technologies has become increasingly common. These technologies offer invaluable tools for students, particularly in locating scholarly journal articles and enhancing the efficiency of literature review processes. AI technologies play a pivotal role in the context of literature review writing. They

Table 2.4 In-Text Citation Examples for a Paper Written in APA Style

Description of citation	Type of citation	Explanation	Example
Quote with author's name in text with designated page numbers	Narrative citation	The author's name is in the text with the date immediately after the author's last name in parentheses. At the end of the sentence, add the page number in parentheses. Use the abbreviation "p." for the page.	Sweeney (1995) demonstrated how to ". . ." (p. 36).
Paraphrasing with the author's name in the text	Narrative citation	The author's name is in the text with the date in parentheses after the author's last name.	Sweeney (1999) shared the same theories as well.
Paraphrasing with the author's name in parentheses	Parenthetical citation	Add the author and date in parentheses.	The findings were also shared in other journal articles (Sweeney, 2000).
Source with two authors in the text	Narrative citation	List both authors in the text. Separate the authors with the word "and." Add the date in parentheses immediately after the last name of the second author.	Sweeney and Odgen (1993) argued . . .
Source with two authors in parentheses	Parenthetical citation	List both authors and date in parentheses. Separate the authors with an ampersand (&).	The authors proved the facts were true (Sweeney & Odgen, 1993).
Source with no author in parentheses	Parenthetical citation	Give the title of the work in place of the author. Abbreviate a few words if the title is long and complicated. Italicize a book title.	This book describes a historical event (*Effective Management*, 2018).
Quote from a website or electronic source with no page number	Parenthetical citation	Include the author's name, the date, and the paragraph number.	Furthermore, the research found that ". . ." (Sweeney, 2024, para. 4).

Note. Adapted from The College of St. Scholastica. (2021). *Citation help for APA, 7th edition: In-text citations.* https://libguides.css.edu/APA7thEd/Citations.

aid in synthesizing information from a variety of sources. Tools such as text mining and sentiment analysis help students identify trends, patterns, and gaps in existing literature. This facilitates a more nuanced understanding of communication strategies within the field of strategic communication.[6] By automating the extraction of key concepts and themes, AI-powered tools expedite the identification of relevant arguments. This fosters a more structured and comprehensive literature review. Furthermore, advanced AI-driven content summarization tools assist students in condensing lengthy articles into concise summaries, aiding in the synthesis of complex information.

While the integration of AI technologies in literature review processes presents numerous advantages, it is crucial to acknowledge potential challenges. Overreliance on AI tools may result in algorithmic biases, which could limit the diversity of perspectives within the synthesized literature.[7] Additionally, the ethical implications of AI use in research, such as data privacy concerns and potential misuse, require careful consideration. AI systems' ability to process complex search queries and provide tailored recommendations can save students valuable time and effort in identifying relevant articles for their research projects. Furthermore, AI-powered citation and reference management tools can assist students in organizing and citing their sources accurately, contributing to the overall quality of their academic work.

The incorporation of AI technologies in the exploration of scholarly journal articles and the writing of literature review sections equips students in strategic communication research with powerful tools to enhance efficiency and accuracy. As technology continues to advance, it is essential for students and researchers alike to responsibly embrace these innovations, recognizing the opportunities and challenges they bring to the academic landscape.

Application of an AI-Powered Tool

Box 2.2
Microsoft Copilot's Advice for Better Writing

Using an AI-Powered Tool (Microsoft Copilot) to Explore the Possibility of Better Writing

Command syntax: Offer college students some advice on how to create error-free and well-written papers, including any writing assistance they could get from Microsoft Copilot, websites, apps, and new technology instead of writing center tutors.

Answer:

1. Use Microsoft Copilot for writing assistance: You can ask me for help with rewriting, improving, or optimizing your content. Simply type in your request and I'll provide you with suggestions on how to improve your writing.

2. Use grammar and spelling checkers: There are many websites and apps that can help you check your grammar and spelling. Some popular options include Grammarly, Hemingway, and ProWritingAid. These tools can help you identify and correct errors in your writing.
3. Use citation generators: Properly citing your sources is important to avoid plagiarism. There are many citation generators available online that can help you create citations in the appropriate format for your paper. Some popular options include EasyBib, Citation Machine, and BibMe.
4. Use new technology: There are many new technologies available that can help you improve your writing. For example, voice-to-text software can help you dictate your thoughts and ideas, while text-to-speech software can help you listen to your writing and identify errors or awkward phrasing.
5. Understand the assignment: Read the instructions carefully and understand what is expected of you.
6. Research with ruthless efficiency: Use credible sources and take notes while researching.
7. Create a flat outline: Organize your ideas into an outline before you start writing.
8. Create the perfect writing environment: Find a quiet place to write and eliminate distractions.
9. Follow a standard structure: Use an introduction, body paragraphs, and conclusion.
10. Focus on quality over quantity: Write clear and concise sentences that convey your ideas effectively.
11. Draft and edit separately: Write your first draft without worrying about errors, then edit it later.
12. Write the conclusion and introduction last: Write the body of your paper first, then write the introduction and conclusion.

I hope these tips are helpful!

Summary

- ✓ Research in strategic communication pursues practical findings that can be used by government, corporations, and any type of organization.
- ✓ Research topics in strategic communication can be related to the subjects of advertising, social and traditional media, public relations, marketing, and communication technology.
- ✓ Selecting and narrowing a research topic requires pre-research questions to answer.
- ✓ Research models such as deductive reasoning and inductive reasoning contain theory and data.
- ✓ The academic research paper structure has specific sections of introduction, literature review, method, results, and discussion/conclusion.
- ✓ Primary and secondary sources are both used for research papers.
- ✓ Boolean search is a way of finding scholarly journal articles.
- ✓ Scholarly, trade, and popular publications have different characteristics.
- ✓ A literature review is a study of scholarly sources.
- ✓ A literature review has different forms such as summary, chronological, theoretical, and pros and cons.
- ✓ Scholarly journal articles serve as the main source for the literature review section.
- ✓ The APA style is widely practiced in social science writing.
- ✓ Researchers in strategic communication adapt to the latest version of the APA style in the 7th edition released in October 2019.
- ✓ References include only cited sources in the research paper.
- ✓ In-text citations correspond to entries in the references section.
- ✓ The incorporation of AI technologies in the exploration of scholarly journal articles and the writing of literature review sections equips students in strategic communication research with powerful tools to enhance efficiency and accuracy.

Key Terms

1. Research topic
2. Deduction versus induction
3. Scholarly journal articles
4. Boolean search

5. Primary sources
6. APA style
7. Research paper structure
8. Literature review
9. Reference
10. Peer review

Chapter 3

Ethics of Research in Strategic Communication

Chapter Learning Outcomes

- Become aware of historical cases of unethical research.
- Recognize principles of ethical research.
- Apply ethical codes to protection for participants.
- Describe philosophical foundations for research ethics.
- Explain the process of going through IRB approval.
- Practice IRB proposal writing.
- Recognize the format of informed consent.
- Describe the concepts of fabrication, falsification, and plagiarism.
- Discuss several advantages of online research.
- Apply AI tools to screen plagiarism.

Strategic communication research aims to explore and provide answers for specific groups or organizations in society. It seeks to offer practical solutions and suggestions for communication issues that individuals encounter daily. Humans communicate in various settings, both physical and virtual, whether in person or through communication technologies. Communication researchers study all forms of communication, including verbal, nonverbal, written, and visual. These forms of communication revolve around humans and their communication activities.

Research in Ethical Situations

Strategic communication research is a broad and constantly evolving field, with new communication technologies and social media platforms emerging regularly. Strategic communication researchers play a vital role in helping people communicate more effectively in this rapidly changing world. When studying people, researchers have a responsibility to protect their research participants from physical and psychological harm. For a strategic communication researcher, ethical considerations play a pivotal role in conducting scientific research right from the very beginning of the research process. Ethics in research is not an absolute science but rather involves essential guidelines and behavioral generalizations accepted in the practice of communication research. These guidelines serve as a strong reminder to prioritize human safety while conducting research.

Consider the following hypothetical situations from an ethical perspective:

- To develop a curriculum module to educate college students about the consequences of alcohol abuse, a researcher recruits 10 freshmen and makes them drink a bottle of whiskey a day for a month.
- To study the impact of pornography on human brains, a researcher recruits 20 fraternity members on campus and forces them to watch nothing but pornographic movies for 16 hours a day for a week.
- To test the effect of fake news, a researcher posts a fake video on the college's official Instagram page saying that the college bookstore is about to give away 500 new iPhones on a first-come, first-served basis.
- To prove students' obedience to professors, a researcher recruits an entire class of 50 students in a communication course and asks them to answer a questionnaire with 300 lascivious questions if they do not want to receive an F.
- To objectively observe students' online shopping behavior, a researcher moves into a campus dorm and installs IP address tracking devices in the building, but the dorm residents have no information about the devices.
- To test the power of social media influencers, the researcher asks 50 TikTok influencers to post short videos of themselves smoking marijuana and tell their followers to do the same.

These scenarios highlight the importance of ethical considerations in strategic communication research. They serve as reminders of the potential ethical dilemmas researchers may face and the need for ethical guidelines to navigate these challenges, including such questions as: How do you feel about such hypothetical situations if you are a researcher? Do you think the procedures should be considered acceptable in pursuit of scientific research? Where is the line you should draw at ethical research? Who should have the authority to make an ethical decision in the middle of conducting research? More importantly, how would you know whether you conducted ethical or unethical research?

Historical Background of Research Ethics

Research ethics in most academic fields has largely been shaped by issues related to the use of human subjects. When a researcher, whether a professional or a student, conducts research, the outcomes typically stem from the analysis of data obtained through intervention or interaction with real people. Throughout the history of research involving human subjects, several cases provide valuable insights into the current state of research ethics.

The Tuskegee Syphilis Study (1932–1972)

The U.S. Public Health Service (PHS) conducted a syphilis study in Macon County, Alabama, an area known as the "Black Belt" where most residents were Black sharecroppers. The study, officially titled the "Tuskegee Study of Untreated Syphilis in the Negro Male," aimed to examine untreated cases of latent syphilis in humans to determine the "natural course" of the disease.[1] Nearly 600 low-income African American males were recruited, 399 of whom were infected with syphilis and monitored for 40 years, along with 199 noninfected Black males.[2] Free medical examinations were given to those infected with syphilis, despite the lack of proven treatments for the disease in the 1930s when the study was conducted. Even after penicillin became the recommended treatment for syphilis in the late 1940s, the researchers, hoping to track the disease's full progression, decided not to provide effective care. The study continued until 1972, resulting in 28 participants dying from syphilis, "100 more passing away from related complications, at least 40 spouses being diagnosed with it, and the disease being passed to 19 children at birth."[3]

This tragic event could have been halted sooner when Peter Buxton, a PHS venereal disease investigator, filed an official report on ethical grounds to his superiors in 1966. However, his protest was declined in the name of the incomplete study. The study continued until Buxton leaked information about it to the media in 1972. A class-action lawsuit was filed the following year on behalf of the study's surviving participants and the heirs of those who had died, resulting in a $10 million out-of-court settlement. Congress found the study ethically unjustified, and President Bill Clinton issued an apology in 1997, stating, "The United States government did something that was wrong—deeply, profoundly, morally wrong," and the researchers who conducted the study at Tuskegee diminished "the stature of man by abandoning the most basic ethical precepts."[4]

The Milgram Experiment

In 1963, Yale University psychology professor Stanley Milgram sought to understand the concepts of obedience and authority. He tested the extent of humans' willingness to obey orders from an authority figure. He instructed the participant, dubbed "the teacher," to read out strings of words to his partner, dubbed "the learner," who was hooked up to an electric shock machine in another room. Each time the learner answered incorrectly by repeating the words, the teacher was asked to deliver a shock of increasing intensity, starting at 15 volts (labeled "slight shock" on the machine) and going up to 450 volts ("danger: severe shock").[5] In the experimental setting, the learner was an actor, a part of Milgram's research team, while the teacher was a real participant in the research. Located in a separate room from the teacher, the learner purposely gave the wrong answer to receive fake shocks with painful screams, even though the voltage was not connected to the learner's body. The teacher was forced to give a higher shock to the learner with each wrong answer during the process, and some of the teachers refused to continue the shocks due to emotional distress.

Some of the participants wanted to quit, but they stayed because the professor in charge insisted that they continue shocking the learner. Many participants, however, did not protest and even administered what they considered the highest and potentially lethal shock to the learner, even when the learner yelled about his poor heart condition and then fell alarmingly silent. Milgram found that 65% of the teachers were willing to progress to the maximum voltage level, even though many of them begged for the experiment to stop but continued the shocks. Milgram concluded that many people, but not all, tend to obey even the most abhorrent of orders by authority.[6] Some of the teachers even transferred the blame to the learner, claiming that the learner was too foolish and stubborn. The Milgram experiment drew heavy criticism on ethical grounds because the teacher was not informed about the fake shocks and was led to believe that the learner was harmed by their choices.

The Stanford Prison Experiment

In 1971, Professor Philip G. Zimbardo of Stanford University intended to measure the effect of role-playing, labeling, and social expectations on behavior, with the hypothesis that brutality reported among U.S. prison guards stems from the violent personalities of the guards, and if not, the prison environment causes the guards to be brutal to prisoners. Zimbardo converted a basement of the psychology building into a mock prison on campus and recruited 24 research participants who would play the roles of guards and prisoners, randomly dividing them into equal groups of 12 each. The group of guards, wearing sunglasses and khaki uniforms, had the freedom to do "whatever they thought was necessary to maintain law and order in the prison and to command the respect of the prisoners."[7]

Soon after the prisoners were transported to the mock prison, the guards searched them naked, gave them prison uniforms, and booked them into prison cells. Zimbardo, who acted as the prison warden, allowed the guards and prisoners to interact in any way they planned. On the first day, the guards began to awaken the prisoners at 2 a.m. for counts and inflicted physical punishment. In response, the prisoners staged a rebellion the next day, removing their stocking caps and ripping off their prison uniform numbers. However, the guards became violent and used fire extinguishers to quell the riot. After the incident, the guards became more aggressive and abusive toward the prisoners, while the prisoners became passive and submissive. Several days later, the guards expected greater obedience from the prisoners, and the prisoners tried to please the guards by telling on other prisoners. The experimental research resulted in emotional breakdowns

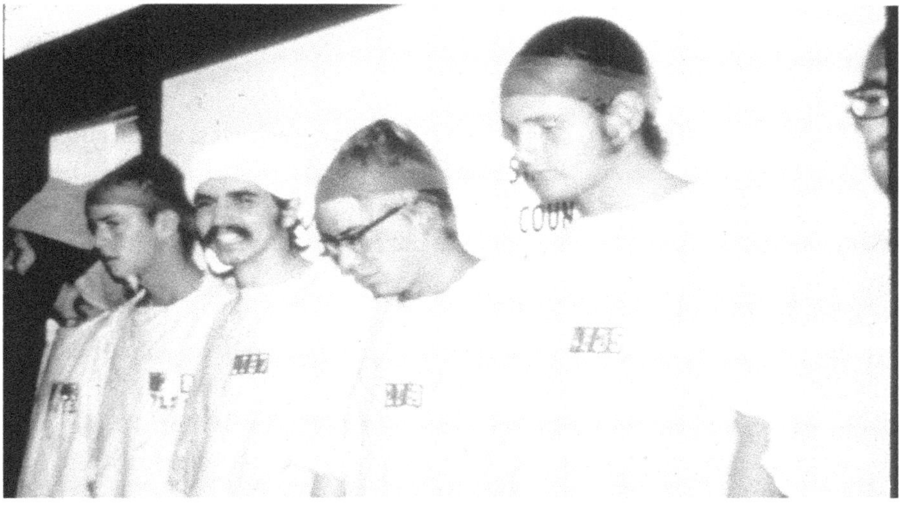

Figure 3.1 Lineup photo from the Stanford Prison Experiment movie
Source: From PrisonExp.org.

of prisoners and excessive hostility from the guards, so Zimbardo had to end the process on the sixth day instead of continuing the 14-day plan.

Professor Zimbardo concluded that innocent people in a situation where they have power over others tend to abuse that power, while people in powerless situations tend to behave submissively. The Stanford prison experiment, cited as a notorious example of unethical research, was made into a movie with the same title in 2015. More strikingly, it turned out that Zimbardo purposely increased tension between the guards and the prisoners with strategies such as sleep deprivation and physical abuse to elicit the conclusion in a way that he wanted, where societal roles and expectations can influence a person's behavior. See figure 3.1.

All three cases of historical research on ethical grounds were not academically scrutinized while being conducted in those days. Regarding the safety and well-being of human research participants, they raised the question of whether the end goal of the research justifies the means to find new groundbreaking outcomes despite the danger of harming people. These unfortunate research practices on human beings raised public awareness of ethical issues:

- lack of informed consent
- coercion or undue pressure on volunteers
- exploitation of a vulnerable population
- withholding information and available treatment
- putting subjects at risk

- deception
- violation of rights[8]

The U.S. government's official involvement in human research ethics began in the mid-1970s. This led to the creation of the Office for Protection from Research Risks (OPRR) and the development of Subpart A, also known as the Common Rule. This rule established the fundamental ethical guidelines for all human research conducted in the country.

Philosophical Foundations of Ethics

As researchers, we contemplate research and ethics, evaluating beliefs about which ethical perspective best aligns with our research practice. The field of ethics or moral philosophy guides us by suggesting concepts of right and wrong behavior in human activity. Ethical research can be seen as an expression of how we should behave as researchers in society. Ethics and research are deeply intertwined in the research process of moral judgment, and various philosophical foundations guide us to make ethical research decisions. We will discuss three guiding foundations to explore philosophical boundaries in ethics: utilitarianism, Kantianism, and virtue ethics.

Utilitarianism

Utilitarianism provides an answer to the practical question: "What ought a person to do?"[9] The answer is that an individual should act in a way that maximizes happiness or pleasure and minimizes unhappiness or pain. English philosophers Jeremy Bentham and John Stuart Mill popularized utilitarianism, which emphasizes results rather than rules. Utilitarian philosophers believe that the ethically correct course of action is the one that leads to the greatest amount of utility or usefulness. Utilitarianism, a form of consequentialism, is exemplified by the adage "The end justifies the means." It guides people to choose the right action in a situation where an action is right if and only if the sum of utilities produced by that action is greater than the sum of any other action available to us. In brief, utilitarianism suggests that the ideal ethical choice is the one that creates the greatest good for the greatest number in society. However, such a choice is often criticized for justifying military force, war, and greedy business practices. Utilitarianism can resonate with research practice in which the researcher is willing to sacrifice one participant to benefit a greater number for significant research outcomes.

Kantianism

Developed primarily by Immanuel Kant, a German philosopher, Kantianism posits that human life is valuable because humans are capable of rational behavior. Kantianism suggests that an action is only good if it is guided by a universal moral law, and humans have a sense of the categorical imperative as a way of evaluating motivations for action. Kant emphasized that certain types of wrongdoing committed by human—including deception, murder, and robbery—must be prohibited, even in cases where the action would bring about good consequences. Kant also argued that because humans are free rational beings capable of rational behavior, they see themselves as understanding subjects of the natural law with the autonomy of free will, by which they must act under the universal law. The categorical imperative, as the moral yardstick, emphasizes that every act we commit should be based on "maxims," which are essentially the "why" behind our actions. This raises the question of whether we would want maxims to be universal laws.[10] Kantianism tells us to only choose an act if we would want every person on earth to act in a way that demonstrates respect for others. In the research process, Kantianism can resonate with the practice that the researcher respects the autonomy and dignity of participants.

Virtue Ethics

Living and acting virtuously requires possessing moral characteristics known as virtues. The founding fathers of virtue ethics, Plato and Aristotle, believed that helping others is a charitable act for a virtue ethicist, as opposed to a utilitarian who considers the consequences of helping others for their benefit. This philosophical foundation emphasizes the importance of virtuous qualities rather than fulfilling one's duty or acting to bring about good consequences. According to Aristotle, a virtuous individual is someone who has developed internal traits that align with living a life of moral character. To nurture virtue, Aristotle suggested practicing honesty, bravery, justice, kindness, and generosity toward others, allowing an honorable and moral character to develop naturally into a permanent virtue. While virtue ethics does not provide specific guidance on how to be virtuous, it leads individuals to pursue rational reasoning for excellence and become morally admirable. In the research process, virtue ethics can inspire researchers to conduct morally righteous research.

To illustrate the difference among the three philosophical foundations of ethics in a *New York Times* column, ethics scholars Mark White and Robert Arp used the film *The Dark Knight*.[11]

- Utilitarianism, based on the work of Jeremy Bentham and John Stuart Mill, would probably endorse killing the Joker, based on comparing the many lives saved against the one life lost.
- Kantianism, stemming largely from the writings of Immanuel Kant, would focus on the act of murder itself, rather than the consequences. Kant's position would not support any person (such as Batman) killing the Joker.
- Virtue ethics, dating back to the ancient Greeks (such as Aristotle), would highlight the character of the person who kills the Joker. Does Batman want to be the kind of person that takes his enemies' lives? If he killed the Joker, would he be able to stop there, or would every two-bit thug get the same treatment?

Ethical Codes and Principles

Conducting research involving human beings often presents complex and evolving ethical considerations. While researchers may rely on their intuition and moral values to guide their work, determining what is ethically right or wrong can be challenging. This issue affects the global research community, leading to the development of various guidelines and codes of research ethics worldwide. One landmark document in this field is the Nuremberg Code, developed in response to abuses in medical experimentation on humans. Originating from the Nuremberg trials of Nazi physicians and investigators, the code sets out explicit requirements for voluntary consent from research participants as follows:

- Informed consent is essential.
- Research should avoid all unnecessary physical and mental suffering and injury.
- Only qualified researchers must conduct research.
- The results must hold the promise of benefit to society.
- Voluntary withdrawal of subjects is allowed.
- Research will be terminated at any stage if research subjects are likely to be harmed.[12]

Although now viewed as a fundamental ethical standard for human research, the Nuremberg Code was not initially well received by researchers in the United States, primarily because it was created to condemn the heinous actions of Nazi doctors. Instead, the Declaration of Helsinki, which outlines ethical principles for medical research involving human subjects, gained universal acceptance. The World Medical Association developed the declaration in 1964 and has since revised it multiple times, most recently in 2013. To summarize, the declaration provides a set of ethical guidelines for medical research involving human subjects:

- Research should be reviewed by an independent ethics committee.
- Informed consent should be required.
- Research should be conducted by qualified individuals.
- Potential benefits must outweigh risks of harm, and risk can be managed.
- Research should protect human dignity.
- Participation is voluntary and subjects are fully informed.[13]

The Declaration of Helsinki provides a set of ethical guidelines for medical research involving human subjects and laid the foundation for the establishment of the institutional review board (IRB).

In the United States, following the Tuskegee study, Congress passed the National Research Act of 1974, creating the National Commission for the Protection of Human Subjects of Biomedical and Behavioral Research. This commission published the Belmont Report in 1979, while scholarly associations for academic disciplines have introduced more customized ethical guidelines relevant to their research areas. The Belmont Report identifies three basic ethical principles:

- Respect for persons: Individuals should be treated as autonomous agents, and second, persons with diminished autonomy are entitled to protection.
- Beneficence: Two general rules have been formulated as complementary expressions of beneficent actions in this sense: (1) do not harm and (2) maximize possible benefits and minimize possible harms.
- Justice: Fair procedures and outcomes in selecting research subjects should be applied to each person with an equal share, according to merit.[14]

Whereas the Belmont Report was created by the government and Congress, scholarly associations for academic disciplines introduce more customized ethical guidelines relevant to their research areas. For example, the Association for Education in Journalism and Mass Communication (AEJMC) outlines eight ethical guidelines for research practices and research papers:

1. Plagiarism and conflict of interest violate ethical research standards.
2. Knowingly causing harm to research participants is unethical.
3. Data collection, processing, and analysis must be undertaken with integrity.
4. Research studies must be reported accurately and objectively.
5. Authorship credit must be fair, accurate, and without conflict of interest.
6. Only original work may be submitted for publication.
7. Ethical research principles should guide the supervision of students and mentoring of junior faculty.
8. Ethical research standards should guide the handling of manuscripts by editors, editorial boards, research chairs, and reviewers.[15]

Strategic communication researchers now have an abundance of ethical guidelines and codes to consider when conducting research involving human beings. When referring to the people who participate in strategic communication research, various descriptive terms are available, such as *subjects*, *informants*, *respondents*, and *participants*, as follows:

- In traditional experimental designs, research subjects are often treated as pawns in the pursuit of knowledge, rather than as individuals with their own agency and autonomy.
- Informants are considered naive, so they must be instructed by the researcher about what is going on in a setting, about cultural rules, and so forth.
- Respondents are those who answer questionnaires in survey designs, telling the researcher exactly what the research asks: no more, no less.
- Participants indicate the most active role of the people who are being researched, and most researchers in strategic communication prefer "research participants" over other terms.[16]

Regardless of what research participants are called, the number-one priority of ethical research can be summarized as doing no harm to them. However, most codes appear a bit vague or too general to provide researchers with specific information on a case-by-case basis. Thus, college students and professors conducting research turn to institutional review boards for detailed instructions.

Institutional Review Boards

The institutional review board is a formal committee tasked with reviewing and monitoring research involving human subjects and animals. The IRB oversees all research proposals of institutions that receive federal funding. Most colleges and universities in the United States have review boards for research conducted on campus. The primary purpose of the IRB is to ensure that appropriate measures are taken to protect the rights and well-being of humans participating in research. Therefore, academic institutions engaged in research involving human subjects typically have their own IRBs to oversee research procedures conducted within the institution or by its faculty, staff, and students. Most college IRBs share a similar mission statement: To ensure that all research participants are treated fairly and ethically while assisting researchers in including research participants in their study designs and implementation.[17]

Although the policies and procedures of the IRB may vary among colleges or universities, all research projects involving human subjects conducted by students and professors are expected to be reviewed and approved by the campus IRB. According to the U.S. Department of Health and Human Services, a human subject is defined as "a living individual about whom an investigator (whether professional or student) conducting research obtains data."[18] Prior to beginning the research, it is important to recognize the authority of the IRB, which can approve, require modifications for approval (pending), or disapprove your research project. Generally, after completing the Collaborative Institutional Training Initiative (CITI) program, you as a student researcher are required to write a research proposal to obtain IRB approval for your research project. The research proposal, which describes your study plan, typically includes:

- research questions and/or hypotheses
- background information on the research
- relevant literature on the topic
- research design with methodology and data analysis
- research procedures, including information on participants and informed consent
- a statement of privacy and confidentiality
- a statement of benefits and risks of the research

After writing your proposal and developing supplemental materials such as consent forms and data collection instruments, the next step is to submit the proposal to the IRB, which will process the proposal and consider it for approval or disapproval.

Informed Consent

One of the most important responsibilities for researchers is to obtain informed consent from potential research participants. Individuals who are willing to participate in human research agree to a process of communication with the researcher, who should explain what is involved in advance of the research practice. The concept of informed consent is to educate potential research participants about the key components of the research, as the informed consent process aims to achieve ethical conduct of research with human subjects. Obtaining the consent of potential participants means that the researcher cannot force individuals into participating in research against their will. The federal standard requires that potential participants are given all related information that might reasonably influence their willingness to participate in a form of research. As the concept and practice of informed consent have evolved in ethics and research, a checklist of the U.S. Department of Health and Human Services for informed consent is considered the most notable guidance available, as follows:

- a statement that the study involves research, including an explanation of the purposes
- the expected duration of the subject's participation;
- a description of the procedures to be followed, including foreseeable risks;
- a description of any benefits to the subject or to others, including any compensation;
- a statement describing the extent, if any, to which confidentiality of records identifying the subject will be maintained;

- an explanation of the research subjects' rights, and whom to contact in the event of a research-related injury to the subject;
- a statement that participation is voluntary and that refusal to participate will involve no penalty or loss of benefits to which the subject is otherwise entitled.[19]

Informed consent creates responsibilities for the researcher to provide research information in writing for potential participants. The written form of informed consent is commonly provided by the college's IRB. Box 3.1 provides an example of an informed consent form for college students and professors:

Box 3.1
INFORMED CONSENT FORM

UNIVERSITY OF XXXXXXXXX
INFORMED CONSENT FORM

Study title:
Name of participant:
Principal researcher: Telephone: xxx-xxxx

KEY INFORMATION ABOUT THE STUDY

- Take your time and ask to have any words or information that you do not understand explained to you.
- What will you do if you agree to be in the study?
- Can you be harmed by being in this study?
    - Risks to your personal privacy and confidentiality: Your participation in this research will be held strictly confidential and only a code number will be used to identify your stored data.
    - You will receive XX for participating in the study.
- What other choices do you have if you decide not to be in the study?
    - You can stop participating at any time.

How will my privacy be protected?

- Your information will be stored with a code instead of identifiers (such as name, date of birth, email address, etc.).
- No published scientific reports will identify you directly.

Who to contact regarding your rights as a participant

This research has been reviewed and approved by the University of Xxxxxxxxx Institutional Review Board for Human Subjects Protections (IRB). If you have any questions about your rights as a participant, please contact the IRB at (xxx) xxx-xxxx or irb@xxxxxxxxx.edu.

Signatures

By signing below, you indicate that you are voluntarily agreeing to participate in this study and that the procedures involved have been described to your satisfaction. To participate, you must be at least 18 years of age. If you are under 18, please inform the researcher.

____ ___/___/___

Participant's Signature Date

Most cases of strategic communication research with human participants simply require informed consent signed by the participants, but some exceptional cases require more than signed forms. For example, if you as a researcher are interested in exploring the relationship between elementary school students and their dream of becoming YouTubers, you might need to obtain permission from superintendents, principals, teachers, and parents of the children. When uncertain about any informed consent issues, you should consult with the IRB on campus. Before the research begins, you must inform the participants of what the research is about and how it will proceed. After gaining informed consent, you must conduct your research while upholding participants' rights to confidentiality and privacy. Confidentiality refers to an agreement about the maintenance of and who has access to identifiable data, and privacy is a right to be protected belonging to the participant, not the researcher.

Upon the completion of their involvement in your study, participants may anticipate a debriefing session where you share the purpose of the research and the overall findings. Notably, it is imperative to provide a debriefing when participants have been subjected to deception. For example, some research activities involve deceptive scenarios in which the researcher gives misinformation to the participants or purposely misleads them about some key aspect of the research. The Milgram obedience experiment is a well-known example of deceptive research. According to the American Psychological Association (APA), researchers only use deceptive methods when "the use of deceptive techniques is justified by the study's significant prospective scientific, educational or applied value," as well as when effective nondeceptive alternative procedures are not feasible.[20]

Ethical Issues in Reporting Research

Researchers also have a responsibility to adhere to ethical standards when reporting their data after gathering responses from research participants. Reporting data implies conducting scientific and honest analyses of data without research misconduct, which refers to fabrication, falsification, or plagiarism in reviewing research or reporting research outcomes. According to the Office of Research Integrity under the U.S. Department of Health and Human Services, the definitions of these terms are as follows:

- Fabrication is making up data or results and recording or reporting them.
- Falsification is manipulating research materials, equipment, or processes or changing or omitting data or results such that the research is not accurately represented in the research record.
- Plagiarism is the appropriation of another person's ideas, processes, results, or words without giving appropriate credit.[21]

In other words, honesty is the most prominent rule to avoid research misconduct, especially for data analysis and paper writing. Researchers are expected to process the task of data analysis using academically proven qualitative or quantitative methods. Some researchers under pressure are vulnerable to data fabrication or falsification to produce significant or groundbreaking research outcomes. Both omissions of data, information, and results and fabricating sources of information are considered common unethical issues in reporting research. In addition, some researchers are often accused of artificially creating data to make parts of their reporting look important and innovative.

The most concerning ethical issue in reporting research for college students is plagiarism, a common form of research misconduct. Plagiarism occurs when the student directly copies phrases or sentences from a text (e.g., journal articles, books) and fails to provide quotation marks and citations. Other types of plagiarism include paraphrasing or summarizing other people's ideas without giving credit to the sources. In a similar vein, accidental plagiarism happens when students neglect to cite their sources or misquote "their sources, or unintentionally paraphrase a source by using similar words, groups of words, and/or sentence structure without attribution."[22] To avoid plagiarism, the APA suggests that students provide appropriate credit to the sources by adding "author-date in-text citations for direct quotations and ideas"[23] (see Chapter 14 for detailed information).

Online Research Ethics

With a wealth of research conducted online in the digital age, researchers are facing new ethical issues due to the lack of clear guidelines or regulations about online research. Conducting research online involves the collection of information in a way that researchers use online focus groups, online interviews, and online surveys. Two immense merits of online research are (1) having rapid access to a large number of research participants and (2) spending little or almost no money. Researchers use online tools to collect data while asking participants particular questions. Sending research participants a web link for an online survey via email is convenient and easy, but there are key ethical issues that come with online research:

- Informed consent: Although the researcher asks participants to sign the consent form online, some of them will skip the process because they simply ignore or do not see the form. In addition, someone else can sign the form on behalf of the participant, which can raise problems in establishing the authenticity of participants.
- The public/private debate: Research participants may feel more comfortable online because of their expectation of privacy. Sometimes, however, they tend to express more offensive or vulgar language irrelevant to their research responses.
- Anonymity: Research participants are guaranteed their online anonymity by the researcher, but digital footprints and online search engines may allow others to trace back and identify them.[24]

Ethics in research, both online and offline, places great emphasis on the safety of human participants. For online research, it is advisable for students to refer to the ethical research guidelines of their college's institutional review board. However, with the advent of artificial intelligence (AI) and related software (e.g., ChatGPT, Google Gemini, Microsoft Copilot), coupled with the trend of interdisciplinary research for big data, research ethics has become more complex. IRBs and government agencies are grappling with new ethical challenges and are developing fresh guidelines to tackle them. Thus, researchers must stay abreast of the latest regulatory ethical policies.

AI Tools and Plagiarism

In the digital age, AI tools have become increasingly prevalent in various fields, including academic research. Such AI tools can generate text that might be used in research papers. However, in order to maintain academic integrity, it is crucial to understand the ethical implications of using these tools. When using AI-powered tools to create research papers, students must avoid presenting the generated text as their own work. This is considered plagiarism, a serious academic offense.

Plagiarism is not just copying and pasting from a source without citation, but also presenting someone else's work, including work generated by AI, as the student's own original idea. To prevent plagiarism, the student should always cite any sources used, including text generated by AI tools. This includes not only direct quotes but also paraphrased information. Proper citation allows readers to trace the origin of the information and gives credit to the original author or tool that generated the information. Moreover, while AI tools can provide valuable information and insights, they should not replace the student's own ideas and conclusions. Students should incorporate their own critical thinking and analysis into their writing. This not only helps to avoid plagiarism but also contributes to a more robust and insightful research paper.

Understanding the ethical considerations of utilizing AI tools in academic work is essential. These tools should be used responsibly and ethically. They are meant to assist in the research process, not to shortcut it. If students are unsure about whether using an AI tool could be considered plagiarism, they should seek guidance from their professors or institution. Many educational institutions provide resources and guidelines on how to avoid plagiarism and maintain academic integrity when it comes to using AI-generated content.[25] While AI tools can be a valuable asset in academic research, they must be used responsibly and ethically. Always remember to cite your sources correctly, include your own analysis and insights, and, when in doubt, seek guidance. This will ensure that you maintain academic integrity and produce high-quality, original research.

Application of an AI-Powered Tool

Box 3.2
ChatGPT's Advice on How to Use AI-Powered Tools to Avoid Academic Dishonesty

Using an AI-Powered Tool (ChatGPT) to Ask for AI Guidelines to Avoid Academic Dishonesty

Command syntax: There are concerns over AI-powered tools that can encourage college students to engage in academic dishonesty such as plagiarism. How can they use such AI tools academically without being involved in academic dishonesty?

Answer: AI-powered tools have become increasingly prevalent in academic writing, and they can provide valuable support for students without encouraging academic dishonesty. To use these tools effectively without being involved in academic dishonesty, college students should focus on using AI as an "assistant" rather than as a substitute for their own work. Here are some tips on how to use AI tools for academic writing without risking academic dishonesty:

1. Use AI tools for guidance and support: AI tools can be used to help with the research and writing process, but students should view them as assistants rather than replacements for their own work. For example, students can use AI-powered writing assistants to suggest potential topics, generate ideas, or provide feedback on grammar and style, but they should still rely on their own critical thinking and writing skills to develop their ideas and arguments.

2. Use multiple sources for verification: If students use AI-powered tools for research, they should cross-check the results with other sources to verify the accuracy and credibility of the information. Using multiple sources can help students avoid relying too heavily on a single tool or source, which can increase the risk of academic dishonesty.
3. Follow academic integrity policies: Students should familiarize themselves with their institution's policies on academic integrity and plagiarism, and ensure that their use of AI tools does not violate these policies. For example, some institutions may prohibit the use of AI tools to generate entire papers or to paraphrase large portions of existing work.
4. Verify and evaluate AI-generated content: Cross-verify AI-generated content with reliable sources. Students should critically assess the information provided by AI tools to ensure accuracy and relevance in their academic work.
5. Avoid copy-pasting output: While AI can aid learning and exploration of new topics, students should refrain from directly copy-pasting AI-generated outputs. Instead, use AI-generated content as a starting point for further research and original writing.

Overall, college students can use AI-powered tools for academic writing in a way that promotes academic integrity by using these tools as assistants rather than substitutes for their own work, verifying information from multiple sources, and following academic integrity policies. Additionally, students can benefit from personalized learning, feedback, and support provided by AI-powered educational tools while still upholding academic integrity.

SUMMARY

- ✓ Historical research cases on ethical grounds were not academically scrutinized.
- ✓ The safety and well-being of research subjects should always be a priority.
- ✓ Utilitarianism, Kantianism, and virtue ethics offer philosophical foundations for ethical development in research.
- ✓ Human beings are identified as subjects, informants, respondents, or participants in research.
- ✓ The Belmont Report highlights respect, beneficence, and justice in research.

- ✓ The institutional review board (IRB) is a formal group designated to review and monitor research involving human subjects and animals.
- ✓ The research proposal submitted to the IRB will be under consideration for approval or disapproval.
- ✓ Informed consent creates responsibilities for the researcher to provide research information in writing for potential participants.
- ✓ Research misconduct includes fabrication, falsification, and plagiarism in reporting research.
- ✓ Online research helps the researcher to access a large number of research participants and costs little.
- ✓ Many educational institutions provide resources and guidelines on how to avoid plagiarism and maintain academic integrity when it comes to using AI-generated content.

Key Terms

1. Research ethics
2. Debriefing
3. Informed consent
4. Ethical guidelines
5. Milgram experiment
6. Anonymity
7. Philosophical foundations
8. IRBs
9. Plagiarism
10. Online research ethics

Chapter 4

Sampling Techniques

Chapter Learning Outcomes

- Define a sample and a population.
- Recognize the different types of sampling between nonprobability and probability.
- Apply a sample to the population in terms of representative results.
- Discuss mistakes in sampling.
- Describe four methods of nonprobability sampling.
- Describe four methods of probability sampling.
- Explain the process of the sampling frame.
- Carry out the calculations of sampling error and sample size.
- Recognize the confidence interval and level.
- Identify the relationship between sample size and sampling error.
- Apply AI tools to sampling.

The choice of topic in research is often influenced by the researcher's academic interests. However, the selection of study participants is a more sophisticated process, involving various sampling methods and disciplines. This process is governed by sampling theory, a branch of statistics that guides the selection of a subset from a larger population for making inferences about the entire population.[1] Sampling theory provides a framework for understanding the reliability and accuracy of statistical inferences based on sample data. In strategic communication research, the relevance of research samples to research populations is crucial for achieving scientifically valid and reliable outcomes. To comprehend these complex concepts, it is essential to familiarize yourself with the key terms of sampling.

Population and Sample

Strategic communication research serves multiple purposes, one of which involves characterizing the nature of a population. A population encompasses all people or things—such as events, countries, or species—that the researcher studies. For example, if you aim to gather data on college students' preferred social media platforms, your population would be all 40,000 undergraduate students at your college. However, it is nearly impossible to collect data from every individual in a population. Therefore, researchers typically select a sample from the population to conduct efficient and scientific research. Studying an entire population is often unfeasible due to time and budget constraints. For instance, many governments conduct a census every decade to count the entire national population. The U.S. federal government counts all residents and citizens living in the country every decade using the U.S. Census (the U.S. population at the start of 2020 numbered just over 331 million people).[2] However, this approach is impractical for most research situations. Hence, researchers commonly select a representative sample from the population since selecting a representative sample from the population is the most effective approach in terms of conducting efficient and scientific research.

Researchers strive to choose a representative sample, often using a sampling frame, a list from which the sample is drawn. A good sampling frame for a research project involving human participants should be accurate, complete, up to date, accessible to the researcher, and unbiased, that is, not favoring any particular group. By using a representative sample and ensuring a proper sampling frame, researchers can draw valid conclusions about the population and make generalizations based on their findings.

A good sampling frame for a research project involving human participants should:

1. Include all individuals in the target population: for example, you decide to select a sample from your entire college student body of 40,000.
2. Exclude all individuals not in the target population: for example, you will not select anyone who does not attend your college during the semester of your research.
3. Identify accurate and up-to-date information for selected individuals: for example, you make sure that they are undergraduate students and go to class during the semester. (See figure 4.1.)

Following the sampling frame method, a representative sample should accurately reflect the targeted population group's characteristics, even though collecting a representative sample can be challenging.

There are two basic types of sampling among the various methods for selecting a representative sample: probability and nonprobability.

Probability and Nonprobability: The Two Types of Sampling Procedures

The primary distinction between probability and nonprobability sampling lies in randomness, which refers to the lack of pattern or predictability in events. Probability sampling

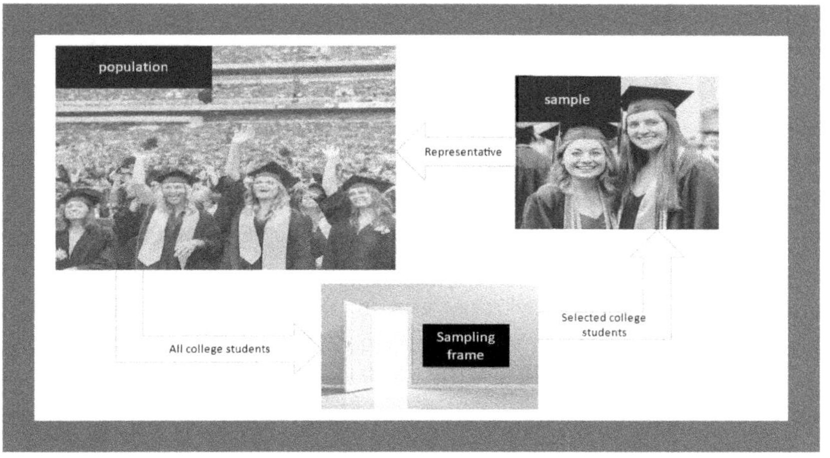

Figure 4.1 Sampling process
Source: Created by author.

allows for a random process in selecting a sample, while nonprobability sampling seldom allows for mathematical randomness. As a researcher, you must select the appropriate sampling procedure, considering the following factors:

- Research method: Qualitative research typically employs nonprobability sampling, while quantitative research favors probability sampling. Therefore, you must decide on the research method before selecting a sampling type.
- Cost and representation: Nonprobability sampling is more cost effective than probability sampling because the sample size is smaller. However, probability sampling offers better chances of producing more generalizable, valuable research outcomes.
- Time and data: Probability sampling allows for a larger sample size and quicker data analysis than nonprobability sampling because probability sampling uses formatted questions and statistical data analyses.
- Representativeness: Nonprobability sampling is less likely to accurately represent the population compared to probability sampling, which can produce statistical evidence for generalization.

Although no sampling method is perfect, it is widely agreed that probability sampling is more representative of the population for strategic communication research. However, this does not imply that nonprobability sampling is less valuable or trustworthy than probability sampling, as both are commonly used in the academic world.

Probability Sampling

Probability sampling is a technique where the researcher selects a sample from the target population using a method based on statistical probability. This method assumes that every member of the population has an equal chance of being selected to participate in the research. Probability sampling uses a statistical basis to randomly select a group of people (sample) from the entire population that the researcher aims to study. The key term for probability sampling is *random*, meaning that the chance of being selected is equal for each member of the population. Random selection reduces the researcher's bias because it does not allow the researcher to pick a sample based on their preference, ensuring that the sample is representative of the population. Because probability sampling primarily utilizes some form of random selection, you need to apply a more specific method to the process of choosing your sample. There are four main methods of probability sampling:

- Simple random sampling: This method is considered easy and quick as it ensures that all members of the population have an equal chance of being drawn. You can use techniques like lotteries or random draws. To perform simple random sampling, you assign each individual a number from 1 and select one person at a time until you recruit all members for your research sample. For example, if your research population is a total of 100 people and you need 10 of them as a sample, assign them numbers from 1 to 100 and randomly pick 10 numbers corresponding to the assigned people. Drawing numbers out of a hat, throwing dice, and lotteries are examples of simple random sampling. However, for a larger population, such as the 40,000 college students, a sample of 4,000 manual drawings can be burdensome. Selecting a random sample from a large population usually requires computer-generated numbers performed by a computerized algorithm.
- Stratified random sampling: One disadvantage of simple random sampling is that it may not select important subgroups in a population. For instance, if you choose 4,000 college students as a sample out of a population of 40,000, there is no guarantee that the 1,000 will be selected from each class standing of freshmen, sophomores, juniors, and seniors. Stratified random sampling, also referred to as proportional random sampling, involves dividing the population into subpopulations to ensure that every subgroup is properly represented in the sample. This sampling method allows separate classifications such as gender, level of income, or level of education. For example, if you need a sample of 10 people from a public relations firm that currently employs 80 female employees and 20 male employees, to ensure gender representation, you randomly select 8 women and 2 men who serve as a representative sample for all 100 employees. In essence, this method of

probability sampling is best used when you aim for precise outcomes that ensure the representativeness of each subgroup.

- Systematic random sampling: Unlike simple random sampling, systematic random sampling allows you to select members of the population at a regular interval (or *k*), determined in advance. You decide on the *n* (sample size) and randomly select an integer *k* after every member of the population is listed with a number. Finally, you take every *k*th unit or person. For example, if your population is 100 people and you want to take a sample of $n = 20$, you assign them a number from 1 to 100. To select 20 people out of 100, the interval size, *k*, is equal to 5, meaning that you select a random integer from 1 to 5. Let's say you decided on 3, and every third person will be selected as the sample with numbers 3, 8, 13, 18, . . . , 93, and 98. You end up with a sample of 20 people. One advantage of this method is that it creates a sample without using technology.
- Cluster sampling: Similar to stratified sampling, cluster sampling divides the population into groups, but it usually takes a large population that is dispersed over a wide geographic area. Cluster sampling involves a two-step procedure: (1) the entire population is selected and separated into different clusters, and then (2) a sample is chosen from these clusters. For example, if your research topic is Walmart and its image among shoppers nationwide, you may find it difficult to select the entire population of Walmart customers for research. So you create a random cluster of each Walmart store in each state (the first step). You select random customers of each Walmart as a sample (the second step). The method of cluster sampling allows you to choose a sample from a large and dispersed population, but it tends to have the potential of producing less accurate outcomes because of the large research scale and less homogeneous population. In other words, sampled clusters nationwide or in dispersed areas are less likely to be representative of the whole population.

Probability sampling maximizes the representativeness of the randomly drawn sample with respect to its population. Although no sampling type is flawless, probability sampling is commonly accepted as more representative of the population for research in strategic communication.

Nonprobability Sampling

Nonprobability sampling is based on the researcher's subjective judgment for choosing a sample, rather than using a random selection process. While random selection is generally recommended for scientific research, there are situations in strategic communication research where nonprobability sampling may provide more benefits than probability sampling. Nonprobability sampling involves nonrandom selection of a sample, meaning that not every individual in the population has an equal chance of being selected. While some researchers consider nonprobability sampling inferior to probability sampling due to the latter's representativeness of the population and objectivity of results, nonprobability sampling is a useful technique for studying small or underresearched populations, such as drug addicts, gang members, and sex workers. Rather than attempting to generalize outcomes and represent large populations, researchers using nonprobability sampling focus on exploring the details of a sample.

Here are four main methods of nonprobability sampling:

- Convenience sampling: A sample is selected from the population only because you choose some people at your convenience, or they are conveniently available to you as research participants. You simply select them as a sample because they are easy to recruit. You might have participated in research as a sample from one of your college classes because your professor conveniently recruited you and your classmates for his research project. In return, you might receive some extra credit. Most researchers have easy access to college students who are cooperative with research projects, but it is hard to generalize that a class of students can represent the entire population of the college. For example, it is unlikely that 20 students in the Introduction to Biology class are representative as a sample of the entire student body of 40,000 for research on college students' attitudes toward dating apps such as Tinder and Hinge. Convenience sampling can be useful when you need to obtain rapid results with a small sample size. Additionally, conducting research with a conveniently selected sample is simple because the sample is easily accessible, making data collection convenient. However, it is important to note that convenience sampling can be biased and may not accurately represent the entire population.
- Purposive sampling: Also known as *judgmental sampling*, purposive sampling is based on the idea that a specific person or communication unit will meet specific criteria the researcher is looking for. A purposive sample is chosen when you decide to select a sample based purely on your prior knowledge and interests regarding the characteristics of the population. To perform purposive sampling, you need to exclude individuals who do not fit a purposive profile when creating the sample. The purposively selected sample enables you to obtain valuable information from the data, as your prior knowledge enriches your research process. For example, if you, a former war veteran who returned to school, want to conduct research on the opinions and experiences of veteran students at your university, you purposefully select a certain number of students involved in campus veteran organizations and collect data on their campus experiences. You purposively selected the veteran sample because you know the war veteran lifestyle from your experience.

- Quota sampling: Almost identical to the stratified random sampling method of probability sampling, quota sampling allows you to divide the population into proportional strata or groups. The main difference between stratified sampling and quota sampling is that the former selects a random sample, and the latter does not require randomness in selecting a sample. In quota sampling, you choose a certain number of people from each of the distinct groups to include in the sample. For instance, if $n = 100$ is the intended sample size, you need to make sure that the age distribution in the sample is representative of the population. The human resources department of your college reports that 10% of the population is 18 years of age or younger, 70% is between the ages of 19 and 24, and 20% is 25 or older. You then sample $n = 10$ students who are 18 or younger, $n = 70$ between the ages of 19 and 24, and $n = 20$ who are 25 years of age and older. Since random sampling is not required for a quota sample, it may not be representative of the population.
- Snowball sampling: Also known as *network sampling*, this sampling technique relies on members of a network to introduce you to other members of the network. Snowball sampling is particularly suitable when the population you are interested in studying is socially marginalized or hard to find. Once you have recruited one participant, more participants can be introduced to you because the first participant acts like a rolling snowball, becoming bigger and bigger. Snowball sampling consists of two steps: (1) try to identify one potential participant in the desired population, and (2) use the potential participant to find and recruit more participants until the size of the sample you wish for is met. For example, if your research is investigating illegal immigrants and their free calling apps on smartphones, most potential participants living in the United States as illegal workers would be unlikely to participate in your research project. However, one potential participant can persuade others about the benefits of your research and reassure them of research confidentiality. The method of snowball sampling is usually chosen when there may be no other way of finding and recruiting the sample. Like other nonprobability sampling methods, snowball sampling is not considered to be representative of the population because the obtained sample consists only of a small number of voluntary participants.

Table 4.1 can help you to conceptualize probability sampling and nonprobability sampling.

Mistakes in Sampling History

Opinion polls, which predict the outcome of significant social and political events, are a popular type of research using samples. The accuracy of these polls, especially those for

Table 4.1 Comparison of Probability and Nonprobability Sampling

Probability sampling	Nonprobability sampling
The sample is randomly selected.	The sample is selected by the researcher's judgment.
Everyone in the population has an equal chance of being selected.	Not everyone has an equal chance of being selected.
The sample is considered nonbiased as the researcher assures the random process.	It is not a concern if the sample is biased or not.
It is used when the researcher pursues generalization of research outcomes.	It is used when the researcher pursues characteristics of particular subpopulations.
The sample is representative of the population.	The sample is not representative of the population.
Methods: • Simple random • Stratified random • Systematic • Cluster	Methods: • Convenience • Purposive • Quota • Snowball

U.S. presidential elections, heavily depends on the chosen sampling method. However, there have been instances of historical polling failures due to biased sampling mistakes. A notable example was the 1936 presidential election.

The *Literary Digest*, an influential American weekly magazine during the early 1900s, had correctly predicted the winner of each presidential election from 1920 to 1932. For the 1936 presidential election, the magazine predicted that the Republican candidate, Governor Alfred Landon of Kansas, would beat President Franklin Delano Roosevelt, the Democratic incumbent, in a landslide. This prediction was made after mailing out a questionnaire to 10 million people about their voting intentions. The *Literary Digest* received replies from 2.4 million voters (a response rate of 24%). Notably, a significant number of responses came from the magazine's readers, registered car owners, and telephone customers in 1936.[3]

However, on November 3, 1936, President Franklin Delano Roosevelt won 46 states, while Landon only won Maine and Vermont (523 electoral votes versus 8 electoral votes). Roosevelt also won the popular vote by over 24%.[4] Thanks to the loyal support of farmers, labor workers, and the poor, Roosevelt declared a landslide victory. So what went wrong with the magazine's prediction? The main factor in the failure of the *Literary Digest*'s poll was the sample frame. The poll year was 1936, when the United States was still suffering from poor economic conditions after the Great Depression. People who were affluent enough to afford cars, telephones, and magazine subscriptions in 1936 were relatively wealthier than the average person. The rich in the middle of the Great Depression tended to be Republican voters. The sample frame for the poll, which employed a set of lists of rich voters, was biased. The significance of the magazine's faulty prediction ended up ruining the magazine's credibility. As a result, the magazine with impressive records for predictions went out of business less than two years after the election, and its subscriber list was acquired by *Time* magazine.

The 1936 presidential election was a catastrophic event for the *Literary Digest*, but it was a blessing for another polling organization, the American Institute of Public Opinion, founded by George Gallup. Acknowledging that a large sample would not always predict precise outcomes, Gallup conducted polls using more systematic, scientific sampling techniques than the *Literary Digest* did.[5] Gallup correctly predicted that Roosevelt would win the Depression Era election after using a relatively smaller sample size of 50,000. Gallup sent out hundreds of interviewers across the country and asked them to use the method of stratified random sampling within subgroups of the population of voters, such as middle-class urban women and lower-class rural men.[6] The 1936 Gallup election poll put the new era of scientific surveys on the map thanks to probability sampling. The accuracy of sampling for Gallup stemmed from the random list of stratified subgroups he used, while the *Literary Digest*'s sampling frame was closer to convenience sampling obtained from groups of magazine readers, car owners, and people with home telephones.

Sample Size

Determining the best sample size for scientific research is a complex task. There is no fixed number or answer for an ideal sample size. The sample size refers to the number of participants or observations used for research, including public surveys and experiments. A group of participants selected from the general population should represent the real population. For example, if you want to predict how a specific ethnic group will respond to a new TV commercial, you need to test the commercial on a sample size that should be representative of the real population.

The right answer to the question of sample size depends on your research method. Some argue that around 1,500 people is an adequate sample size in most national research cases, so long as they are randomly chosen.[7] However, few researchers can afford a sample size over 1,000, or even over 100. So a better question about sample size is, "How small a sample can result in scientific results?" The answer depends on research topics, research questions, research methods, and analytical types of measurement. For example, qualitative research tends to select a smaller sample size than quantitative research.

As a researcher, you first determine how big or small a sample to obtain from the population. Generally, in terms of sample size, the bigger the sample the better. As the sample size increases, the margin of error (sampling error) decreases. In statistics, a larger sample size is supposed to reduce sampling error. If you have a larger sample size, it means that the sample is closer to being representative of the population. However, a larger sample does not always guarantee greater precision. Though there is no absolute answer that fits all research situations for the right sample size, there are decent guidelines to consider when you determine your sample size:

- Decide your research method: If you use the methods of focus group studies or in-depth interviews, either may require about 10 people for the sample. In contrast, for the method of a commercial marketing survey, you may typically need over 1,000 people. However, these are not definite numbers.
- Consider your resources: Research is a time-consuming and often expensive process for you. You can dream big with a sample of 1,000 for your research, but you should consider time and budget. In addition, a sample of 200 could possibly result in almost the same scientific outcomes.
- Choose a better sampling method: Instead of simple random sampling with a sample of 1,000, opting for stratified sampling with a sample of 100 could yield more accurate outcomes. A sample of 100 college students can be stratified into 4 groups of academic standings with 25 each representing the entire population on campus.
- See what other researchers did: Scholarly research articles relevant to your research topic and questions offer you a decent size for the sample. If reputable corporate communication articles used a sample of 200 for research on brands, you could use this to justify a similar sample size for your research.
- Refer to statistical suggestions: The optimal sample size varies based on statistics, such as the margin of error, confidence level, population, and sample proportion. For example, a 5% margin of error, a 95% confidence level, a population of 100,000 people, and a 50% sample proportion/ratio would lead you to choose a sample of 383 people. For your particular circumstances, you can use a sample size calculator available online (https://www.calculator.net/sample-size-calculator.html, see figure 4.2).

Although we plan to delve into fundamental statistics for strategic communication research in later chapters (Chapters 9 and 10), it is beneficial to have a preliminary understanding of sample size calculation. It is crucial to understand that there is no simple answer for the perfect sample size. However, statistical suggestions, especially for quantitative research, can be made with key terms and formulas as follows:

- Margin of error: This term expresses the size of the random sampling error in the results of research or surveys, providing you with the percentage points by which your results will differ from the real population value. When the sampling

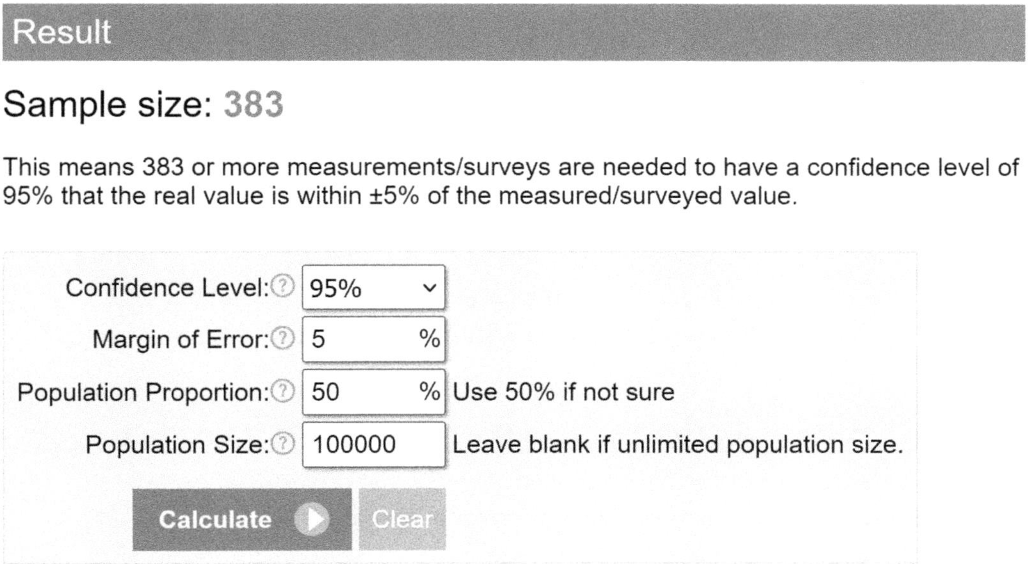

Figure 4.2 Using an online sample size calculator
Source: From Calculator.net

is random, the maximum likely size of the sampling error is called the margin of error, which is the plus or minus number that is often reported with an estimated proportion and is also called the confidence interval (e.g., ±5%).

- Confidence level: This is the probability that the interval estimate (the range of values likely containing the true population value) captures the true population parameter. It tells you how confident you can be that your research findings represent the actual population. For example, a 95% confidence level implies that 19 times out of 20 (95 times out of 100), the results would fall within the ± confidence interval. Most social science and communication researchers use the 95% confidence level.
- z score: This is a number that corresponds to the confidence level. A z score is a value that indicates the placement of your raw score on a normal distribution curve. One thing you need to know about a z score at this moment is that it is given numbers corresponding to the confidence level, and $z = 1.96$ is what researchers in strategic communication commonly use:
  - 90% confidence level: $z = 1.645$
  - 95% confidence level: $z = 1.96$
  - 99% confidence level: $z = 2.576$

- Sample proportion/ratio: This is the estimated proportion of a particular characteristic within the sample. It is assumed that the characteristics of the sample are representative of the population, expressed as a percentage such as 10%, 48%, or 87%. If you do not know what the sample proportion might be, use a standard estimate of 50%, as this maximizes the margin of error and ensures a more conservative estimate.

BOX 4.1
EXAMPLE OF SAMPLE SIZE CALCULATION

Sample Size Calculation

Now that you know what goes into determining sample size, you can calculate sample size either online or the old-fashioned way—by hand.

The formula for the sample size for known proportion is:

$$\frac{\frac{Z^2 \cdot p(1-p)}{e^2}}{1+\left(\frac{Z^2 \cdot p(1-p)}{e^2 N}\right)}$$

Sample size $z = z$ score
for known $= e =$ margin of error
population $p =$ proportion
$N =$ population

For practice by hand, let's assume there are 1,000 households in the target population for your research, with a 95% confidence level, 5% margin of error, and proportion unknown. You want to calculate the sample size (n).

$$n = \frac{\frac{(1.96)^2 \times 0.5(1-0.5)}{(0.05)^2}}{1+\frac{(1.96)^2 \times 0.5(1-0.5)}{(0.05)^2(1000)}}$$

You will need a sample size (n) of 276.6 or 278.

What if you do not know the population? How do you calculate the sample size? Calculate the sample size necessary to estimate the proportion of people watching Netflix at work who identify as binge-watchers, with 95% confidence, a margin of error of 5%, a proportion of 50%, and an unlimited population size.

$$\frac{Z^2 \times \hat{p}(1-\hat{p})}{\varepsilon^2}$$

Sample size z = z score
for unknown = ε = margin of error
population $\hat{p}$ = population proportion

$$n = (1.96^2 \times .5[1 - .5]) / .05^2 = 384.16$$

The sample size is 384.

Based on the known population formula and thanks to the sample size calculator, we can standardize sample sizes if we desire a 95% confidence level and we assume a 5% margin of error (sampling error) and a 50% sample proportion. See table 4.2.

SAMPLING ERROR

From a population, a sample is chosen to represent some traits of the population. If, for instance, a sample of 100 students at your college expressed their happiness with their college education, the 40,000 total students would do the same. Does this appear believable or scientific? Perhaps not. Results from a sample typically diverge somewhat from the population. The term *sampling error* or *margin of error* refers to the estimated discrepancy between the sample and the population. Sampling errors can affect research and surveys that use a random sample of individuals. The definition of *sampling error* is "a calculation of how closely the results reflect the attitudes or characteristics of the full population that's been sampled."[8]

The sampling error reveals how near the data in a sample are to the population. In statistics, sampling error is defined as a discrepancy between the sampled value and the true population value. Even a randomized sample is far from free of sampling error because a sample is merely an approximation of the population. However, sampling error in your research endeavor does not imply that you chose the wrong individuals for your sample. Rather, it means that sampling error is unavoidable when dealing with any random sample. As a result, your focus is on how to reduce sampling error by using a

Table 4.2 Sample Size Based on Population Size

Population size	Sample size	Population size	Sample size
50	44	1,000	278
100	80	5,000	357
150	108	10,000	370
200	132	50,000	382
500	218	100,000	383

representative sample of the population. Just know that a sample can never fully represent a population, although it can come close.

You might have read some news articles about survey results, reporting that the survey by XXX news agency was conducted November 1 through 10 on a random national sample of 1,100 adults reached on cell phones, including 1,036 likely voters. Results for the full sample have a sampling error of ±2.9 percentage points. Aren't you curious about how the sampling error is computed, which helps your research results gain credibility and accuracy? There are several different formulas for computing sampling error, and we use a simple but popular one used in social science (shown in Box 4.2).

Box 4.2
Sampling Error Practice

Sampling Error Formula

$$SE(p) = z \times \sqrt{}(p \times [1 - p] \;/\; n)$$

z: z score for the confidence level selected

n: sample size

p: proportion or percentage of people surveyed who are expected to respond in a certain way

For practice, suppose you have a sample of 1,000 potential voters for the 2028 presidential election. You do not know the proportion of their voting preferences (Democrats or Republicans), but you can compute the sampling error at the 95% confidence level, which has an associated z score of 1.96, and you can use the proportion of 50% when you do not know

$$SE(p) = 1.96 \times \sqrt{}(.5 \times [1 - .5] \;/\; 1{,}000) = \pm 3.09\%$$

What if you know the proportion? Suppose in the same sample, you found that 600 out of 1,000 people are likely to vote for a Republican candidate. To compute the sampling error, we know 60% is the proportion, or .6.

$$SE(p) = 1.96 \times \sqrt{}(.6 \times [1 - .6] \;/\; 1{,}000) = \pm 3.04\%$$

Thus, you may claim that the proportion of voters who plan to vote for a Republican candidate is 60%, plus or minus 3.04%.

In general, as the sample size increases, the margin of error decreases. What if you had a sample of 2,000 potential voters with a 60% proportion?

$$SE(p) = 1.96 \times \sqrt{(.6 \times [1 - .6] / 2{,}000)} = \pm 2.15\%$$

If you see the computing process as a bit burdensome, you can use online calculators (www.calculator.net):

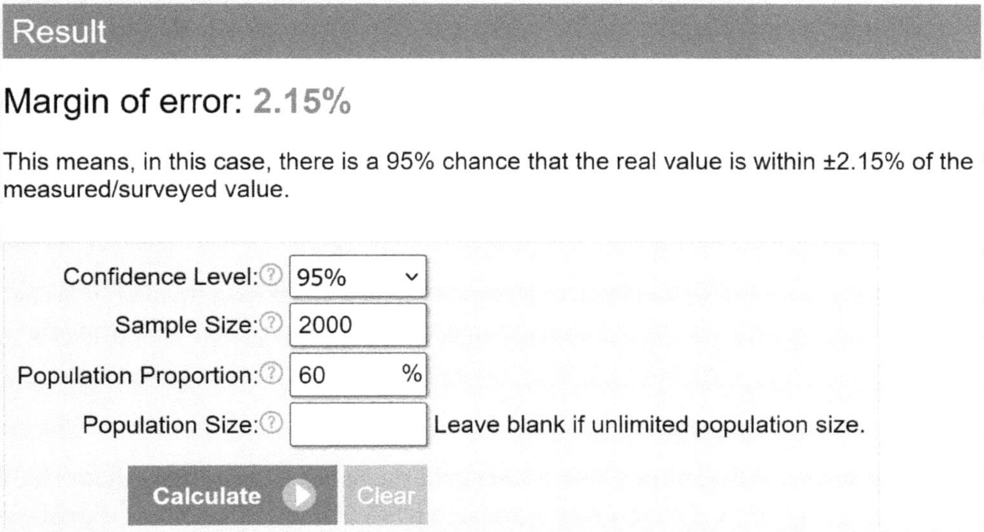

Source: From Calculator.net.

Now, we will incorporate all the skills of sample size and sampling error computation into the final practice problem in Box 4.3.

BOX 4.3
SAMPLING SIZE WITH PROPORTION

Practice for Sampling Size and Error

Suppose you have 1,000 potential voters in the population for the 2028 presidential election in your town. For your survey, you need to determine a sample size at a 95% confidence level and a 5% margin of error. You know the proportion this time instead of the 50% assumption: 60 percent of them will vote for a Democratic candidate. What is your sample size?

$$n = \frac{\frac{(1.96)^2 \times 0.6(1-0.6)}{(0.05)^2}}{1+\frac{(1.96)^2 \times 0.6(1-0.6)}{(0.05)^2(1000)}}$$

Answer: You need a sample of 270 voters to have a confidence level of 95% that the real value is within ±5% of the measured/surveyed value.

On second thought, you would like to reduce the sampling error of 5% to 1% to gain more accurate results for the same case. How many people do you need for the sample?

$$n = \frac{\frac{(1.96)^2 \times 0.6(1-0.6)}{(0.01)^2}}{1+\frac{(1.96)^2 \times 0.6(1-0.6)}{(0.01)^2(1000)}}$$

Answer: You need a sample of 903 voters to have a confidence level of 95% that the real value is within ±1% of the measured/surveyed value. Therefore, the larger sample size in statistics leads to a smaller sampling error.

In many academic disciplines, researchers hold the belief that a sample should ideally represent the population. However, it is important to acknowledge that a sample will never perfectly mirror the population. The presence of sampling error is an inevitable aspect of the scientific research process and is generally accepted by the research community. Therefore, a crucial responsibility for researchers is to meticulously select a sample that best represents the population for their scientific research. This process is vital in ensuring the validity and reliability of the research findings.

Researchers in many academic fields believe that a sample should be representative of the population, but the population will never be 100% correctly represented by a sample. In this sense, the existence of sampling error is unavoidable and acceptable in the scientific research process. In sum, one important responsibility for researchers is to optimally choose a representative sample for their scientific research.

How to Apply AI Technologies to Sampling

Mastering the principles of sampling is fundamental in scientific research, encompassing the selection of a representative sample, calculating the sample size, and acknowledging sampling error. In the era of AI, these processes can be significantly enriched through advanced technologies, providing invaluable support for college research students.

1. Guidance in the sampling process: AI technologies offer students step-by-step guidance, interactive tutorials, and real-time feedback. For instance, platforms like AI-Google AI Hub provide interactive modules, assisting students in navigating the intricacies of diverse sampling methods.[9]

2. Understanding sampling error and size calculation: AI tools automate sample size and sampling error calculations, mitigating human error. Utilizing tools like Omni Calculator enhances efficiency, offering visualizations and interpretations to foster a deeper understanding of these complex statistical concepts.[10]

3. Data collection and analysis: When dealing with extensive data sets, AI streamlines data collection, cleaning, and preparation. AI tools automate these processes, enabling efficient analysis. AI-driven data analytics platforms such as Dynatrace identify intricate patterns and trends, providing insights that may elude manual examination.[11]

4. Enhanced learning experience: AI-powered educational platforms, such as Absorb, tailor learning experiences to individual styles and paces. Offering instant feedback and recommendations, these platforms contribute to a more profound understanding of sampling and research methodologies.[12]

Incorporating AI technologies into the learning and research process not only enhances efficiency but also allows students to focus more on their conceptual understanding and interpretation of results. As we move forward in the digital age, the integration of AI in research methodologies like sampling will continue to evolve, opening new avenues for scientific exploration and discovery.

APPLICATION OF AN AI-POWERED TOOL

BOX 4.4
SAMPLING STRATEGY AND TACTIC RECOMMENDED BY MICROSOFT COPILOT

Using an AI-Powered Tool (Microsoft Copilot) to Select a Sample of College Students

Command syntax: Explain strategies and tactics to select a sample of college students to strengthen scientific validity with an example.

Answer: Sure! Here's an example scenario:

Imagine you want to conduct a survey to find out if college students want to buy products from socially responsible companies. You have a target population of 10,000 college students from various universities across the country.

First, you can use a sample size calculator to determine the right sample size for your survey. Let's say the calculator suggests a sample size of 500 students. Next, you can use a simple random sampling method to select your sample. This involves randomly selecting 500 students from your target population of 10,000 college students. You can use online tools like SurveyMonkey Audience to help with this process.

Once you have selected your sample, you can conduct your survey with those 500 students. The results from this representative sample can then be used to make inferences about the entire target population of 10,000 college students.

To strengthen the sampling process in terms of validity and scientific research, you can follow several best practices. These include:

1. Defining your population and sampling frame clearly: Make sure you have a clear understanding of the group of people you want to draw conclusions about and the list of individuals that the sample will be drawn from.
2. Using appropriate sampling techniques and tools: Choose a sampling method that is appropriate for your research design and target population. Use tools such as sample size calculators to help with this process.
3. Calculating your sample size and margin of error: Use a sample size calculator to determine the right sample size for your survey. This will help ensure that your sample is large enough to be representative of the target population.
4. Ensuring your sample diversity and inclusion: Make sure your sample is diverse and inclusive, representing all relevant subgroups within your target population.
5. Checking your sample validity and reliability: Evaluate the validity and reliability of your sample to ensure that it accurately represents the target population.
6. Evaluating your sampling bias and error: Be aware of potential sources of bias and error in your sampling process, and take steps to minimize them.

By following these best practices, you can strengthen the validity and scientific rigor of your sampling process.

SUMMARY

- ✓ A population refers to all units of people or things like events, countries, and species studied by you as the researcher.
- ✓ A sample is a specific group or a subset of the population.

- ✓ The size of the sample is always smaller than the total size of the population.
- ✓ Probability sampling is a sampling technique in which the researcher chooses a sample from the targeted population using a method based on statistical probability.
- ✓ Simple random sampling uses techniques like lotteries or random draws.
- ✓ Stratified random sampling divides the population into small subgroups that simple random sampling might miss.
- ✓ Systematic random sampling selects members of the population at a regular interval (or *k*) determined in advance.
- ✓ Cluster sampling takes samples from a large population that is dispersed over a wide geographic area.
- ✓ Nonprobability sampling is based on the subjective judgment of the researcher rather than random selection.
- ✓ In convenience sampling, a sample is selected from the population only because the researcher selects some people at her convenience.
- ✓ Purposive sampling is based on the idea that a specific person or communication unit will meet specific criteria the researcher has.
- ✓ Quota sampling allows the researcher to divide the population into proportional strata or groups.
- ✓ Snowball sampling relies on the members of a network to introduce the researcher to other members of the network.
- ✓ There is no perfect answer for an ideal sample size.
- ✓ Sample size can be computed with a margin of error, confidence level, z score, and the sample proportion.
- ✓ Sampling error is a calculation of how closely the results of research reflect the attitudes or characteristics of the full population that has been sampled.
- ✓ In statistics, as the sample size increases, the margin of error decreases.
- ✓ The integration of AI in research methodologies like sampling will continue to evolve, opening new avenues for scientific exploration and discovery.

Key Terms

1. Probability
2. Nonprobability
3. Population

4. Sample
5. Stratified sampling
6. Representativeness
7. Sampling error
8. Sample size
9. Quota sampling

Chapter 5

Survey Design and Implementation

Chapter Learning Outcomes

- Define a survey.
- Discuss how a questionnaire differs from a survey.
- Explain the difference between cross-sectional and longitudinal types of survey.
- Recognize the advantages and disadvantages of a survey.
- Apply basic questions of demographics to a questionnaire.
- Discuss doing a mail survey versus a telephone survey.
- Describe the process of in-person surveys.
- Practice the use of online survey templates.
- Create an online survey.
- Recognize tactics for enhancing response rates.
- Implement AI technology for conducting a survey.

Surveys are a widely used method for data collection in both academic and corporate environments. They come in various forms, including consumer surveys, brand surveys, employee satisfaction surveys, presidential job-approval surveys, and television rating surveys. Researchers in strategic communication often employ surveys to gather timely and valuable insights into public opinions or sentiments about specific products, corporations, or public policies. Due to their cost effectiveness and efficiency, surveys are a preferred tool for government agencies, news outlets, scholars, and corporations seeking to understand the desires and thoughts of the public, an audience, or customers.

What Is a Survey?

A survey is a research technique for gathering information from a specific group of individuals. It involves a set of structured questions presented to a representative sample from the group. The set of questions, whether printed or oral, is referred to as a questionnaire.

The aim of a questionnaire is to collect responses from participants who are provided with a range of answer choices. In essence, a survey is a data collection process facilitated by a questionnaire. To conduct a survey, you first design a questionnaire intended to extract information about the population via a sample. Once your questionnaire is prepared, you initiate your survey activities by distributing the questionnaire to the sample, collecting their responses as data, and subsequently analyzing them. Surveys are designed to uncover what people want, know, and think, and they can also track changes in attitudes, beliefs, and values over time.

Surveys can be categorized into two types: descriptive and analytical. A descriptive survey aims to depict the current conditions or attitudes of a population, focusing on gathering direct information. For instance, advertising agencies might use a descriptive survey to determine which television commercials resonate most with Super Bowl viewers. Corporations also utilize descriptive surveys to gauge customer satisfaction with their products or services. Conversely, an analytical survey seeks to understand why certain situations arise or why specific behaviors occur. This type of survey necessitates a more structured academic research process, including a hypothesis or data derived from a descriptive survey. While descriptive surveys provide immediate and straightforward information, analytical surveys are employed to investigate and elucidate the relationships between certain characteristics of individuals and their resulting behaviors. Instead of merely describing the phenomenon, the analytical survey guides the researcher in explaining why people behave or think the way they do. For instance, as a researcher, you might conduct a survey to explore the influence of TikTok on college students during the ongoing war in Ukraine. The survey could analyze why and how students use TikTok to cope with the mental health effects of the war, such as anxiety and stress. While some social media use can negatively impact mental health, TikTok may also provide a platform for students to connect with others facing similar challenges, share information and experiences, or find support and humor.[1]

The two types of surveys should be recognized and discussed in relation to the temporal aspect of surveys:

- A cross-sectional survey, for example, collects data from a defined population at a specific point in time, offering a snapshot of its characteristics. Some key features of a cross-sectional survey include that (1) it occurs at a single point in time; (2) it examines multiple characteristics simultaneously, such as age, gender, and education; (3) it gathers information about the population; and (4) it has a specific duration with defined start and end points. For instance, strategic communication researchers may use cross-sectional research to determine the level of interest among Hispanic housewives aged 25–45 across the United States in purchasing beauty products promoted by Jennifer Lopez on her Instagram. As a one-time survey, cross-sectional research is relatively quick to conduct and is suitable for descriptive analysis to identify prevailing characteristics in a population.

- A longitudinal survey involves repeated observations of the same population or variables over an extended period. Instead of collecting data from one population at a specific point in time, longitudinal research gathers data from multiple subjects on various issues over time. This type of research tends to require more time and resources due to its comprehensive approach. Longitudinal research allows researchers to track changes over time and better understand cause-and-effect relationships. For example, if you survey Gen Z's views on news media and religious organizations in 2025, 2029, and 2033, you can observe how their attitudes change over time. You may find that Gen Z's opinions toward these subjects become more negative and can explore why this is the case. If possible, you could also compare their views with those of the baby boomer generation. Thus, longitudinal research enables researchers to examine changes over time but can be costly in terms of time and resources.

Advantages and Disadvantages of Survey Research

Surveys offer several advantages:

1. They provide a relatively easy and cost-effective way to examine a sample of individuals from a population in realistic settings.
2. They can be conducted via various mediums, including online, mail, email, or telephone.
3. They can be administered remotely, overcoming geographical barriers.
4. They can collect data from a large sample size.
5. They can include numerous questions about a specific subject or topic at one time.
6. They can collect a wide range of characteristic data such as attitudes, beliefs, and opinions.
7. They allow for fast processing of data with advanced statistical techniques.[2]

Researchers favor surveys for their convenience, practicality, affordability, and simplicity. Surveys are a prevalent method for collecting data or gathering information from a defined population, particularly when respondents are comfortable answering survey questionnaires. It is important to note that surveys allow researchers to gather information that can be quantitatively analyzed using precise statistical tests for reliable results. The defined population for surveys can be any group of people with specific characteristics, such as college students planning to buy electric cars, female bankers who read the *Wall Street Journal*, or millennials and Gen Z who value recycling and clean air.

However, surveys also have several disadvantages:

1. Not all respondents tell the truth or provide honest opinions.
2. Not all respondents may fully understand the survey questions.
3. Not all respondents even want to participate in surveys.
4. Some respondents purposely answer the opposite of what they think.
5. Some respondents refuse to return survey answers, so response rates may be low.
6. Some respondents cannot give exact answers because of a lack of memory.
7. Some respondents complain about the format of questions that have only yes or no options for answering.[3]

Many surveys are ignored or deleted in emails by respondents. Even when they respond, there is no guarantee that the answers are truthful and credible. Many respondents find surveys annoying and irritating, and they are often reluctant to provide personal information.

Organizing Survey Questionnaires

Most college students are likely to have experience answering survey questionnaires distributed by professors, graduate students, or college administrators. While these questionnaires may seem simple and easily written and formatted, it takes significant effort, practice, and energy to create a questionnaire that complies with the following principles:

> A good questionnaire should be valid, reliable, clear, succinct, and interesting. It is important to design the questionnaire based on a conceptual framework, scrutinize each question for relevance and clarity, and think of the analysis you are going to perform at the end of the day. A final touch-up will make a difference in the response rate and always pilot-test the questionnaire to perfect the questionnaire.[4]

A well-designed questionnaire should be valid, reliable, clear, concise, and engaging. Since the success of a survey largely depends on the questionnaire, it is essential to learn how to design a questionnaire that accurately reflects the survey's topic and purpose. A good questionnaire will be able to extract the information the researcher seeks to capture from respondents. The format, structure, question types, and wording of the questionnaire play a significant role in eliciting sincere answers and active participation from respondents, leading to successful survey outcomes.

Before including specific and customized questions in the questionnaire for a particular field of study, such as public relations or advertising, most researchers begin their questionnaires with general demographic questions: gender, age, ethnicity, location, education, marital status, income, and employment. These demographic questions provide useful background information about the survey respondents. Table 5.1 presents basic demographic questions commonly included in most surveys.

Asking questions is an important part of collecting data when a researcher conducts a survey. There are two basic question types the researcher uses:

- Closed-ended questions: Closed-ended survey questions prompt respondents to select one answer from a finite set of options. While this type of question may offer limited insights to the researcher, the data obtained can be readily analyzed using statistical tests. Closed-ended questions are also advantageous for respondents, as they are straightforward to understand and answer, requiring minimal time to read and respond. However, a potential drawback is that respondents may not find an option that accurately represents their desired response among the provided choices, which could potentially skew the survey results.
- Open-ended questions: To mitigate this issue, researchers may employ open-ended survey questions, which allow respondents to elaborate on their answers. Examples of open-ended questions include "How can the company improve its reputation?" "What challenges have you faced during and after the pandemic?" and "Why do you prefer watching Netflix over Max or Hulu?" Open-ended questions enable respondents to answer in an open-text format, allowing them to express their comprehensive knowledge, feelings, or understanding. Research employing open-ended questions can gather more detailed and candid information on a topic from respondents. However, it requires more time and effort to analyze the data compared to research using closed-ended questions.

There are six additional survey question types that researchers commonly use in questionnaires besides open- and closed-ended questions. These are described in Table 5.2.

Creating a Questionnaire

As a researcher, crafting effective survey questions is a crucial part of your role. The creation of a good questionnaire can be considered an art form. The survey questions you create and place in your questionnaire should adhere to the following principles:

- Questions are clear and direct, not ambiguous.
- Questions are short and simple.
- Questions are written using correct grammar.
- Questions are easily understood by respondents.

Table 5.1 Demographic Survey Questions

Demographic categories	Answer choices
Gender: "What is your gender?"	A. Female B. Male C. Other ________ (please specify) D. Prefer not to answer
Age: "What is your age?"	A. 0–18 years old B. 19–30 years old C. 31–50 years old D. 51+ E. Prefer not to answer
Ethnicity: "Please specify your ethnicity."	A. White B. Black or African American C. Latino or Hispanic D. Asian/Pacific Islander E. Native American F. Two or more G. Other/unknown H. Prefer not to answer
Location: "You are currently located in?"	A. North America B. South America C. Europe D. Africa E. Asia F. Australia G. Other: ______ H. Prefer not to answer
Education: "What is the highest degree or level of school you have completed?"	A. Some high school B. High school C. Bachelor's degree D. Master's degree E. PhD or higher F. Other (please specify) G. Prefer not to answer
Marital status: "What is your marital status?"	A. Single, never married B. Married C. Domestic partnership D. Widowed F. Divorced G. Separated F. Prefer not to answer
Household income: "What is your annual household income?"	A. Below $10,000 B. $10,000–$30,000 C. $30,001–$ 75,000 D. $75,001–$100,000 E. More than $100,000 F. Prefer not to answer

Demographic categories	Answer choices
Employment: "Are you currently . . . ?"	A. Employed full time B. Employed part time C. Seeking opportunities D. Out of work and looking for work E. Unable to work F. Retired G. Prefer not to answer

- Questions are logically structured (from broad to specific).
- Questions ask for only one piece of information at a time (no double-barreled questions).
- Questions avoid showing bias.
- Questions are not loaded.
- Questions are not leading.

It is essential to create a well-designed questionnaire that includes clear, specific, and straightforward questions written in simple language. When formulating survey questions, you should try to avoid wording that may cause respondents to misinterpret or misunderstand the questions. Confusing questions can negatively impact survey results, so researchers use carefully chosen words and sentences to ensure clarity. The way questions are written and structured can influence respondents' views on the survey topic or encourage dishonest answers. Researchers suggest avoiding four common survey question mistakes:

1. Leading questions: Some researchers create leading questions that subtly prompt the respondent to answer in a particular way. For example, a survey question may read: "Many patriotic citizens enjoy working overtime without overtime pay. How do you feel about this?" Another example: "What do you think about Kim Kardashian? Many people worship her as an Instagram goddess, by the way." Leading questions are based on the researcher's personal bias. If any words reflect the researcher's preference, the question with biased wording should be changed or removed.
2. Loaded questions: Some researchers incorporate implicit assumptions into their questionnaires, creating questions written in a way that forces the respondent into an offensive or unjustified answer. Examples of loaded questions include "Where do you enjoy watching adult or pornographic movies, at home or at the office?" or "When did you stop abusing your spouse?" The easiest way to avoid writing loaded questions is to remain neutral about respondents' characteristics and steer clear of presumptions.

Table 5.2 Survey Question Types

Survey question types	Examples
Dichotomous type: Respondents choose one of two possible answers	Do you like to use Snapchat? ___ Yes ___ No
Multiple choice type: Respondents choose one or more answers	I am willing to pay more for? ___ Netflix ___ Hulu ___ Showtime ___ HBO ___ Apple TV ___ Amazon Prime ___ Disney+
Rank-order type: Respondents rank their choices in order	Please rank your choices by writing "1" next to your first choice, "2" next to your second choice, and so on. My future husband should be: ___ Rich ___ Romantic ___ Good looking ___ Powerful ___ Intelligent ___ Considerate
Rating scales type: Respondents select the number that represents their response	How likely is it that you would ask your parents to vote for Matthew McConaughey as governor? Not at all Extremely 1 2 3 4 5 6 7 8 9 10
Likert scale type: Respondents locate their level of agreement	How satisfied are you with shopping at Walmart online? ___ Very dissatisfied ___ Not satisfied ___ Neutral ___ Satisfied ___ Very satisfied
Semantic differential scale type: Respondents mark between bipolar adjectives with five or seven scale points	You downloaded the Chase Bank app a month ago. How would you rate it on the following criteria? Innovative _ _ _ _ _ _ _ Dull Interesting _ _ _ _ _ _ _ Uninteresting Successful _ _ _ _ _ _ _ Unsuccessful

3. Double-barreled questions: Some researchers incorporate more than one topic in a single question, forcing respondents to answer only one of two questions. If a single question contains two topics, the respondent, being allowed only one answer, can hardly decide which one should be answered. Examples of double-barreled questions are "How satisfied are you with the pay and work environment of your current job?" or "Should the government spend more money on space projects and less money on Medicaid?" These questions require two answers each. A good survey question targets one clear answer.
4. Double negatives: When the researcher uses two negative forms in the same question, it can confuse the respondent. As a result, the answer may reflect the opposite of what the respondent intended. Here are some examples: "Do you not agree that housewives who play baseball are not uncommon?" or "Isn't Lady Gaga's X difficult to retweet unless you are not allowed to use the search bar?" Unless the survey uses double negatives for special research like poetic lyrics, they will not do any good in a questionnaire.

The art of creating a good questionnaire lies in the ability to craft clear, concise, and unbiased questions that accurately capture the information the researcher seeks to obtain. Avoiding common pitfalls like leading questions, loaded questions, double-barreled questions, and double negatives can significantly enhance the quality of your survey data. Remember, the goal is to gain insights from your respondents, not to confuse or mislead them. In other words, if the respondent cannot understand your survey questions, your data will be useless. The priority in forming a questionnaire is to ensure that it consists of understandable and simple questions written in clear language with direct relevance to the topic. It is highly recommended that you review the questionnaire several times and avoid the four common mistakes above. One easy way of creating a survey questionnaire is to get some help from AI tools such as ChatGPT and Microsoft Copilot. For example, when asked to generate a questionnaire about college students' use of TikTok, ChatGPT responded with the 10 questions in Box 5.1.

Box 5.1
Example of Using ChatGPT for a Questionnaire

Here are 10 survey questions about the use of TikTok among college students:

1. How often do you use TikTok?
2. What type of content do you usually watch on TikTok?
3. Have you ever created and posted a video on TikTok?

4. Do you follow any specific TikTok creators or hashtags?
5. How much time do you spend on TikTok per day?
6. Have you ever used TikTok for educational purposes?
7. Do you think TikTok has influenced your behavior or opinions in any way?
8. Have you ever participated in a TikTok challenge or trend?
9. Do you think TikTok is a positive or negative influence on college students?
10. Would you recommend TikTok to a friend?

Is there anything else I can help with? ☺

Instructions for the Survey

Once you have a group of respondents for your survey and a questionnaire ready for them to answer, be sure that you provide clear instructions. Even if the questionnaire contains well-written questions, it will not yield meaningful responses without a clear introduction and instructions. According to SurveyMonkey, an online survey company, an introduction should briefly explain the topic and purpose of the survey, assuming that most respondents have little knowledge about the survey's topic.[5] The introduction should include the goal of the survey, a privacy protection statement, and the expected contribution from the respondent. For example, an introduction for a market survey might read as follows:

> Hello, my name is ________, with the University of ________. I am conducting research on environmental health campaigns concerning college students' soda consumption and disposable drinking straws. I would like to ask you some questions, and all your answers will be completely anonymous. Please answer as honestly as possible to make positive environmental changes in the United States of America. This survey should only take less than 10 minutes. I really appreciate your help.

Since many respondents find surveys annoying and are suspicious of marketing ploys, some researchers also add a statement to highlight its academic purpose: "I am not trying to sell anything through this survey; this is only used for academic research." Between questions in the questionnaire, some procedural instructions may be necessary to help the respondent complete it. An example is given in Table 5.3.

After putting in considerable effort, you will have a complete questionnaire ready for distribution. However, before distribution, one more step is needed: pretesting. Pretesting

Table 5.3 Instructions for the Survey

- What are your favorite social media platforms in order?
  1.______ 2. ______ 3. ______ 4. ______ 5. ______
  Write names of the platforms. You don't have to name five, but try to name at least three.
- Do you read the daily news from Facebook News Feed?
  ___ Yes ___ No

  ____

  If yes, please explain how long you've been using it and what news you pay attention to. If no, please move on to Question 4.
- If you have posted at least one TikTok video in the past month, please continue with Question 5. If not, please skip to Question 9.

involves testing your questionnaire with a small group of people to identify any problems before conducting the actual survey. You can select about 10 people from your target group to pretest the questionnaire. While they are answering your questionnaire, observe them to identify any issues that cause hesitation or confusion. After they complete it, ask them about any major problems they encountered. Address these problems to finalize the questionnaire. Depending on the scale and complexity of pretesting, you could also run a pilot study, which is a trial run of the entire survey. To conduct a pilot study, you need to run the survey process from start to finish with a reasonably large sample of about 50. You may need to hire several data collectors for a pilot study to distribute and collect the questionnaires exactly as you would do in real surveys. One significant advantage of conducting a pilot study, besides identifying questionnaire problems, is that you can identify practical issues that may arise while implementing the larger survey.

Choosing Survey Methods

After deciding to use a survey for data collection and finalizing your questionnaire, the next step is to decide on the right audience of respondents and find a practical way to reach them. Respondents can be reached via mail, telephone, in person, or online. You can use all these methods to reach a large number of respondents, but you should consider your budget and time resources before distributing your questionnaire.

Mail Survey

A mail survey is useful when respondents are geographically dispersed. It involves sending questionnaires enclosed with postage-paid or stamped reply envelopes to a sample of respondents. The respondent is usually asked to answer a long list of questions at their convenience, without time restrictions. They can be given enough days to return the survey through the mail on their own schedule. A mail survey is straightforward and comprehensible, with both open- and close-ended questions. Mail surveys are especially popular among market researchers who view them as an effective and cost-friendly data collection method. Moreover, conducting a mail survey is typically low cost since the researcher alone can oversee the entire survey process. However, not every researcher prefers mail surveys due to certain limitations. According to the National Public Research Center, a mail survey can only be successful in collecting data if:

- You know or have access to the complete name and home address of the members of your target population.
- Your respondents must be able to read and write well. It is also ideal if their educational level is above average.
- Your respondents are likely to be concerned or interested in the goals of the research (e.g., improving the quality of the brand).
- The survey does not have time constraints, as sending and receiving a mail survey can be a monthlong process.
- The instructions on the questionnaire can be easily followed, and the questions are simple and can be understood without difficulty.[6]

As some respondents feel more comfortable offering answers through writing, mail surveys tend to yield more honest feedback, as opposed to other survey methods. For you as a researcher, a mail survey is easy to implement as long as you enclose the questionnaire with the reply envelope. Professional survey organizations also use mail surveys, such as the Nielsen survey for television ratings and J. D. Power for customer satisfaction. For example, the Nielsen mail survey includes a set of multiple-choice questions: (1) Which types of TV shows do you watch regularly? (2) What is your favorite TV show or channel? and (3) Do you or does anyone in your household work for a radio, TV, or cable company? Race, gender, and age demographic questions are also included.[7]

Some respondents reported that they received a dollar bill that came in Nielsen's mail survey envelope. Nielsen motivated the respondents to return the survey questionnaire with the cash reward. This is an effective tactic to increase the response rate, although the response rate for mail surveys is low among young people, who rarely go to the post office to send a letter.

Telephone Survey

A telephone survey employs a standardized questionnaire administered by trained interviewers who gather information from respondents over the phone. These surveys often involve randomly contacting individuals who agree to participate. Previously, researchers selected telephone numbers from directories such as the white pages. However, with the majority of the American population now owning individual cell phones, many researchers have shifted to using random digit dialing (RDD). This method, which involves computer systems arbitrarily selecting phone numbers, has become a popular approach for conducting phone surveys. Before initiating a telephone survey, you as a researcher need to hire and train phone interviewers. Their phone etiquette and communication skills can significantly impact response rates. Therefore, providing comprehensive training and instructional modules is essential. The success of phone surveys largely depends on the interviewer's ability to engage in friendly conversation while demonstrating excellent reading, listening, and recording skills.

If you serve as a telephone survey interviewer, you are expected to introduce yourself and your organization at the beginning of each call and explain the survey's topic and process. These instructions should be included in your questionnaire. A significant challenge is persuading respondents to stay on the line and complete the survey. To overcome this problem, common strategies include emphasizing the survey's importance and assuring the respondent that the survey will take minimal time and contribute to the community. Once the respondent agrees to answer your questions, you should adhere to the script of the questionnaire, reading each question verbatim and recording each response accurately. The telephone survey concludes with a thank-you to the respondent for their time and effort.

While telephone surveys may seem straightforward and scientifically rigorous due to their use of randomly selected samples, they do have their limitations. Traditionally, these surveys used landline telephones. However, as many people now exclusively use cell phones, the potential for bias in landline surveys has increased, according to the Pew Research Center.[8] As a result, more researchers are attempting to use cell-phone numbers for surveys. However, caller identification and automatic call screening apps often discourage respondents from answering survey calls. If you are planning to conduct a telephone survey, some researchers recommend calling on Wednesday or Thursday, especially between 4 and 5 P.M. or between 11 A.M. and noon.[9] It is advisable to avoid conducting telephone surveys early in the morning or during dinnertime.

In-Person Survey

In an in-person survey, you, as the interviewer, are required to be physically present at a specific location and time. Despite seeming more inconvenient compared to mail and telephone surveys, in-person surveys offer several advantages. These include obtaining accurate information through direct questioning and assisting respondents in a face-to-face setting. Unlike mail and telephone surveys where respondents can choose not to return or answer questions, in-person surveys often result in higher completion rates once initiated.

To conduct an in-person survey, you travel to the respondent's location. In some cases, this may involve going from house to house, where many residents may refuse to participate. To maximize respondent cooperation, arranging the survey at a predetermined time and place is crucial. Your presence allows for control of the environment and ensures that the respondent does not skip any questions. If the respondent has any concerns or confusion about the questionnaire, you are there to clarify the process. However, this method can be time consuming and energy intensive due to the one-on-one approach.

One efficient practice of conducting an in-person survey is a classroom survey. With your questionnaire ready, you can ask teachers or professors for about 10 minutes of class time for your survey. If granted permission, you can distribute the questionnaire to the students with instructions. You assist those who have questions about the survey, and depending on the class size, you may collect dozens of completed surveys. However, this convenience typically comes at the cost of biased data, as most student respondents in a classroom are not randomly selected.

Online Survey

In the digital age, online or internet surveys have emerged as the most popular data collection method. These surveys are efficient and user friendly, with respondents receiving online questionnaires through various digital channels such as email, websites, and social media platforms. The widespread accessibility of the internet allows for any type of survey to be conducted online. The low cost of conducting surveys, the simplicity of answering surveys with a few clicks, and the dramatic popularity of the internet provide a wide range of advantages for both researchers and respondents.

Creating an online survey has become easier with professional survey companies such as SurveyMonkey and Qualtrics offering hundreds of online survey templates, including customer satisfaction, training evaluation, product evaluation, and health care satisfaction. Most colleges in the United States purchase online survey software from these companies and allow students and employees to use it for their online research. With various types of questions in different templates offered by online survey companies, you can easily create your own online survey from scratch. Every section of your online survey can also be customized (e.g., colors, fonts, background themes). If you want to research college students' online shopping behavior, you can use a premade questionnaire from survey software. For example, JotForm.com shares survey questions on the topic as follows:

- How frequently do you purchase things online?
- Why do you prefer online shopping? (Choose as many as applicable.)
- If you do not purchase things online, why? (Choose as many as applicable.)
- How much have you spent on online shopping in the past year?
- What is your preferred payment method?[10]

Most online survey software allows you to customize your questions and a list of answers from the template you choose. Hence, whatever kind of online survey you conduct, you will obtain a great deal of help from such software. When your online questionnaire is ready to be distributed, you decide which online channel to use. SurveyMonkey suggests various ways of sending your survey and collecting responses:

- Web link: Create a URL or QR code linking to your survey so you can send or post your survey anywhere you want.
- Email invitation: Send customized email invitations to your contacts through the online survey software to track who responds and send follow-up emails.
- Social media: Post your survey on Facebook, X, or LinkedIn.
- Website: Embed your survey or show a pop-up invitation to your survey on websites.
- Text message: Text your contacts a link to your survey. Survey takers can tap the link to take your survey in their mobile browser.[11]

Increasing Survey Response Rates

The survey response rate, defined as the percentage of individuals who successfully complete the survey, is a critical metric for researchers. While a 100% response rate is ideal, it is often unrealistic, except perhaps in the case of in-person surveys. A low response rate results in a smaller sample size for analysis, and if the number of respondents is too small, their answers may not accurately represent the target population. Regardless of the survey distribution channel or method used, increasing the response rate is a significant challenge for researchers.

While there is no definitive answer to what constitutes an acceptable survey response rate, survey statistics suggest that the average response rate ranges from 18% for telephone surveys to 29% for online surveys, 30% for email surveys, 50% for mail surveys, and 57% for in-person surveys.[12] The high response rate for mail surveys can be attributed to factors such as the inclusion of a small cash reward in the survey envelope and a preference among older generations to respond to mail surveys.

College students and professors often receive numerous survey invitations via email each semester. However, while understanding the importance of research, they often ignore or delete these requests instead of responding. When conducting their own research or surveys, they strive to increase the response rate, knowing that low response rates can undermine their survey efforts. Here are some strategies to increase the survey response rate:

- Use monetary incentives: Placing a dollar bill in the survey envelope has proven effective at boosting the response rate. For online or email surveys, some researchers offer a lottery opportunity: "As a thank-you for helping us with this survey, you will be entered into a drawing to win one of five $20 Amazon gift cards" (see Box 5.2).
- Personalize the survey: Using the respondent's name in the survey and customizing the introduction with information you know about the respondent can

increase the response rate. Although it consumes more of your time and energy, the goal of receiving more responses will be met with the personalization tactic. An example might be, "Dear Dr. Cooper, we hope you like your new car. Please allow us to ask you some questions about your shopping experience with us."

- Choose the right channel: Depending on your sample, you should pick the right survey distribution channel. For college students as a sample, email or a cellphone text can make the response rate high. Mail surveys can be a better fit for improving survey participation among housewives or househusbands.

BOX 5.2
EXAMPLE OF AN EMAIL SURVEY AIMING TO INCREASE THE RESPONSE RATE

Hi Professor Lim,

I hope the semester is going well! I'm just following up as I don't believe you've had a chance to complete (Company Name)'s "Professor Vibe" survey. (Company Name) offers a comprehensive teaching platform. You may have heard of us from colleagues around campus. We are collecting feedback on the current state of higher education from professors.

We have over 9,600 responses so far but would love to hear from you. Your answers will remain confidential, and the results will be compiled into an interactive report, which we will deliver straight to your inbox. *You can take the survey here.* It should only take about five minutes to complete, and as a thank-you for your time you will automatically be eligible to win $100.

Thank you in advance!

Regards,
(Name of the survey sender)
Education Outreach Director of (Company Name)

Surveys are undoubtedly one of the most valuable research methods in the field of strategic communication. Despite the complex procedures involved in some surveys, they serve as an effective method of collecting research data. Surveys should be conducted with well-prepared questionnaires, samples, methods, and tactics, based on the research topic.

THE EVOLUTION OF SURVEY RESEARCH: THE PROFOUND IMPACT OF AI

As we proceed into the 21st century, the advent of AI technology has ushered in a paradigm shift, particularly within the realm of communication research. Prominent tools like Microsoft Copilot, Google Gemini, and ChatGPT are at the forefront, creating novel possibilities for conducting surveys and analyzing data.

- Consider the creation of survey questionnaires: AI tools extend beyond mere assistance, actively suggesting questions aligned with the research topic.[13] This ensures a comprehensive questionnaire that captures the necessary facets, coupled with assistance in crafting clear and unbiased questions—integral elements for securing reliable survey results.
- Unleashing analytical prowess: The analytical prowess of AI tools becomes evident in data processing. Swift and accurate, these tools navigate through vast data sets, uncovering patterns and trends that might elude manual analysis.[14] The output is not just raw data but comprehensive reports, embellished with charts and graphs for intuitive visual representation.
- Elevating response rates strategically: AI tools serve as strategic allies in boosting survey response rates. They contribute to the design of personalized survey invitations and reminders, a proven tactic for enhancing engagement. Additionally, by facilitating the testing of different survey versions, these tools empower students to identify the most effective approach for maximizing response rates.[15]
- Responsible AI utilization: However, with great power comes great responsibility. Students must wield AI tools judiciously, critically evaluating suggestions for alignment with research objectives.[16] Ethical considerations, such as privacy and data security, should remain at the forefront of the use of AI technologies.

The advent of AI technology creates thrilling possibilities for elevating survey research. As students adeptly harness tools like Microsoft Copilot, Google Gemini, and ChatGPT, they not only conduct more efficient surveys but also make significant contributions to the progress of communication research.

Application of an AI-Powered Tool

Box 5.3
Google Gemini's Creation of a Questionnaire and Advice for a Survey

Using an AI-Powered Tool (Google Gemini) for the Creation of a Questionnaire and Survey

Command syntax: Create a questionnaire about college students' use of YouTube regarding its influence on their college life, including demographic and psychographic questions, and pros and cons of using YouTube over television or other social media platforms, and strategize how to distribute it and a get a higher response rate.

Answer: Sure, here is a sample questionnaire that you can use to survey college students about their use of YouTube:
Demographic Questions

- Gender:
- Age:
- Year in school:
- Major:
- College:

Psychographic Questions

- How often do you use YouTube?
- What are your favorite types of YouTube videos?
- How do you use YouTube in your college life?
- Do you think YouTube has a positive or negative influence on your college life?
- Why?

Pros and Cons of Using YouTube

- What are the pros of using YouTube over television or other social media platforms?
- What are the cons of using YouTube over television or other social media platforms?

Other Questions

- Any other comments or suggestions?

To distribute your survey, you can use a variety of methods, such as:

- Emailing it to a list of college students
- Posting it on social media
- Distributing it in person on campus

To get a higher response rate, you can offer incentives, such as:

- A chance to win a prize
- The opportunity to be featured in a research study
- A small amount of money

It is also important to make sure that your survey is easy to complete and that it is clear what you are asking.

Here are some additional tips for getting a higher response rate:

- Make sure that your survey is well designed and easy to complete.
- Keep your survey short and to the point.
- Offer incentives for completing the survey.
- Personalize your emails and messages when inviting people to take the survey.
- Follow up with people who have not yet completed the survey.

By following these tips, you can increase the chances of getting a high response rate for your survey.

Summary

- ✓ A survey is a system for collecting information about certain groups of people.
- ✓ A descriptive survey attempts to describe the population's current characteristics.
- ✓ Analytical surveys are used to examine and explain relationships between certain characteristics of people and their behavioral consequences.
- ✓ A cross-sectional survey evaluates data from a defined population at one specific point in time.
- ✓ A longitudinal survey is used to take multiple observations of the same population or variables over an extended period of time.
- ✓ Researchers take advantage of surveys because of their convenience, practicality, inexpensiveness, and simplicity.
- ✓ A good questionnaire should be valid, reliable, clear, succinct, and interesting.
- ✓ Leading questions are used to persuade the respondent to select a particular answer.
- ✓ Loaded questions based on problematic presumptions are phrased in a way that the respondent is put in a disadvantageous and defensive position.
- ✓ Double-barreled questions simultaneously force the respondent to answer only one of two questions.
- ✓ A survey introduction briefly explains the topic and purpose of the survey with the assumption that most respondents have little knowledge about the topic.
- ✓ Respondents are most often reached for surveys via mail, telephone, in person, or online.

- ✓ A survey response rate is the percentage of people who successfully complete your survey.
- ✓ AI tools extend beyond mere assistance, actively suggesting questions aligned with the research topic.

Key Terms

1. Survey
2. Questionnaire
3. Cross-sectional survey
4. Longitudinal survey
5. Demographics
6. Mail survey
7. Telephone survey
8. In-person survey
9. Online survey
10. Response rate

Chapter 6

Qualitative Research Methods

Chapter Learning Outcomes

- Define qualitative research.
- Discuss how the method of qualitative research differs from that of quantitative research.
- Explain ontology, epistemology, and axiology.
- Recognize the data collection tools of qualitative research.
- Discuss the roles of researchers in qualitative research.
- Identify the paradigms of qualitative methods.
- Apply a conceptual framework and a theoretical framework to the literature review section.
- Create a research design.
- Recognize the process of finding meaning.
- Discuss analytic techniques of qualitative research.
- Apply AI technology to the practice of qualitative research.

Strategic communication relies on two primary research methods: qualitative and quantitative. Methodology refers to the overall approach to research, encompassing methods of data collection and analysis.[1] Researchers can choose qualitative, quantitative, or mixed methods depending on their research goals. Qualitative methods in strategic communication delve deep into understanding human motivations, behaviors, and experiences in specific social contexts. They aim to provide rich, contextual insights that reflect how people make sense of communication and interact with strategic messages. In contrast, quantitative methods focus on collecting numerical data to measure variables and test hypotheses. They provide statistical evidence to support broad generalizable claims about communication effectiveness. In short, both qualitative and quantitative methods play crucial roles in strategic communication research, offering different but complementary perspectives.

Qualitative Researchers

Equipped with a fundamental understanding of research philosophy, theory, and practice, qualitative researchers in strategic communication employ various methods to uncover deep insights into human attitudes, opinions, and motivations. They conduct interviews, observe interactions, and analyze texts, such as social media posts, news articles, and campaign materials. These methods enable researchers to explore research topics relevant to human intuitions, ideologies, events, and values in strategic communication contexts. Simply put, the qualitative approach allows researchers to interpret the meaning behind human behavior and uncover unique characteristics that shape communication dynamics.

From a philosophical perspective, the qualitative method is guided by three philosophical assumptions:

- Ontology is the philosophical study of existence or being. It involves long-standing questions, such as the existence of God or a higher being. Ontology's main components are concepts, relations, and instances, which represent a set of entities in a specific domain. Ontology helps researchers understand that there is no absolute truth in the existence of entities and that there is no single reality. Truth emerges within the independent human mind, and reality exists according to how individuals experience it at any given time and place. Therefore, multiple truths and realities exist in human interactions and engagements, and researchers strive to unveil each layer of human existence.
- Epistemology is the study of knowledge. It seeks to understand what it means to know, how sources of knowledge are accessed, and under what conditions knowledge can be acquired. Epistemology guides researchers in the right direction of seeking knowledge. As knowledge is developed through individually experienced subjectivity, research procedures based on epistemology involve intuitive, logical, and empirical knowledge to explore phenomena in which people make and communicate meaning in specific situations. Every individual is positioned as having important knowledge about human behavior, and epistemology suggests how the relationship between the researcher and research participants should build knowledge as cocreators.
- Axiology is the study of the nature of value. It seeks to understand how individuals make ethical judgments derived from their values. Axiology encompasses both ethics (goodness) and aesthetics (beauty) in its attempt to understand what is valuable and why it is valuable in human behavior. The term *value* originally referred to the monetary worth of something, mainly in the business sense of trade value,

> but its meaning has expanded to include studies of morality, religion, and logic. In research, axiology helps researchers make their own judgments about value during the implementation of research. The values of researchers, such as their methods of collecting and interpreting data, affect how the research is conducted. More importantly, the researcher's values lead to the final outcomes of the research, as the value from a research perspective influences how meaning and characteristics are analyzed.

The qualitative method has evolved into a broad and complex range of approaches, incorporating interdisciplinary practices (e.g., communication, business, philosophy, psychology, political science, and history). As a result, qualitative researchers in strategic communication adopt a holistic approach to examining how ontological, epistemological, and axiological perspectives impact research procedures and outcomes.

Paradigms of Qualitative Methods

Qualitative research is designed to explore and interpret the meanings that inform human behavior and outcomes. Researchers interested in investigating social meaning aim to explore, describe, and explain a particular societal phenomenon. They acknowledge several paradigms central to qualitative research:

1. Researcher as instrument: In qualitative research, the researchers are active participants in the research process.[2] They use their own senses to observe and interact with participants, integrating their subjectivity, attitudes, and personality into the research. This means the researcher plays a key role in shaping the research findings and must be aware of their own biases and how these may influence the research.
2. Participant–researcher relationship: Qualitative research emphasizes the idea that researchers are tools for data collection, providing them with ethical guidelines for observing or researching people. A relationship between the researcher and the participant forms as soon as they engage in the research process. The participant–researcher relationship is crucial as they share the research space where they interact, communicate, and shape reality together. The researcher captures every moment and scene of the interactions within the boundaries of not harming the participant, which is a critical ethical rule in strategic communication research.
3. Contextualization: Qualitative research aims to understand and analyze complex human behavior through contextualized interpretation. Circular definition make sense of it in a particular situation where people exchange information with real meaning. Reality is a central concept in contextualizing the way people create social meaning, share personal experiences, and communicate different views. This methodological paradigm of qualitative research seeks verifiable interpretation from

socially interwoven contextualization of information in the real world. Qualitative researchers focus on analyzing their data by embracing multiple aspects of human attributes.

4. Skill sets of the researcher: Researchers in qualitative research possess special skills in detailing events or phenomena in words. They should be able to elaborate on complex research procedures in descriptive and explanatory language. After actively observing, interviewing, and listening to participants, researchers need high-skill analytic techniques to complete the process of interpreting contextualized and interconnected human behavior in reality.
5. Real-world setting: As qualitative research emphasizes an in-depth understanding of human behavior, the researcher plans fieldwork to engage with participants in a particular place, such as organizations, communities, and homes. The researcher collects data from the behavior of the participants who are observed and recorded. Based on the combination of the researcher's knowledge and the participants' answers and behavior, the results are drawn in the context of a real-world setting.

The qualitative research method enables the researchers to use all their available physical and mental functions for the research activity. The researcher's focus while conducting qualitative research remains in the process of making meaning and sharing meaning among the participants. This entails a deep inquiry into how humans socially and individually share constructed meanings in a real-world setting.

Conceptual/Theoretical Framework of Qualitative Research

In Chapter 2, we discussed the paths of inductive and deductive reasoning. If a hypothesis or a research question is developed based on theories and then data are collected, we refer to this process as deductive reasoning. Conversely, if data are collected and patterns are established to build a theory, we call this process inductive reasoning. Conceptually, quantitative research follows the path of deductive reasoning with hypotheses, while qualitative research takes the route of inductive reasoning with research questions (see Figure 6.1). However, most academic qualitative researchers use the deductive reasoning route to conduct scholarly research, although some researchers adopt the inductive reasoning route to create a theory or theoretical model. Departing from theories or theoretical models, qualitative researchers typically conduct a literature review (theoretical and conceptual framework), formulate research questions, and collect data for analysis.

In qualitative research, the literature review section guides researchers in formulating research questions. It is important to note that the literature review section in qualitative research places a high value on theoretical and conceptual frameworks to move to the next step of formulating the research question. For academic research purposes, qualitative research papers in the field of strategic communication commonly include a theory

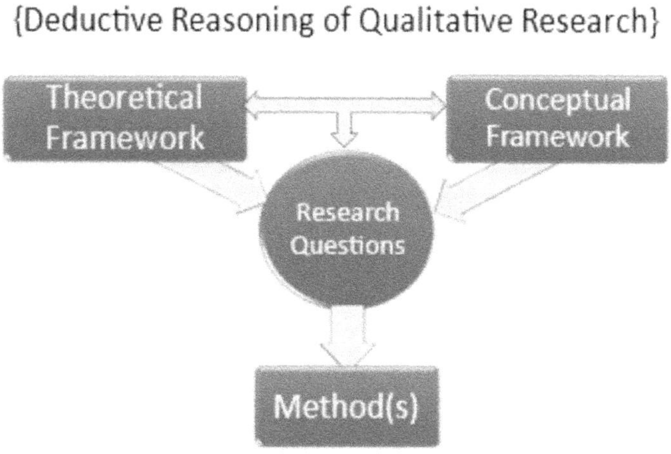

Figure 6.1 Frameworks to research questions
Source: Created by author.

or theories and a conceptual framework in the literature review section to formulate research questions. This is a customary practice in writing qualitative research papers, and we are expected to apply this practice to our research papers to be part of the academic community. If you intend to write a qualitative research paper as a researcher, your paper should contain a theory or theories (theoretical framework) relevant to your research topic and a conceptual framework that explains the fundamental concepts and key terms related to the research topic. As you have already taken or are taking a theory class, we will focus on discussing what a conceptual framework is.

The term *conceptual framework* is a confusing concept with various definitions, as it is still being conceptualized and developed by researchers who often use it in vague ways and interchangeably with other terms, including *logical models*, *the background of the study*, *conceptual maps*, and *theory*. These terms are used in the literature review section in qualitative research papers for headings or subheadings to explain key terms related to the research topic. For clarity, we will focus on two kinds of frameworks popularly used in literature reviews in the field of strategic communication: conceptual and theoretical.

- A conceptual framework showcases your comprehension of the literature, synthesizing it to elucidate the research topic. It identifies the key concepts necessary for the mapping process, encouraging you to integrate insights, knowledge, and arguments from other researchers into your perspective relevant to the research topic. Essentially, the conceptual framework is designed to pinpoint the most critical concepts about the research topic. You need to articulate the concepts that sparked your interest in conducting the research. When constructing the conceptual framework, you draw ideas from other scholarly articles that have already explored your topic and key concepts. These serve as references for your conceptual framework and aid in the development of new research questions that other scholars have yet to answer. For instance, if your research topic is "ethical concerns about ChatGPT via TikTok," your conceptual framework should identify and explicate key concepts such as the impact of ChatGPT on the public, the ethical debate about TikTok, and the government's policy on artificial intelligence's manipulative information. The conceptual framework represents your case for why your research is significant and relevant to the topic, and even to ongoing social phenomena. Therefore, the conceptual framework serves two roles: (1) it highlights multiple contexts of the topic, enabling you to take a comprehensive approach to examining any relevant issues and positions in your research process, and (2) it guides you not only to adopt a theory or theories to develop a theoretical framework but also to formulate research questions. For example, while conceptualizing ChatGPT and ethics as key concepts, you might find the artificial theory of mind useful in developing your theoretical framework. For qualitative research, using a theory or theoretical framework enhances the quality of your academic research paper.

- A theoretical framework is a collection of interrelated theoretical concepts, including a theory, theories, or theoretical models. Theories of communication and social science are built to explain, describe, criticize, and understand a particular phenomenon caused by human behavior or social systems. The theoretical framework for research papers can be viewed as the structure that supports the theory behind your research, introducing the theory and explaining why your research topic exists in association with the theory. For example, if you are interested in studying juvenile delinquents' use of communication tools, you might choose the labeling theory for the theoretical framework, which explains how society can negatively label a group of people whose behavior is deemed to deviate from the social norm. You could also add the uses and gratification theory to explore why the group members communicate with each other through a particular communication tool. Like the conceptual framework, the theoretical framework strengthens your research in three ways: (1) it connects you to an understating of the research topic under special circumstances, (2) it guides you to specify the particular phenomenon related to your research topic, and (3) it helps you formulate research questions based on the link between theoretical assumptions and human behavior in reality.[3]

Both conceptual and theoretical frameworks take up an important portion of a literature review in the structure of a qualitative research paper. Your research questions should be supported by the logic of the framework development process. You will likely explain several concepts, theories, or theoretical models in the literature review section to build a strong background for your research topic. In addition, the two frameworks separately or together enable you to reach the step of formulating the most crucial research questions that need to be answered to maximize understanding of the topic.

In practice, you can visualize the process of frameworks by placing all concepts and phenomena first and then specifying a topic with more narrowly tailored frameworks. For example, let's conceptualize the general term *strategic communication* for practice. The term is no longer unique or vague in the digital age since a wide range of entities and people from business, government, and academia used and developed the concept and practice of strategic communication. Over the last decade, a wide variety of industrial, academic, governmental, and nonprofit institutions have used the term according to their interpretation and application, which leads to a convoluted confusion as they attempt to assume the utmost authority in terms of the agreed-upon meaning of *strategic communication*.[4] So we look at previous research on strategic communication and take a comprehensive approach to conceptualizing it, as visualized in Figure 6.2.[5]

We select the four main entities that facilitate the practice of strategic communication (nongovernmental organizations, government, business, and academics) and identify the fundamental concepts of strategic communication, including persuasion, psychology, technology, information, channels, and media. After identifying the concepts, we can continue explaining some of them based on our research topic (e.g., diplomatic strategic communication of government, strategic communication tactics of food delivery companies, and psychological operations of strategic communication for charity organizations). In addition, we add a theoretical framework to formulate research questions (e.g., cognitive dissonance theory to develop the link between eating disorders and YouTube content

Figure 6.2 An example of conceptualizing strategic communication

Source: Created by author.

creators' food porn strategies). As we see here, both conceptual and theoretical frameworks in qualitative research can only be used when you have sufficient basic knowledge of theories and the literature to lay the foundation for the formulation of research questions. It should be mentioned that your research questions should be as specific, feasible, and relevant as possible to your topic.

Designing Qualitative Research

A research design serves as the blueprint for a research project, guiding the researcher toward obtaining relevant scientific data or evidence related to the research topic. It involves five key processes: (1) topic identification, (2) literature review, (3) formulation of research questions and/or hypotheses, (4) data collection, and (5) data analysis methods. While quantitative research designs aim to collect numerical data that can be generalized, qualitative research designs focus on exploring, describing, and explaining specific human behavioral phenomena. Researchers generally select one of these designs based on their confidence and academic comfort. Qualitative research design seeks to answer the whys and hows of the phenomenon under study. It provides a systematic approach to conducting qualitative research. Unlike quantitative research, which focuses on numerical data analysis, qualitative design adopts a comprehensive approach to the phenomenon. Let's discuss the step-by-step design from initiating to concluding qualitative research.

Choosing a Topic

Before doing anything, just know your positionality (the relationship of you and your characteristics to choosing a topic and setting expectations). The inception of most research projects is an idea or interest. The question "What research topic are you interested in?" often guides researchers in deciding their topic. In qualitative research, most topics are closely tied to contemporary social phenomena impacting individual lives. Strategic communication researchers often stay abreast of the media to explore intriguing research topics. Their personal values and beliefs intertwine with their research positionality, influencing their choice of research topic. In essence, the interest in researching a particular phenomenon relevant to the researcher's positionality stems from their political preference, cultural background, sexuality, ethnicity, or social status. For instance, a researcher from a wealthy, interracial celebrity family might be interested in exploring the relationship between affluent interracial couples and the marital crises they experience triggered by social issues like racial profiling. If you are a qualitative researcher struggling to choose your research topic, consider these questions: (1) Am I interested in current events, government, politics, world affairs, or any specific social issue? (2) Is there something that conflicts with my values and beliefs, motivating me to learn more about it? (3) What do I aim to understand, explain, or discover, and why? (4) What benefits will I gain from conducting this research? Most researchers find their topics rooted in their personal experiences and positionality, reflecting the stance they have chosen within the given research topic.[6]

Formulating Research Questions

In qualitative research design, researchers typically formulate research questions rather than hypotheses, which are more common in quantitative research. Qualitative research questions often start with "What is happening here?" reflecting an interest in exploring social phenomena. We aim to describe how individuals interpret their experiences and explain their behaviors in real-world settings. Once an interesting societal phenomenon is identified, we develop a specific topic and setting, which then guides the development of research questions. The formulation of research questions in qualitative research is often an evolving process. The questions can be reformulated as the topic is conceptualized or even as data are collected. Some researchers successfully formulate research questions immediately after selecting the research topic, while others delay this step until after completing a theoretical framework and literature review. Both approaches are valid, and as a qualitative researcher, you can choose the path that suits you best. However, ensure that your literature review, including the conceptual and theoretical frameworks, directly relates to your research questions and aligns with ongoing discussions, existing theories, and previous findings in the field of strategic communication.

Assessing Qualitative Research Methods for Data Collection

Once you have your research question(s), the next step is to determine the qualitative research method you will use to answer them. In other words, you strategize how to collect data as evidence for the answers. Primary data collection methods for qualitative research include in-depth interviews, focus groups, ethnography, case studies, and qualitative surveys (refer to Chapter 7 for more information). You select one or two of these methods to plan your data collection process. For instance, if you choose in-depth interviews, you identify a specific group of people who can answer your research questions in a one-on-one interview setting. When selecting a qualitative method, consider factors such as your academic abilities, attitudes, and resources. An objective assessment of these factors can lead to successful data collection. Since qualitative research often requires researchers to be in the field where participants live, it is important to consider the resources available for fieldwork, including time and money, before finalizing your data collection method.

Selecting your Research Participants

In qualitative research, the selection of research participants is a critical step that follows the choice of research method. This process involves considering who to study and where and when to do it. The aim is to examine a specific group of individuals who form a sample of the target population. To devise an effective sampling strategy, prioritize the path to answering your research questions. Selecting the right group of people who can respond to your questions becomes a key strategy in your sampling decision. This means you should carefully seek research participants who can relate to the full range of your research questions, ideally forming a homogeneous sample. Homogeneous sampling involves selecting similar individuals or cases in order to understand and describe a particular group in depth. For instance, if your research focuses on communication barriers between female coaches and male athletes, you would select only current male college athletes and female college coaches as the homogeneous sample. After deciding whom to sample, consider potential places to gather data, such as single or multiple sites, or online or offline, depending on how you plan to question or observe the participants.

Determining Data Analysis Instruments

After gathering data from a homogeneous sample, the next step is to analyze and interpret the data. Unlike quantitative data, which are typically analyzed with statistical tools, qualitative data are analyzed using methods such as qualitative content analysis, narrative analysis, discourse analysis, conversation analysis, and grounded theory analysis. These analytical methods focus on describing and explaining the meanings of words, images, phrases, symbols, and signs used in social or individual settings. As most qualitative data stem from communicated words and symbols with people or organizations, researchers begin the analysis process by reading the data and uncovering particular patterns or themes. They aim to identify the most common responses to questions and interpret meaning in context. Qualitative research gathers spoken or written word-based data, and qualitative researchers delve into the meaning of the data, aiming to identify and interpret how and why people behave in a particular way within their cultural and societal context. For example, analyzing how and why spectators of the National Hockey League (NHL) swear a lot during games is an example of qualitative research.

Addressing Validity

Validity, viewed as the academic trustworthiness of the research process and its outcomes, is highly valued in qualitative research. In qualitative research design, researchers strive to demonstrate that their research outcomes will be credible and acceptable through scholarly explanation and interpretation of the phenomenon they plan to research. Several approaches to academic validity for qualitative research include (1) truth value—establishing confidence in the truth of the findings, (2) applicability—the extent to which the findings have usefulness in other contexts, (3) consistency—whether the findings can be repeated, and (4) neutrality—the degree to which the findings are determined by the research participants, not the researcher.[7] In qualitative research, the choice of methods is crucial to achieving some degree of validity because the processes used in collecting data greatly influence academic approval from other scholars. If the data were collected from invalid participants or sources, leading to invalid outcomes, the entire research could be deemed a failure. A key to achieving validity is triangulation, which reduces fundamental biases from the use of a single method. Triangulation, referred to as the use of multiple methods or data sources, is an effort to help explore and explain complex human behavior using a variety of methods to offer a more balanced explanation to the audience of your research paper.[8]

Writing the Research Design Paper

The research design outlines your research plan, demonstrating that your project is both feasible and capable of answering your research questions with evidence from the data you plan to collect. When writing a research design paper, consider it as a concise version of your entire research paper. This paper provides an opportunity to strategize your research process. The length of a research design in your paper can vary depending on the level of detail in your description. However, your research design paper should include the following elements, according to the librarians of the University of Southern California:

1. Identify the research topic clearly and justify its selection, particularly in relation to any valid alternative designs that could have been used.
2. Review and synthesize previously published scholarly literature associated with the research topic.
3. Clearly and explicitly specify research questions central to the topic.
4. Describe the information and/or data that will be gathered from participants.
5. Explain how such information and/or data will be obtained.
6. Describe the methods of analysis to be applied to the data in answering the research questions and interpreting meaning.[9]

In essence, the research design serves as a guide, providing an overall sense of what to do for your research project in the form of an outline or blueprint. While the structure and contents of the research design vary, students of strategic communication can use the outline given in Box 6.1 for a research design paper.

Box 6.1
Qualitative Research Design Paper Format

Research Design Paper Format

Important Notice: The student is expected to write a research design paper (double-spaced) in the academic writing format of the APA. There should be no typos, grammar/punctuation errors, or APA format discrepancies.

Student Name:

1. **Introduction (between three and four paragraphs)**
    - Introduces the topic in broad terms
    - States field's (discipline's) recognition of the topic
    - Briefly summarizes the context and significance of the project
    - Shows the connection between strategic communication (the field) and the problem area (topic)
2. **Literature Review and RQ(s): Between three and five paragraphs**
    - Relates the proposed project to specific issues and areas of inquiry within the field
        - ▪ Conceptual framework
    - Delineates the major and relevant theoretical position(s) pertaining to your problem
        - ▪ Theoretical framework
    - Explains how your project will extend, revise, or complicate what is already known
        - ✓ Draws on previous material, explain the issues you plan to investigate
        - ✓ Must include research questions (hypotheses are optional if necessary)
3. **Methods (between one and two paragraphs)**
    - This section contains an overall description of your approach, materials, and procedures.
        - ◦ What method will be used?
        - ◦ How will data be collected and analyzed?
        - ◦ What materials will be used?

THE ALL-INCLUSIVE APPROACH TO QUALITATIVE RESEARCH

Qualitative research and quantitative research differ fundamentally: the former focuses on words, while the latter emphasizes numbers. Researchers further distinguish what academic research is and how it is conducted by comparing aspects such as sampling selection and presentation of findings.

- Sampling selection: Sampling can be categorized into two types: probability and nonprobability. Qualitative research often relies on or includes nonprobability sampling, focusing on identifying research participants, events, organizations, and written or oral documents that serve the purpose. The researcher aims to understand a social phenomenon or specific individual behavior embodied in social structures in order to interpret their meaning. Qualitative research is commonly viewed as subjective, in contrast to the objective nature of quantitative research. Instead of aiming for a large sample size, qualitative researchers select a small subset of the population that aligns with the purpose of the study. This means participants are chosen as the sample because their specific characteristics can purposefully answer the research questions. The sample is biased and nonrandomly selected. Therefore, the researcher should explain why the sample is special or important, justifying the sampling process in terms of settings, activities, and the unique characteristics of the sample. For instance, if you recruited nine participants from a rare religious cult that has never been researched before, you need to justify why these seven individuals are so important or unique to your research project, given the small sample size.

- Presentation of findings: To present the results or findings of qualitative research, the researcher provides a detailed context of the entire research journey, including quotations, field notes, or other data that should be identified in a way that enables the reader to judge the range of evidence being used. The presentation should include detailed explanations of how the sample was observed and recorded, what patterns or themes were generated, and who else was involved in conducting and analyzing the research. The qualitative research method requires more articulate work to integrate individual behavior into social phenomena in the context of research evidence, contrasting with the quantitative research method, which allows numbers to speak for scientific results. The researcher should present clear distinctions between the data and the interpretation, backed by sufficient original evidence justified by the sample size. This is a critical process in achieving validity for any qualitative research findings.

Data Analysis in Qualitative Research

Data analysis in qualitative research can be challenging unless researchers are equipped with strong writing and transcribing skills. Unlike quantitative researchers who analyze data based on statistical tests, qualitative researchers interpret data based on written or spoken accounts, which include detailed outcomes in the form of words or texts. When it comes to qualitative data analysis, you first classify the data into qualitative techniques of language analysis such as discourse analysis, narrative analysis, grounded theory analysis, conversation analysis, and content analysis.

- Discourse analysis: This technique focuses on analyzing written or spoken language in relation to its social context. It is especially useful for explaining how language is used to create meaning in real situations where humans communicate their values, beliefs, and assumptions to others in a social, political, historical, and cultural context.

- Narrative analysis: Stories told by people or organizations can be understood through narrative analysis. Researchers interpret the construction of stories from what participants narrate, helping them make sense of their lives and represent themselves to others in society.
- Grounded theory analysis: In this approach, the researcher constructs their own theory about a topic based on the data collected during the research process. After data collection and analysis, the researcher can build a theoretical assumption or model derived from the data. This technique is limited to the use of inductive reasoning.
- Conversation analysis: This technique focuses on explaining the systems of human conversations, which follow social rules and patterns. It aims to explore an underlying body of social talk-in-interaction by examining words.
- Content analysis: Texts, images, and visual content can be qualitatively analyzed using this technique. It is viewed as a systematic and objective means of making sense of the data. It requires special procedures such as coding, categorization, or theme identification, which is the content of communication (see Chapter 13 for detailed information).

Among these qualitative analysis techniques, you will choose one based on your analytical skills and preference. However, you can generalize the steps of analyzing qualitative data and interpreting data regardless of the specific techniques:

1. Prepare your data: Transcribing research data is the first and most important step in organizing your data analysis process. The transcribed data are a critical element in the meaning-making process because you will translate what your participants said and how they behaved into a context of qualitative analysis.
2. Review your data: You read the transcribed data several times to get a sense of what the data imply or to uncover meaning in the data. As the data may contain metaphors, sarcasm, and unspoken agendas, it is your responsibility to highlight some keywords, significant phrases, and unique ideas from the data.
3. Categorize your data: Departing from the reviewed data, you categorize them into the specific actions and feelings of the participants. Their particular actions and feelings expressed in your data can be captured and categorized by your understanding. You can sort them out with several themes in categorization, and you discover specific patterns in the data.

4. Interpret your data: With the patterns, you explain the process of meaning-making. As most qualitative researchers assume that a certain type of particular human behavior stems from meaningful actions in some way, you interpret these actions with the meaning given by your scholarly insights.

To ensure the validity of your qualitative research findings, the data you analyze and interpret can be easily understood and agreed upon by other researchers or readers. Additionally, the analysis and interpretation should provide compelling evidence that answers your research questions within the appropriate context.

Applying AI Technologies to Qualitative Research Practice

AI technologies have the potential to greatly enhance qualitative research practices. From data collection to analysis, AI can streamline workflows, enhance insights, and unlock new avenues for exploration. Let's delve into some recent examples of how AI is being used in qualitative research:

1. Automated transcription services: AI-powered transcription services such as Assembly AI and Otter.ai, which identify emotions and speaker nuances in audio recordings, can transcribe audio and video data into text, saving researchers considerable time and effort. This can be particularly useful for interviews or focus group discussions.
2. Text analysis tools: AI can help analyze large amounts of text data. Natural language processing (NLP) techniques can identify patterns, themes, and sentiments in the data, providing valuable insights for the researcher.[10]
3. Data visualization tools: AI can help visualize data in meaningful ways, making it easier to understand and interpret complex data sets. This can enhance research presentations, facilitate stakeholder discussions, and deepen understanding of complex findings.
4. Predictive analysis: AI can help predict future trends based on existing data, which can be useful in longitudinal studies. Tools like Amazon Forecast and Google Cloud can analyze historical qualitative data to predict future trends and behaviors.[11]
5. Participant recruitment: AI can help identify and recruit potential participants for a study. For example, it can analyze social media data to find individuals who match the study's criteria. As a result, using AI-powered clustering algorithms to segment qualitative data based on key characteristics enables researchers to tailor communication strategies and interventions to specific audience segments.[12]

AI is transforming qualitative research, offering exciting possibilities and raising ethical considerations. By critically evaluating and responsibly integrating these tools, researchers can gain deeper insights, enhance research efficiency, and contribute to more informed and impactful communication strategies.

APPLICATION OF AN AI-POWERED TOOL

BOX 6.2
EXAMPLE OF USING GOOGLE GEMINI FOR FRAMEWORKS OF TIKTOK

Using an AI-Powered Tool (Google Gemini) for Conceptual and Theoretical Frameworks

Command syntax: Write a conceptual and theoretical framework about the use of TikTok and the uses and gratifications theory.

Answer: Sure. Here is a conceptual and theoretical framework for the use of TikTok and the uses and gratifications theory:

The uses and gratifications theory (UGT) is a media effects theory that was developed in the 1940s and 1950s. The theory argues that people use media to fulfill their needs and wants. The needs and wants that people use media to fulfill are called gratifications.

The UGT has been used to explain a wide range of media use, including the use of TikTok. Some of the gratifications that people may use TikTok to fulfill include:

- Passing time: TikTok is a great way to pass the time when you're bored or have a few minutes to spare.
- Entertainment: TikTok is a great way to be entertained. There are videos on TikTok about everything from funny memes to cooking tutorials.
- Social connection: TikTok is a great way to connect with friends and family. You can share videos with your friends and family, and you can also follow other users who share your interests.
- Information: TikTok is a great way to learn new things. There are videos on TikTok about everything from history to science.
- Escape: TikTok can be a great way to escape from the stresses of everyday life. You can watch videos about funny animals or travel destinations, and you can also listen to music and watch funny videos.

The UGT is a useful theory for understanding why people use TikTok. The theory helps us to understand the motivations behind people's media use, and it can also help us to predict how people will use media in the future. It is important to note that the UGT is not a perfect theory.

The theory does not take into account the individual differences between people, and it also does not take into account the social and cultural context in which people use media. However, the UGT is a useful tool for understanding why people use media, and it can also help us to develop effective media interventions.

Summary

- ✓ Qualitative researchers seek in-depth knowledge about people's attitudes, opinions, and motivations in a particular social environment.
- ✓ As the study of being or what it is in existence, ontology seeks the entities in the universe.
- ✓ As the study of knowledge, epistemology is concerned with attempts to understand what it means to know.
- ✓ As the study of the nature of value, axiology seeks to understand how individuals make ethical judgments derived from their values.
- ✓ The phrase *researcher as instrument* refers to the researcher as an active participant in research.
- ✓ Qualitative research aims to understand and analyze complicated human behavior through contextualized interpretation.
- ✓ Researchers in qualitative research have special skills in using words to describe events and phenomena.
- ✓ A conceptual framework demonstrates the researcher's understanding of the literature in a synthesizing manner.
- ✓ A theoretical framework is a collection of interrelated theoretical concepts, including a theory, theories, or theoretical models.
- ✓ A research design is the framework of research methods and techniques chosen by a researcher.
- ✓ A research design specifies at least five processes: (1) topic identification, (2) literature review, (3) research question and/or hypothesis formation, (4) data collection, and (5) data analysis method.
- ✓ The qualitative research method differs from quantitative research with regard to sampling selection and presentation of findings.

✓ Transcribing research data is the first and most important step to organizing the data analysis process.

✓ AI can help visualize data in meaningful ways, making it easier to understand and interpret complex data sets.

Key Terms

1. Ontology
2. Epistemology
3. Axiology
4. Researcher as instrument
5. Contextualization
6. Conceptual framework
7. Theoretical framework
8. Research design
9. Data analysis
10. Interpretation

Chapter 7

Applications of Qualitative Research

Chapter Learning Outcomes

- Explore expectations of in-depth interviews.
- Apply journalistic interview skills to the practice of qualitative interviews.
- Discuss different structures of in-depth interviews.
- Explain the difference between online and offline focus groups.
- Recognize the process of conducting a focus group study.
- Discuss why marketing/business research prefers focus groups.
- Identify the characteristics of ethnography.
- Describe the different roles of ethnographic researchers.
- Explain the goals of case studies.
- Recognize the practical advantages of case studies.
- Leverage AI technology in qualitative research data collection.

Qualitative researchers acquire data to interpret or construct meaning. The data they collect are often detailed and rich, enabling them to gain a profound understanding of the subjects and phenomena under study. Qualitative research is a flexible approach that empowers researchers to delve into complex and sensitive topics, such as human behavior, social interactions, and cultural practices. By employing methods such as in-depth interviews, focus groups, ethnography, and case studies, qualitative researchers can glean nuanced insights into their participants' experiences, perspectives, and motivations. These methods are especially useful when the goal is to comprehend the rationale behind people's actions or to explore new or emerging phenomena.

In-Depth Interviews

In-depth interviews are a tool used by qualitative researchers to gain insights into the unique knowledge about human behavior that is conveyed through individual and social communication activities. The aim is to gather vivid, personalized, and contextualized information from participants. The primary objective of qualitative in-depth interviews is to obtain a deep understanding of a specific group of people's unique perspective on the research topic. During the interview, the researcher focuses on gathering information about the interviewees' experiences, their understanding and perception of reality relevant to the topic, and the reasons behind their constructed perspective. In-depth interviews are a customized form of communication between the researcher and the interviewee in a research setting. The researcher poses questions, and the interviewee responds and expresses their thoughts. This process is seen as an information exchange initiated by the researcher and responded to by the interviewee.

In qualitative research, in order to better understand the research topic, the researcher delves into the interviewee's experiences and perspectives, which the interviewee describes and explains. In this context, the interviewee—not the researcher—is the expert on the topic, and the researcher serves as a facilitator who encourages the expert to provide valuable and rich information about the topic. For instance, the group of interviewees being interviewed will decide what to share and how much to share about the topic based on their opinions and experiences. Their information sharing can be limited and may not be fully transparent due to personal issues and concerns. However, the researcher can incorporate all the information acquired to gain a more comprehensive understanding of the topic after interviewing all chosen interviewees.

In-depth interviews enable the researcher to collect exploratory, explanatory, and descriptive information provided by the interviewees while looking for patterns that emerge from their narratives. The researcher plays the dual role of questioner and listener to make interviewees feel comfortable in sharing their personal information. The process of exchanging questions and answers throughout an in-depth interview aims to yield a wide range of descriptions, realities, and phenomena through the perspective lenses of each interviewee. The interactive communication between the researcher and each interviewee helps the researcher assemble all the information and convert it into primary data for qualitative research, which the researcher later decides how to use, analyze, and interpret.

By conducting an in-depth interview, the researcher expects to

- Obtain an insight into the interviewee.
- Learn how each interviewee constructs and interprets meaning differently about the topic.
- Gain more knowledge about the topic.
- Understand each interviewee's context and motivation.
- Gather high-quality data from interviewees as they are interviewed one-on-one.

- Integrate multiple perspectives into the formation of the meaning of the topic.
- Build a holistic understanding of a particular group of people about the topic.[1]

Three Structures of In-Depth Interviews

In-depth interviews involve asking each interviewee a series of questions primarily related to a single topic. The organization and structure of the questions can significantly impact the information obtained from the interviewees. Therefore, it is crucial to carefully structure the questions and plan the interview process. Generally, in-depth interviews are conducted using one of three different structures, depending on the research questions and expected outcomes. When designing an in-depth interview, you might consider using one of these structures to gather valuable information for your research data (see also figure 7.1).

- Structured interview: This type of interview adheres strictly to an interview protocol, guiding the interview process with a comprehensive list of questions. Often referred to as *survey interviews*, structured interviews present each interviewee with identical questions in the same order. This approach leaves no room for interviewees to bring up additional conversations. They only answer the questions

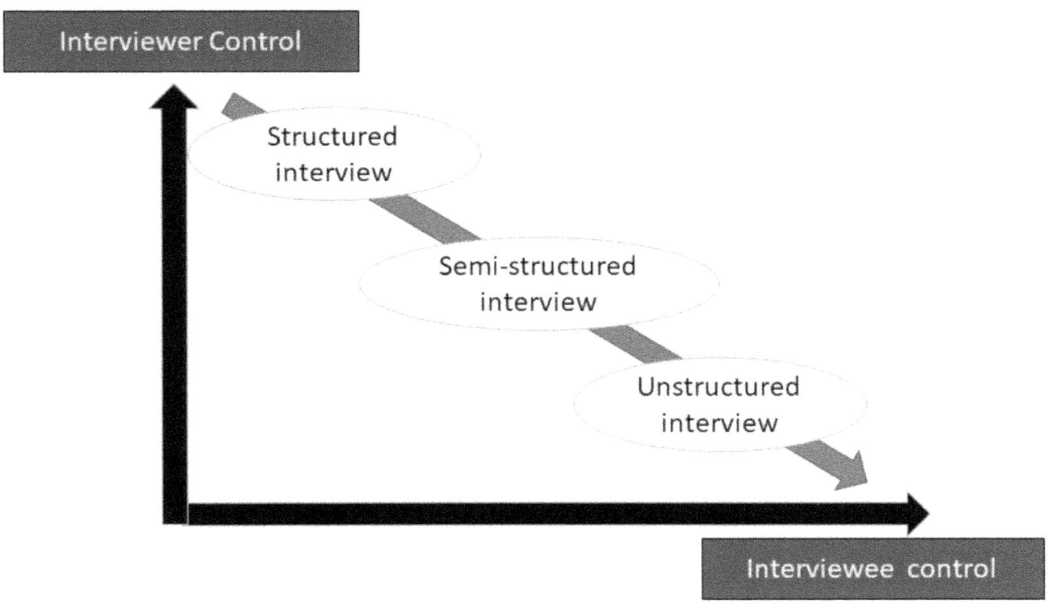

Figure 7.1 In-depth interview structure
Source: Created by author.

asked, and you do not pose any follow-up questions that are not already in the set of questions. This structure leverages uniformity across interviews to expedite the interview process efficiently.

- Unstructured interview: This type of interview allows each interviewee to feel comfortable while having a normal conversation relevant to the research topic. You inform the interviewees of the topic and let them discuss anything about the topic without any specific protocol. Since there is no set of questions, their answers can deviate from the scope of the topic, and it may take a longer period with more sessions to complete the interview in terms of information gathering. You need to be patient with participants' talking and strive to have more friendly conversations.
- Semistructured interview: This type of interview lies between structured and unstructured interviews. It uses a certain list of questions, allowing each interviewee some freedom to discuss other ideas and opinions not covered by the questions but still relevant to the topic. During or after answering questions, the interviewee and you have a topic-related natural conversation. You even allow the interviewee to digress. This process can yield new knowledge or information you never anticipated. In this structure, you have the opportunity to seek clarity with follow-up questions based on what the interviewee actually meant. If you need to conduct an in-depth interview in a short amount of time, a highly structured and organized process is best. On the other hand, an unstructured interview allows the conversation to flow wherever the interviewee takes it within the topic. In this case, you would simply listen and watch for any patterns that emerge. A semistructured interview combines both conversational and guided elements, providing flexibility for both you and the interviewee.

Conducting an In-Depth Interview with Skill

Historically, an in-depth interview in qualitative research is seen as a conversational method that elicits information reflecting the interviewee's perspective toward reality. It can be likened to an academic form of investigative journalism, where journalists strive to produce large-scale news stories with multiple sources and extensive data. Both investigative news reports and research based on in-depth interviews aim for an in-depth understanding of a single topic. Good journalists are acknowledged for their excellent interview skills to gather newsworthy information, and they strive to master essential interviewing techniques. For news interviews, journalists are advised to follow these principles:

- Prepare carefully, familiarizing yourself with as much background as possible.
- Establish a relationship with the source conducive to obtaining information.

- Ask questions that are relevant to the source and that induce the source to talk.
- Listen and watch attentively.[2]

As a qualitative researcher conducting an interview, you can apply these journalistic interview principles to your research practice: (1) before posing questions, prepare and familiarize yourself with the background of your topic and the interviewee; (2) explain the interview process to the interviewee, outlining expectations and protocols; (3) pose questions and allow the interviewee to respond; and (4) listen and record responsively. However, in-depth interviews necessitate additional academic skills since an in-depth interview is a two-way partnership in a meaning-making process between you and the interviewee. While the interviewee shares a story over a range of topics, pay attention to the information-sharing conversation in the process of constructing meaning. The primary reason to conduct an in-depth interview is to gain information about specific human behavior as a result of people's feelings, opinions, knowledge, perspectives, and senses. You need to capture the moment while interviewing. Here are practical criteria to enhance your interviewing skills as a qualitative researcher:

- Handling: Influence the course of the interview to prevent digression from the topic. Assist the interviewee in focusing on answering questions or telling a story directly related to the topic.
- Patience: Be understanding and sensitive to what the interviewee says. Allow the interviewee to speak, and listen patiently to any provocative or unorthodox opinions.
- Clarity: Be simple and clear with questions. Pose spoken questions to the interviewee that can be easily understood.
- Knowledge: Know the topic and the characteristics of the interviewee. Ensure your own deep knowledge of the topic so the interviewee feels reassured about having the conversation.
- Interpretation: Make an interpretation of what the interviewee meant. Apply all your research skills to the meaning-making process.[3]
- While conducting an in-depth interview, record the information provided by the interviewee, either by taking notes or by using recording devices with permission. If taking notes, you need to be unobtrusive while trying not to lose eye contact with the interviewee, who could be less talkative with no eye contact. If using a video recorder or voice recorder app on your smartphone, ensure that the interviewee has your full attention at the moment, which will result in the interview yielding more information.

Academic Issues With In-Depth Interviews

Before the interview, it is essential to familiarize yourself with the fundamental background of the topic and the interviewees. While the topic is chosen by you and is thus familiar, gathering background information on the characteristics of the interviewees can be challenging until you interview them. The primary reason to know your interviewees before the interview is to ensure that they belong to the selected group for your research sample. Some of them could be dishonest from the very beginning of the sampling process. If they misrepresented their identification to become one of your interviewees, your research data could be significantly distorted. However, even without a prescreening process, you can still validate your data by verifying and assessing their information. They could overemphasize or hide information, or simply provide you with false or partially true information due to traits of lying, exaggerating, or having faulty memory. In such cases, gaining insight into the topic becomes impossible.

Like most investigative reporters, qualitative researchers conducting in-depth interviews carry out a process of fact checking. Depending on the interviewee's characteristics, the data can be biased, and you could discover discrepancies in the data. To clarify this information, contact your interviewees again with follow-up questions and key ideas to verify the credibility of the information you gathered for use as data. As soon as you filter out any inaccurate information, you may begin to analyze and interpret the data. An in-depth interview is recognized as an effective qualitative research type for gaining practical knowledge about particular phenomena involving specific groups of people. Its core lies in a process of communicative interaction that forms a two-way conversation between you and the interviewee, and your well-honed interviewing skills will maximize the likelihood of gaining insightful data.

Focus Groups

In research, a focus group is a qualitative data collection method that involves gathering a group of people to discuss their thoughts and opinions about a product, idea, or public figure. Focus groups are often used by corporations for market research on their products and services, or by political strategists investigating the viability of candidates running for governmental positions. For instance, a focus group study in 1959 recommended that Mattel produce Barbie, one of the first fashion dolls. In 2014, another focus group suggested that the company introduce a new "curvier Barbie to appeal to a more varied audience."[4]

Focus group research is similar to group interviews, but instead of interviewing people one-on-one, the researcher invites multiple people to a location to generate data in a group setting. For example, a focus group researcher might select 10 participants, place them in a room at the same time, and interview them about a topic. A focus group is also considered a type of group discussion about a topic, led by a trained group moderator, usually the focus group researcher. Organizations in the field of strategic communication—such as market research firms, advertising agencies, and opinion research institutions—invest significant amounts of time and money to conduct focus groups as a group-based data collection technique.

In a focus group setting, participants are encouraged to interact with and influence each other while expressing actionable insights based on their specific knowledge about the topic. In other words, each participant can respond to each other's comments relating to their thoughts and attitudes toward a series of questions asked by the moderator. While sharing their opinions and thoughts about the topic, participants may become involved in the process of creating a context of groupthink, which occurs when all participants think similarly to generate a group understanding of the topic. To avoid groupthink, the focus group moderator needs to create a safe and supportive environment where participants feel comfortable sharing their thoughts and opinions. The moderator should also be careful not to lead the discussion or to influence participants' answers.[5] If the researcher offers a group setting that ensures participants feel comfortable sharing their thoughts and opinions, a focus group serves as a great tool for capturing the moment as meaning is shared through the specific group of people in the same space. As a result, interactive communication is produced in the group context.

Since focus groups and surveys are among the most popular market research methods, researchers in strategic communication should familiarize themselves with the procedural components of focus groups. This includes how to select focus group participants, how to act as a moderator, and how to analyze focus group data. See figure 7.2.

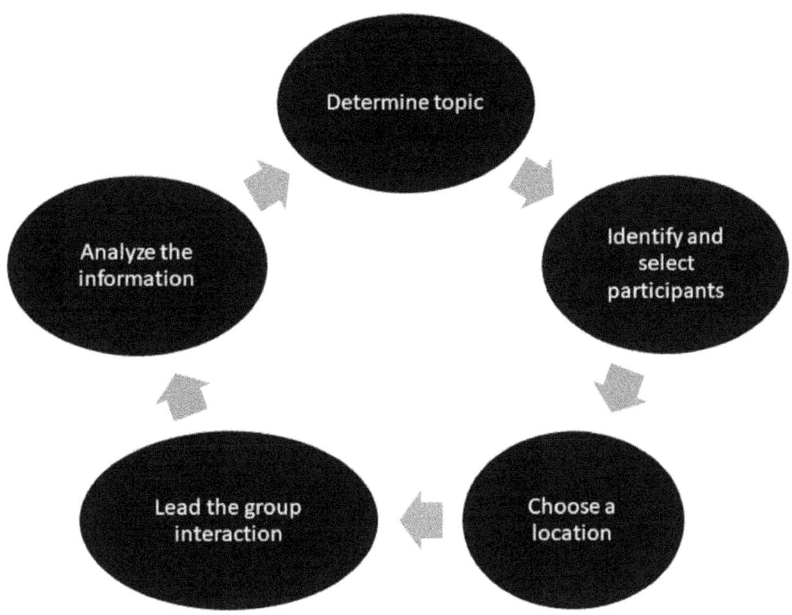

Figure 7.2 Focus group process

Source: Created by author.

How to Select Focus Group Participants

When selecting participants for a focus group, keep in mind that the aim of a focus group is to gain insight about how a specific group of people in a forum think or feel about a topic or situation. The participants are selected based on your research purpose and with the characteristic of homogeneity, meaning that they must have something in common. For example, if you conduct a focus group on the topic of the design of baby formula containers, the homogeneous participants could be those who became parents of babies in the last year. Here is another example: if you are organizing a focus group to discuss iPhone beauty apps with female baby boomers, all participants should have been born before 1964 to maintain age homogeneity. Ideally, a focus group should range in size from 6 to 10 participants, but there is no definitive range for the number.

Although the ideal number of participants varies based on the focus group type, the traditionally recommended size for a focus group in commercial research is 10–12 participants, and for noncommercial research it is 5–8 participants.[6] You can imagine them sitting in a seminar class where a small number of people have enough time for an in-depth discussion about the topic. A large group of more than 10 people would not be recommended because it can deter each participant's opportunity to express independent perspectives across the questions and topics. On the other hand, if the group is smaller than 5, the participants can feel pressured to talk more to fill any vacant silence. They could end up offering unfruitful information. Hence, the size of the participant group should be carefully determined by you based on your research purpose.

How to Act as a Moderator

One unique characteristic of a focus group is that you decide to become either the researcher or the moderator, or both. This means that if you hire a moderator to interact with the participants, you observe and record their conversations and activities from a distance. If you decide to play both roles, which is likely to save money, you lead the discussion with the group and take notes simultaneously. This role could be challenging, especially the part about taking notes, but recording devices can be a solution. You conduct your focus group study, acting as the moderator, while recording the conversation. Another important piece of advice is that after selecting and inviting all participants to a safe and comfortable room, you should offer them a conversation-friendly environment where all participants feel included in the process of an open-ended discussion. You allow each participant to share independent ideas and perspectives to contribute to the focus group research. Because of the open-ended discussion method, each participant answers, and others respond or interact. Some disagreements can arise when participants exchange heated or emotional comments, especially from dominating participants.

Your primary duty as the moderator is to keep the conversation flowing in the right direction and to make the group's time as productive as possible.[7] Since leading the group and taking notes simultaneously can be challenging, you should focus on guiding the conversation to stay with the research topic. Let the recording device handle the note-taking part. Ensure that you hear from every participant and that all participants have the right to respectfully refute each other's opinions. You can also allow them to question and answer each other to obtain more information. The moderator plays a critical role in engaging all participants in active conversation about the topic, and if the moderator fails to foster constructive conversation, the entire research session will end up being futile. Hence, the moderator should be able to

- Ask questions to all participants.
- Listen to answers from each participant and conversations between all participants.
- Keep the focus group on the right track.
- Run a fair and friendly focus group for all participants.
- Treat all participants with respect.

Again, you should make sure to keep the group talking and sharing in-depth qualitative data by making them feel comfortable in the environment.

How to Analyze Focus Group Data

The primary reason focus group research has become one of the two dominant forms of data collection in market research (the other being surveys) is its utility in gathering in-depth information that stems from the interaction between group participants who exchange ideas and opinions. After recording the entire process, you analyze what they said and how they responded to your questions and requests. It is now time to take notes from the recorded data, which can be voluminous and overwhelming. You screen and select valuable information, noting what is said word for word. In dealing with such an arduous effort, you should attempt to detect the main concepts, ideas, or patterns on the topic.

One crucial task in analyzing focus group data is to write down direct quotations that highlight the importance of your research topic and bring interesting perspectives on behalf of your research purpose. Conflicting opinions also enrich the analysis as they demonstrate the diversity of focus group findings from multiple viewpoints. More importantly, since the group interaction is what makes a focus group different from other forms of data collection, you need to include nonverbal cues and nontextual moments from the participants in the data analysis. For example, facial expressions, pauses, eye gazes, and interruptions during the group interaction can be described and explained if they are worthy of interpretation and meaning construction. Like in-depth interviews, a focus group is designed to collect data in a group context that allows humans to identify and explore socially embedded perceptions and values toward a product, idea, or candidate. The data collected from a focus group are used to uncover ideas and opinions from a homogeneous group of people.

Online Focus Groups

More researchers are shifting their focus group locations from offline to online. An online focus group is conducted via an online platform, enabling researchers to conduct focus group research with participants remotely. Popular video conferencing platforms like Zoom or Microsoft Teams are commonly used for online focus groups, allowing the moderator to direct the online conversation and keep it flowing. Rapidly advancing communication technology makes online focus groups easier, more cost effective, and more accessible to people all around the world. Additionally, the sudden popularity of online classes during the coronavirus pandemic has encouraged college students to become familiar with online platforms like Zoom, Microsoft Teams, or Google Meet. Such phenomena have enhanced the trend of conducting and participating in online focus groups for both researchers and participants. Compared to offline or traditional focus groups, online focus groups have several advantages:

- Time: The moderator and participants do not need to travel to a particular place. They can access an online focus group from anywhere connected to the internet. Time is saved as there is no place to drive.
- Geography: An online group is useful when the participants are spread over a wide geographical area. The moderator living abroad or participants from other continents can share and express their opinions and ideas in the group context.
- Representativeness: There is no limit to finding an appropriate and representative sample for the moderator, who can reach any kind of people without regard to geographical barriers or physical restrictions.
- Honesty: Instead of being face-to-face with each other in an actual place, participants, especially younger ones, feel more natural and comfortable in an online environment. Hence, the answers and information the moderator receives can be more honest and spontaneous.[8]

One unique disadvantage of online focus groups is the reduced ability to detect nonverbal cues. However, the moderator can overcome this by encouraging and engaging each participant during the interactive online conversation.

It is noticeable that technology and globalization have opened doors for global online research, and the outbreaks of the coronavirus inadvertently invigorated the use of online focus groups. This qualitative research method has gained momentum among global corporations that study global audiences and promote products and services to global markets. This trend is likely to continue in the future as technology continues to evolve and become more integrated into our daily lives.

Ethnography

Ethnography aims to establish a comprehensive understanding of how individuals in different or unique situations interpret their reality. Ethnography is predicated on cultural diversity, as the term *ethnography* literally means observing and describing culture. The academic fields of anthropology and other social sciences, including communication and sociology, adopt ethnography as a qualitative research method. Ethnographic researchers, or ethnographers, seek a detailed, in-depth description of everyday life and the practice of cultural differences among specific groups of people all over the world. Like investigative journalists, ethnographic researchers in strategic communication focus on reporting human behavior in detail and going beyond the thick description of the experience to find meaning from a cultural perspective that leads to cultural interpretation.

Ethnographic researchers search for "cultural understandings of human behavior through representation of the 'insider's point of view.'"[9] This means that ethnographers immerse themselves in the research setting to observe and record the particular life of individuals as a group. If you decide to use ethnography as your method of collecting data, you will live with your observed group of people while exploring their cultural context and daily activities. You will attempt to record a detailed account of the group in terms of their communication styles, social structures, family relations, and religious and customary materials and activities within the cultural setting. While observing and recording their lives, you will gain information and use it as your research data regarding the engaged relationship between you as the ethnographic researcher and the participants in their particular culture. See figure 7.3.

There are two key approaches to understanding and practicing ethnography: emic and etic. The emic approach refers to the intrinsic cultural distinctions that are meaningfully embedded inside the group of people in the specific cultural setting. In other words, ethnographic research guided by an emic perspective generates the description of an insider's view, including rich explanations of context and social meaning in the specific culture. Taking the emic approach indicates that you place yourself within the cultural setting to delve further into the details of the physical and psychological phenomena of the group that may otherwise be ignored by other researchers. Hence, the emic approach has the purpose of writing descriptive in-depth reports about how individuals who belong to a particular group behave and act in their culture.

The etic approach, on the other hand, refers to ethnography from an outside rather than an inside perspective. It enables you to describe beliefs, behaviors, or ways that a

Figure 7.3 A photo of ethnographic research
Source: Public domain

particular group of people behaves from the perspective of an outsider who is not embedded in the culture. You look at the group as an outsider from a distance. For example, if you as an American ethnographer went to Mongolia to research a nomadic tribe, your findings would stem from the etic approach where you observed and recorded their lives while trying not to disturb their daily routines. From a distance, you carefully observe them and record information about their physical activities, although it could be more challenging to describe and interpret their thoughts and understandings.

Before deciding to live with or observe a particular group of people in their natural environment or habitat, you as an ethnographer need to determine what your research intends to seek with the following questions:

- How does the group of people you decide to research understand and view their world?
- What stories could you discover in their cultural settings?
- How is meaning constructed within the cultural setting?
- How do they live and behave with respect to their customary and cultural practices?

Ethnographic research allows you to choose a group of people and live with them. With their permission, you are invited and allowed to observe them for a certain period in hopes of discovering their characteristics, habits, and differences from a cultural perspective. However, some other preliminary agreements may be required before your ethnographic journey begins. Despite the invitation and permission from the group of people, you and they should work on specified rules for the research setting. For example, if your research topic is the visual communication of illegal immigrants from a Latin American country being detained in a detention center in the United States, you need permission from the center officers and the group of immigrants in the center. If allowed, your next step is to consider accessibility and reactivity as they relate to your role as researcher.

Accessibility refers to the physical distance between you and the researched group of people. The accessibility of your ethnographic group is influenced by many different factors, including disagreement among group members, limited time and space, and even bad weather. For example, if you are permitted to reside within a detention center and observe its inhabitants 24/7, you enjoy 100% accessibility. Conversely, if you must remain outside the center and observe only during specific hours (such as after lunch), your accessibility becomes restricted. Reactivity refers to the problem that the observed people may react to the fact of being observed, thus altering their behavior from what it normally would have been. They could act unnatural when aware of your observation of them. As an ethnographer, your role is to manage both accessibility and reactivity within the research context. There are four different ways that you can conduct your ethnography to maximize the information you want to gather:

- Complete participant: You conceal your identity from the group of people you observe from the very beginning of your research, trying to engage with them in the setting. If you decide to go undercover, you become one of them, looking like them and acting like them. In so doing, there are obvious ethical considerations of being part of the group without revealing your role as an ethnographer. For example, you may join an online chat room of male high school students to explore their communication topics while chatting like one of them, and then write your research paper.
- Complete observer: Your identity is hidden from the people for your ethnographic research. You do not interact with them in the environment or setting; you only make observations of their behavior while trying to be a covert researcher. This might be appropriate in a situation where the group has many members, such as passengers older than 60 in a cruise ship casino. Observing the behavior and the way they communicate as a complete observer allows you not to disturb the casino setting, and the observed will not alter their normal behavior because they do not know you are there to research them. As the complete observer role minimizes reactivity, you can gather valid research information.
- Observer as participant: You reveal your identity in the setting and participate in some or limited activities of the group of people. This observer-as-participant role allows you to focus on your role as a researcher since the group has acknowledged what you are looking for in the setting and why you are there with them. They

may be cooperative with your observation, but it is hard for you to get engaged with them emotionally. Market and business ethnographers adopt this role to analyze how consumers interact with products or services and to establish better business strategies.

- Participant as observer: You are fully engaged with the group of people that knows you are conducting ethnographic research. You become more of a friend than a researcher, immersing yourself in their activities and culture. This role allows you to gain a deeper understanding of the group's dynamics and cultural nuances. For example, if you want to observe a newsroom, you initiate your ethnographic journey as a journalist who finds a story and reports it. After all the work is done, you go out with the newsroom people for dinner and drinks. Your ethnography continues until you gather enough information on the people in the newsroom setting. However, maintaining objectivity can be challenging in this role, and you must be careful not to let your personal involvement with the group affect your observations and interpretations.

Ethnography is used to record and analyze what you see, hear, and feel about a group of people, offering cultural information in a specific setting. You make an effort to capture their interactions in words, sounds, and gestures. As a result, you gather authentic qualitative data that describe particular patterns of human behavior.

Case Studies

A case study is a popular research method used across various disciplines such as law, medicine, business, and marketing. It involves an in-depth examination of a single case, such as an individual, and event, a campaign, an organization, or a phenomenon. A case study directs qualitative researchers to explore complex issues from multiple sources for data collection. Unlike in-depth interviews, focus groups, and ethnography in qualitative research, a case study has yet to develop its methodological standards and conceptual characteristics for research in strategic communication because it evolves from a wide range of different academic fields. However, we can learn how to facilitate a case study as a qualitative research type from a marketing/business communication perspective.

A case study consists of such integrated research concepts as being holistic, empirical, and interpretive, meaning that its approach to a research topic requires researchers to employ all qualitative research methods in collecting and analyzing data. Interviews, focus groups, and ethnography can all contribute to an in-depth case study as a means of gathering information and analyzing data. In addition, any content published in the media or on social media can be used as case study sources, including news articles, Instagram posts, corporate reports, and private and public documents. As a researcher, you ensure that your case study topic is derived from a real situation and is well analyzed via the identification of different factors interacting with each other.[10] The most important task for you regarding a case study is to select a real single case (phenomenon) that seems important to your research and the academic community or some particular industry.

The primary purpose of a case study is to generate an in-depth analysis of a specific phenomenon. Conducting a case study leads to a comprehensive understanding of the phenomenon within a socially realistic context. From a marketing communication perspective, a case study is a piece of research published by marketing professionals who evaluate communicative success or failure in dealing with target audiences. The professionals analyze why a specific phenomenon became successful or unsuccessful from data gathered from multiple sources via diverse methods of data collection. For example, when the $3.99 chicken sandwich at Popeyes gained overnight fame in the summer of 2019, a wealth of social media feeds and content about the new menu went viral while sales and store traffic skyrocketed. Many case studies about the sandwich were published to analyze its success, especially focusing on the competition against the biggest chicken sandwich competitor, Chick-fil-A.[11] Such case studies offer real-life examples to the marketing and business community to strategize and perform effective operations since they can learn from specific cases from the past and present for the future.

One of the main aims of a case study is to highlight practical and nuanced views of the case. With a case study, you offer suggestions and ideas to those involved in the field of your case. Similar to other qualitative research methods, completing a case study in strategic communication follows a step-by-step approach, as follows:

1. Determine where your interest is headed: Are you interested in researching an ongoing social phenomenon such as immigration, discrimination, disease, cyber hacking, poverty, violence, technology, or the stock market? What motivated you to be interested in the phenomenon? What aspects of the phenomenon would you like to highlight and discuss?

2. Make an academic approach to your case study: After choosing a phenomenon as your case study topic, you strategize how to gather information about the case. First, read all news articles and social media comments about the topic to educate yourself. Second, read scholarly journal articles and conceptualize the topic with theories if necessary.

3. Choose your case study design: A compelling way of developing your case study is to use the tactic of telling a story. Your case has a story to tell, and you describe how the case began, evolved, and ended. Choosing your design means that you will decide how to collect your case study data. Do you plan to interview or observe people in the case, do you give an online survey, or do you collect all written online documents?

4. Collect data: The key practice for a valid case study is data triangulation. You are responsible for using multiple techniques to collect data and clarify meaning. If necessary, you facilitate the use of different types of available data sources, including interviews, documents, public records, social media posts, and observations to exhaust the triangulation process, which enhances the validity of the case study.
5. Interpret the case and offer effective suggestions: You conducted a case study because you wanted to provide an opportunity for the in-depth study of a phenomenon and investigate it in far more detail than might otherwise be possible. Because of your in-depth, triangulated approach, your case study shed light on aspects of practical and effective contributions for those engaged in your case. Your case study should include a comprehensive and accurate description of your interpretation and evaluation. In essence, the goal of a case study is not to generalize findings to a larger population but to provide a deep understanding of a specific case within its real-life context.[12] The insights gained from a case study can be valuable for understanding complex phenomena and can contribute to theory development and practice.

For a case study in strategic communication, some researchers choose popular or provocative media campaigns to identify and analyze as a specific phenomenon in society. Media campaigns aim to recommend solutions or call for social or political change while identifying primary factors that contributed to the success or failure of the campaign. For example, Nike's campaign with Colin Kaepernick in 2018 was a great topic for a case study in strategic communication, where the phenomenon involved a large corporation, a football star, a social justice issue, social media platforms, and a consumer boycott movement. The case could be analyzed using a wide range of sources and intensive efforts of triangulation with fundamental case study skills. Among many case studies about the Nike campaign with Colin Kaepernick, one case study's abstract states:

> Nike's selection of politically polarizing Colin Kaepernick as the spokesperson for the 30th anniversary of its iconic "Just Do It" campaign catapulted the brand into the media spotlight and made it a political flashpoint for consumers across America. Would the choice of Kaepernick positively or negatively affect Nike's business results or just generate a lot of social media chatter? After all, on social media, it was easy to say that one would boycott or buycott a brand because of one's political beliefs, but in the marketplace, other purchase criteria often reigned supreme.[13]

A case study concentrates on a singular entity, such as an individual, event, campaign, or organization. The process of conducting the study necessitates a comprehensive description and a well-articulated interpretation of the phenomenon under investigation. The objective is to provide valuable insights and practical recommendations to a specific community or to individuals who would find your analysis beneficial. In a nutshell, the findings or suggestions derived from case studies serve as an excellent reference point for those seeking to understand the successes or failures of others in their business ventures, events, or campaigns. A case study provides you, as a researcher, with the opportunity to employ a variety of tools to examine the phenomenon from a holistic perspective.

Applying AI Technology to Qualitative Research Data Collection

The influence of AI technology on research is transformative, and its application in qualitative data collection can empower college research students. You can effectively integrate AI into your qualitative research practices in the following ways:

- Automated data collection: Utilize AI-powered tools to automate the process of data collection from various sources. These tools can help in gathering and organizing qualitative data more efficiently, saving time and reducing human error.
- Natural language processing (NLP): Implement NLP techniques to analyze and extract insights from textual data.[14] NLP can assist in categorizing, summarizing, and identifying patterns within qualitative data, offering valuable insights for your research.
- Sentiment analysis: Incorporate sentiment analysis tools to understand the emotions and opinions expressed in qualitative data.[15] This can provide a deeper understanding of participant responses and aid in uncovering underlying sentiments within the data.
- Quality assurance: Implement AI technologies for quality assurance in qualitative data analysis.[16] These tools can help in detecting inconsistencies, errors, or biases in your data collection process, ensuring the reliability and validity of your research findings.

By leveraging AI technology in qualitative research data collection, college research students can enhance the efficiency, accuracy, and depth of their research endeavors, ultimately leading to more insightful and impactful outcomes. However, students still need to design their studies, select appropriate methods, and interpret their findings. Furthermore, ethical considerations, such as informed consent and data privacy, remain paramount when using AI in research.

Application of an AI-Powered Tool

Box 7.1
Example of Using Microsoft Copilot for a Case Study

Using an AI-Powered Tool (Microsoft Copilot) for a Case Study

Command syntax: Write a case study on the Budweiser ad and its partnership with a transgender TikTok star in 2023.

Answer: Sure! Here is an elaborated case study of the Budweiser ad and its partnership with transgender TikTok star Dylan Mulvaney in 2023:

In 2023, Bud Light partnered with trans activist and influencer Dylan Mulvaney as a brand influencer. Mulvaney is a TikTok star with more than 10 million followers who posted a video advertising the beer company's March Madness contest offering customers a chance to win $15,000.

The partnership was met with criticism from some social media users claiming the ad campaign is an attempt to push "gender propaganda." Celebrities like John Oliver and Joe Rogan reacted to the Anheuser-Busch and Dylan Mulvaney backlash. Bud Light's parent company, Anheuser-Busch, defended its decision to enlist Mulvaney as part of its efforts to reach consumers from diverse backgrounds.

Anheuser-Busch InBev CEO Michel Doukeris addressed the backlash over Bud Light's partnership with transgender TikTok star Dylan Mulvaney on Thursday. The company is tripling its U.S. media spending in the summer to restore goodwill after learning the hard way that it did not want its beer to be the center of social debate.

The controversy surrounding the partnership highlights the challenges companies face when trying to appeal to a diverse audience while also avoiding backlash from certain segments of society. It also raises questions about the role of corporations in promoting social change and the potential risks and rewards of taking a stand on controversial issues.

Despite the criticism, Bud Light's partnership with Mulvaney can also be seen as a bold move toward greater inclusivity and representation in advertising. By partnering with a prominent transgender influencer, Bud Light is sending a message of support to the LGBTQ+ community and signaling its commitment to diversity and inclusion.

Overall, the case of Budweiser's partnership with Dylan Mulvaney illustrates the complex dynamics at play when companies engage in socially conscious marketing. While there are risks involved, there are also potential rewards in terms of building brand loyalty and connecting with new audiences.

Summary

- ✓ In-depth interviews are a tailored form of communication between the researcher and the interviewee in a research setting.
- ✓ In-depth interviews allow the researcher to collect exploratory, explanatory, and descriptive information provided by the interviewee.
- ✓ By conducting an in-depth interview, the researcher expects to learn how each interviewee constructs and interprets meaning differently on the topic.
- ✓ The semistructured interview lies between structured and unstructured interviews, using a specific list of questions but allowing each interviewee some freedom to talk about other ideas and opinions.
- ✓ A focus group as a qualitative data collection method involves the gathering of a group of people who are asked about their thoughts and opinions.
- ✓ In a focus group setting, the participants are allowed or encouraged to interact and to influence and be influenced.
- ✓ Ideally, a focus group should range in size from 6 to 10 participants.
- ✓ The primary duty of the moderator in a focus group is to keep the conversation flowing in the right direction and make the group time as productive as possible.
- ✓ An online focus group is conducted via popular platforms for online video conferencing.
- ✓ Ethnographic researchers seek cultural understandings of human behavior by adopting an "insider's point of view."
- ✓ There are two key terms for understanding and practicing ethnography: *emic* and *etic*.
- ✓ Accessibility and reactivity determine the researcher's role in ethnography.
- ✓ As a complete observer, the researcher's identity is hidden to the people whom the researcher observes.
- ✓ The key term for a valid case study is *data triangulation*.
- ✓ A case study is an in-depth examination of a single phenomenon such as an event, a person, or an organization.
- ✓ For a case study in strategic communication, some researchers choose popular or provocative media campaigns to identify and analyze a specific phenomenon in society.
- ✓ By leveraging AI technology in qualitative research data collection, college research students can enhance the efficiency, accuracy, and depth of their research endeavors.

Key Terms

1. In-depth interviews
2. Focus groups
3. Ethnography
4. Case studies
5. Meaning construction
6. Interaction
7. Reactivity
8. Phenomenon
9. Interview structures
10. Online and offline research

Chapter 8

Quantitative Research Methods

Chapter Learning Outcomes

- Identify general characteristics of quantitative research.
- Explain independent variables and dependent variables.
- Apply variables to the formulation of hypotheses.
- Discuss different tails of directional and nondirectional hypotheses.
- Describe nominal, ordinal, interval, and ratio scales.
- Apply the four measurement scales to categorical and continuous data.
- Explain reliability.
- Discuss different types of validity.
- Acknowledge the generalization of quantitative research.
- Recognize the popular use of net promoter scores.

Strategic communication researchers find the quantitative research method superbly useful. The method aims to produce findings that can be applied to a broader population beyond the study's participants. Quantitative research can effectively measure the impact of communication campaigns, gauge public sentiment, and identify communication trends. It involves collecting and analyzing numerical data using surveys, experiments, or other means. This makes the method an indispensable tool for researchers in the field of strategic communication.

There are several core concepts and characteristics of quantitative research methods, including the following:

- Measurement: Quantitative research methods rely on the measurement of variables. Variables are concepts that can be measured such as age, gender, income, education, political affiliation, religious affiliation, attitudes, behavior, knowledge, skills, and personality.

- Statistical analysis: Quantitative research methods use statistical analysis to test hypotheses and draw conclusions. Statistical analysis can be used to describe data, to compare groups, and to test relationships between variables.
- Sampling: Quantitative research methods often use sampling, which is the process of selecting a subset of a population to represent the entire population. Sampling is used to reduce the cost and time of research and to improve the accuracy of the results.
- Validity and reliability: Quantitative research methods are evaluated in terms of their validity and reliability. Validity refers to the extent to which a research method measures what it is intended to measure. Reliability refers to the consistency of a research method.

Quantitative research methods can be a valuable tool for strategic communication researchers. They can be used to measure the effectiveness of communication campaigns, to understand the impact of communication on public opinion, and to identify the factors that influence communication behavior.

Concepts and Characteristics of Quantitative Research

Quantitative research follows a deductive process. You begin with a research topic and then examine theories and scholarly journal articles to conceptualize the topic based on this background information. You go through the literature review process. Based on the literature review, you develop hypotheses and/or research questions to guide your collection of data. In the practice of quantitative research, hypotheses are more frequently preferred over research questions because quantitative researchers attempt to make hypothetical predictions. For example, laboratory experiments, content analyses, and surveys are used as popular methods of data collection for hypothesis testing in quantitative research, and quantitative data are statistically analyzed to make the research results valid and reliable. As quantitative research focuses on numerical data from randomly selected samples, it aims to generalize a particular phenomenon across groups of people whose behavior can be objectively measured and statistically analyzed.

The main characteristics of quantitative research are listed below:

- Data are usually gathered using structured research instruments such as surveys and experiments that provide measurable variables.
- The results tend to represent the population because the analyzed data are gathered based on larger sample sizes.
- The researcher can repeat and replicate her research to verify the results in a different setting.
- The researcher has a clearly defined hypothesis to which objectively analyzed answers are sought in numerical data.

- The standardized and pretested design guides data collection to ensure validity and reliability.
- Data obtained via quantitative methods are demonstrated in the form of numbers and statistics, often using tables, graphs, charts, or figures that show relationships or differences among variables.
- The researcher constructs a scenario and predicts future results, using quantitative models or formulas with the aid of computer software.
- The researcher uses digital instruments to measure variables and gather data, making sure that the data were collected through the process of calibration and the comparison of standardized measurement for accuracy.[1]

The quantitative researcher seeks to make a generalization about a specific phenomenon using numerical analysis of data. Exploring the concepts and characteristics of quantitative research, we find several terms to study, including *variables*, *hypotheses*, *validity*, *reliability*, and *measurement*.

Variables and Hypotheses

Independent and Dependent Variables

The numbers used in quantitative research originate from objective scales of measurement of the units of analysis called variables. A variable is a measurable attribute or characteristic that can change in quantity or quality. It can be associated with individuals or units and can assume different values, reflecting variations in amount, volume, number, form, nature, or type. For example, if you as a quantitative researcher select Kim Kardashian's Instagram as the phenomenon you want to research, you begin by developing a topic concerning the phenomenon. Your research topic might be something about her Instagram posts and sponsorship. You gather measurable data by collecting the frequency of her posts on a daily basis, the number of products she promotes, the amount of money for the products she sells, and the number of photos and videos relevant to her Instagram promotions. Such numbers, frequencies, and amounts are changeable and can be measured by a scale.

A variable in quantitative research simply refers to a phenomenon that is measured by you. The best way to understand a variable is to differentiate a dependent variable from an independent variable. The independent variable is the force that may influence or affect the other variable, the dependent variable. In other words, the independent variable is assumed to have a direct effect on the dependent variable, which is dependent on the independent variable. The relationship between independent and dependent variables can be understood with the concept of cause-effect analysis, meaning that the independent variable causes changes in the dependent variable. For example, in the phenomenon of Kim Kardashian and her Instagram account, her Instagram posts about specific products (independent variable) may cause an increase in sales or an increase

Table 8.1 Independent and Dependent Variables for Research Questions

Research questions	Independent variables	Dependent variables
What is the effect of war video games on homicide rates?	The type of war video games (guns or jet fighters)	Homicide rates
How does the use of TikTok before bedtime affect sleep?	The amount of TikTok use before bedtime	Quality of sleep or hours of sleep
How well do different vehicle ads affect car sales?	The type of vehicle ads	Car sales

in boycotts (dependent variable). Another popular example is that time spent studying (independent variable) causes a change in college GPA (dependent variable). You need to master your understanding of variables in order to determine the cause-and-effect relationship and to formulate your research hypotheses and/or research questions. Some examples of research questions are given in Table 8.1.

One more important factor about the independent variable is that the researcher can manipulate or change the amount or level of the variable. For example, if you want to investigate how binge-watching Netflix affects GPA, you can change or manipulate the hours of binge-watching.

Null and Alternative Hypotheses

For quantitative research, researchers are trained to formulate hypotheses to guide the path for data collection and analysis. A hypothesis is an educated guess or prediction regarding what is expected to happen in a particular situation under certain conditions. As a quantitative researcher, you should learn to formulate a good hypothesis that has several characteristics, including a clear rationale, an if-then format, and a clear description of the relationship between the variables of interest in your research. Your development of a hypothesis should cover the following questions:

- Is the language clear and focused?
- What is the relationship between your hypothesis and your research topic?
- Is your hypothesis testable? If yes, then how?
- What are the possible explanations that you might want to explore?
- Does your hypothesis include both an independent and dependent variable?
- Can you manipulate your variables without violating ethical standards?[2]

A good hypothesis relevant to your research topic should include both an independent and dependent variable, and you should outline the prediction and test the hypothesis without any violation of ethics.

A hypothesis is designed to provide a tentative assumption made to draw out and test its logical or empirical consequences between variables. Four different formats of hypotheses in research papers are commonly written in one sentence. Here are some examples of the four formats of a hypothesis—simple, complex, null, and alternative:

1. A simple hypothesis assumes the relationship between two variables, in which the independent variable influences the dependent variable.
2. A complex hypothesis adds more independent and dependent variables that have a certain type of relationship between the variables.
3. A null hypothesis, represented by the symbol H_0, exists when the researcher predicts that there will be no relationship or difference between the two variables.
4. An alternative hypothesis, represented by the symbol H_a, attempts to reject the null hypothesis, meaning that the researcher formulates an alternative hypothesis that predicts a relationship or difference between the two variables.

You can consolidate your understanding of each hypothesis format by looking at the examples given in Table 8.2.

It is critical to notice that the null and alternative hypotheses are two mutually exclusive statements. As quantitative research uses a hypothesis to test sample data to determine whether to accept or reject the null hypothesis, the actual test begins by considering null and alternative hypotheses. The alternative hypothesis (H_a) is a claim about the population that is contradictory to H_0. It is what we conclude when we reject H_0. Hence, the alternative hypothesis is what we might predict to be true or try to prove true.

The alternative hypothesis can be either one tailed (directional) or two tailed (nondirectional). A one-tailed hypothesis, also known as a directional hypothesis, can test for effects in only one direction. In a one-tailed hypothesis, you can specify the direction to be either greater than or less than the hypothesized value. For example, you have survey results showing that a sample of college students nationwide listens to podcasts 12 hours per week. You want to know if college students in Arizona listen to podcasts longer than the national average of 12 hours. A one-tailed hypothesis can be used because you hypothesize that hours of listening to podcasts in Arizona are greater than the national average. You symbolize the hypotheses thus: H_0: $\mu = 12$ versus H_a: $\mu > 12$ (see Table 8.3 about symbols for hypotheses).

The two-tailed hypothesis, also known as the nondirectional hypothesis, can test for effects in both directions. You do not specify the direction where your variable moves in a two-tailed hypothesis. With the same podcast listening example, you are interested in determining whether the hours are either less than or greater than the national average, so you choose neither greater nor less. You hypothesize that there is a difference between

Table 8.2 Formats and Examples of Hypotheses

Common formats	Examples
Simple hypothesis	a. Watching TV news daily may lead to an increase in intelligence. b. Online shopping daily will increase happiness. c. Dating apps on the iPhone will cause narcissism.
Complex hypothesis	a. Parents who (1) value education and (2) seek healthy diet are more likely than other adults to (1) watch more PBS programs and (2) eat less beef. b. Individuals who (1) believe in the apocalypse and (2) live with roommates are more likely than others to experience (1) Twitter addiction and (2) feelings of isolation. c. Overweight college students who (1) eat fast food and (2) consume few vegetables are more likely than others to (1) watch more food channels on YouTube and (2) follow chefs on Pinterest.
Null hypothesis	a. There is no significant change in college GPA when students drink green tea only or whiskey only. b. There is no significant difference between Amazon shopping hours and Walmart shopping hours among male college students. c. There is no significant difference in sales of Tesla Model X if Elon Musk uses Twitter or no social media to promote the car.
Alternative hypothesis	a. College GPA increases if students drink green tea only, as opposed to whiskey only. b. Female college students spend more time shopping on Amazon.com than Walmart.com. c. Sales of Tesla Model X increase if Elon Musk uses Twitter rather than not using any social media platform.

Table 8.3 Symbols Used in H_0 and H_a

H_0	H_a
equal (=)	not equal (≠), greater than (>), or less than (<)
greater than or equal to (≥)	less than (<)
less than or equal to (≤)	greater than (>)

the national average and the Arizona average by symbolizing the two-tailed hypothesis: H_0: $\mu = 12$ versus H_a: $\mu \neq 12$.

To better understand hypotheses and directions, let's practice with the following scenarios:

1. An Apple marketing trial is conducted to test whether or not the new AirPods reduce noise by 12%. State the null and alternative hypotheses.
   - H_0: The AirPods reduce noise by 12% ($H_0 = 12$).
   - H_a: The AirPods do not reduce noise by 12% ($H_a \neq 12$).

2. You want to test if college students take less than two months to get permanent jobs after graduation on average. The null and alternative hypotheses are:
   - H_0: $\mu \geq 2$
   - H_a: $\mu < 2$
3. The U.S. Department of Education wants to test if college students will perform differently from high school students on a memory test without predicting which group of students will perform better. State the null and alternative hypotheses.
   - H_0: college students = high school students
   - H_a: college students ≠ high school students

While a hypothesis predicts what to expect, one goal of quantitative research is to determine whether the hypothesis is right. You must create a hypothesis based on a specific theory or prior research. Assume, for example, that a 2024 study revealed that using Facebook promoted depression among parents with college-aged children who stayed away from home during COVID-19. You might build your own hypothesis based on the results of the previous study: After the COVID-19 pandemic, parents who use Facebook on a regular basis are more likely to feel happy after sending their children to college than parents who still live with children who commute to college from the same house. Another example of hypothesis formation based on a theory is developing a hypothesis from cultivation theory. According to the theory, heavy viewing of crime television shows such as *Dexter*, *Law & Order SVU*, *Fargo*, and *Narcos* leads viewers to believe that the world is a much more dangerous place than it actually is, with higher rates of homicide, drive-by shootings, or gang violence around every corner. Your new theory-based hypothesis could be: Heavy fans of the reality TV show *The Real Housewives of Beverly Hills* are likely to assume that every woman in the country enjoys the affluent lifestyle that only Beverly Hills can supply as long as she finds or marries a wealthy man.

HYPOTHESIS TESTING WITH TYPE I AND TYPE II ERRORS

Most quantitative researchers conduct hypothesis tests by following these standardized steps: (1) formulate a hypothesis, (2) collect data, (3) analyze the data, (4) accept or reject the null hypothesis, and (5) discuss the results. For researchers in strategic communication, nondirectional hypotheses are commonly preferred over directional hypotheses. The null hypothesis states that there is no relationship or no difference between the variables, while the alternative hypothesis states that there is a relationship or difference between the variables. As we note here, there is no particular direction in the two-tailed or nondirectional hypothesis. We do not hypothesize greater or smaller values for the variables but instead that the values will be different.

Although quantitative research using hypotheses and random samples is regarded as objective and less biased than qualitative research, no hypothesis test is 100% flawless. Because a hypothesis is based on predictions or assumptions, there is always a chance of making an incorrect conclusion regarding accepting or rejecting the null hypothesis (H_0). Anytime quantitative researchers in strategic communication make a decision from the hypothesis test based on statistics—the results of their test have to be true within a range of probabilities (typically 95%)—there are four possible outcomes, with two representing correct conclusions and two representing errors.[3] The two representing errors are called Type I errors and Type II errors.

- Type I error: A Type I error occurs when the null hypothesis is true and you incorrectly reject it. This means that your report says that your findings are significant when in fact they have occurred by chance.
- Type II error: A Type II error occurs when the null hypothesis is false and you fail to reject it. This means that your report says that your findings are not significant when in fact they are significant.

Table 8.4 helps us have a better understanding of the four possible outcomes of testing hypotheses.

Table 8.4 Hypothesis Testing and Errors

	The truth about the population in reality	
Decision based on sample	**H_0 is true**	**H_0 is false**
Fail to reject H_0 (accept H_0)	Correct conclusion	Type II error (fail to reject H_0 when it is false)
Reject H_0	Type I error (reject H_0 when it is true)	Correct conclusion

Consequently, researchers view Type I errors as false positives and Type II errors as false negatives. This means that those who make a Type I error will wrongfully assume that the hypothesis testing has worked even though it has not in real-life situations. As a result, Type I errors are generally considered more serious and dangerous than Type II errors—although this is certainly not always the case. (Some researchers argue that Type II errors are more dangerous, depending on the case.)[4] Consider the two error types in the following example.

A medical researcher wants to compare the effectiveness of two coronavirus vaccines: Pfizer and Moderna. The null and alternative hypotheses are as follows:

Null hypothesis (H_0): $\mu_1 = \mu_2$

- The two vaccines are equally effective, with no difference in terms of fighting the coronavirus.

Alternative hypothesis (H_a): $\mu_1 \neq \mu_2$

- The two vaccines are not equally effective, so there is a difference in terms of effectiveness between Pfizer and Moderna.

A Type I error occurs if the researcher rejects the null hypothesis and concludes that the two vaccines show different effectiveness when in fact they are not different. If the vaccines have the same effectiveness, the researcher may not consider this error too severe because those who are about to take either of the vaccines will still benefit from the same level of effectiveness regardless of which vaccine they take. On the other hand, if a Type II error occurs, the researcher fails to reject the null hypothesis when it should be rejected. That is, the researcher concludes that Pfizer and Moderna are the same in effectiveness when in fact they are different.

Measurements in Quantitative Research

After stating a hypothesis with variables, you decide how to collect and measure quantitative data that can be analyzed in numbers or statistics. To perform statistical analysis of data in quantitative research, you should know what to measure and how to measure it. There are four different levels of measurement scales: nominal, ordinal, interval, and ratio. It is important to understand the different levels of measurement of a variable to decide which statistical test you will use, as well as how to interpret the data from that variable. The best way of understanding the four measurements is to see them with examples.

- Nominal scale: This is defined as a scale used for labeling variables into distinct classifications. The labeled variables have no quantitative value or order. In other words, for nominal variables, the numerical values just name or identify people or objects with labels: the unique attribution. For example, if you conduct a survey to gain quantitative information, one of the first questions in your questionnaire is about the sex of your respondents, typically with two categories, male versus female. You could mark a male respondent as 1 and a female respondent as 2. Regarding the sex variable, male is 1 and female is 2. This means nothing in terms of the characteristics of the sexes. You simply assigned the numbers to name each sex, and the numbers have no numerical significance. Another example is jersey numbers in football. A player with jersey number 1 is not more or less of anything than a player with jersey number 99, as they have no numerical significance. See Table 8.5 for examples of variables on a nominal scale.
- Ordinal scale: With the ordinal scale, the values of a variable can be ranked in order. The values are what is important and significant, but the distances between the values do not have any meaning. In other words, you can simply place the variable values in order without respect to how big or small the difference is

between each of the values. For example, you may rank your family as being of the middle-income class, but this does not say anything about how much worse off your family is compared to the family of your best friend who identifies herself as upper class. The ordinal scale is generally used to measure nonmathematical concepts such as customer satisfaction, grades, personal happiness, or degree of pain. For the ordinal scale, it is the order that matters. The most popular example of the ordinal scale is the Likert scale: strongly disagree, disagree, neutral, agree, strongly agree. See Table 8.6 for examples of variables on an ordinal scale.

- Interval scale: Defined by the space in between the values of a variable, the interval scale classifies the order and the difference between variable values, which have familiar, constant, and computable differences. The distance between two values can be identified and quantified on the interval scale. Thus, the interval scale offers the order and the exact differences between values, in contrast to the ordinal scale. For example, temperature scales such as Fahrenheit (F) and Celsius (C) are measured by using the interval scale since the difference between each whole-number value of the variable is the same: the difference between 40 and 30 degrees is a measurable 10 degrees, as is the difference between 70 and 60 degrees. In a similar vein, 50 degrees is equal to 100 minus 50. It shows the correct measurable difference. This capacity of measuring the equidistant difference between variable values makes the interval scale different from the ordinal scale. One important characteristic of the interval scale is that it does not have a true zero value, meaning that the data do not have a starting point of 0. On the interval scale, the value of 0 is arbitrary, and even the 0 degree of temperature does not have a true zero value because of negative values of temperature. Hence, the true zero value refers to the starting point of 0, which is what the ratio scale has. See Table 8.7 for examples of variables on an interval scale.
- Ratio scale: Among all levels of measurement scales, the ratio scale is considered the best because it offers the exact order, difference, and distance from zero of variable values. Data that are measured using the ratio scale produce valuable information on the value of true zero. A true zero point offers the opportunity of calculating the meaningful difference and specific order between the two values of the variable because most research variables with a meaningful fraction are countable from the

Table 8.5 Nominal Scale Examples in Surveys

What is your sex?	What is your political affiliation?	Where do you live?
1. Male	1. Republican	1. Alaska
2. Female	2. Democrat	2. Florida
	3. Independent	3. Virginia

Table 8.6 Ordinal Scale Examples in Surveys

How satisfied are you with our services?	1. Very unsatisfied 2. Unsatisfied 3. Neutral 4. Satisfied 5. Very satisfied
What is your GPA?	1. A 2. B 3. C 4. D 5. F
Out of the five mentioned car brands, rank the order of preference.	() Acura () BMW () Lexus () Mercedes-Benz () Audi

Table 8.7 Interval Scale Examples in Surveys

On a scale of 1 to 7, how likely are you to recommend our Sephora products and services compared with Ulta's to your friends and colleagues?	Very unlikely					Very likely	
	1	2	3	4	5	6	7
Overall, how would you rate your most recent phone call with Chase Bank?	Unacceptable					Outstanding	
	1	2	3	4	5	6	7

starting point of absolute zero. More important, variables on the ratio scale can be meaningfully added, subtracted, multiplied, and divided. Popular examples of the ratio scale are weight, speed, and height. Thanks to the existence of a true zero value, which allows no negative values, the ratio scale provides detailed information for researchers while including the characteristics of the three other variable measurement scales. See Table 8.8 for examples of variables on a ratio scale.

To summarize, (1) the nominal scale is used to name or label a series of variables, (2) the ordinal scale identifies the order or rank of choices, (3) the interval scale provides the order and the ability to quantify the difference between variables, and (4) the ratio scale has the ability to classify, order, and represent the interval between values, plus the ability to calculate ratios with an absolute or true zero. The four data measurement scales in quantitative research are essential to the process of data collection and analysis in order for researchers to apply the right statistical tests. The characteristics of the measurement scales are shown in Table 8.9.

Table 8.8 Ratio Scale Examples in Surveys

How old are you?	___
How many people are in your family?	___
What is your annual income?	___
What is the gas mileage of a Ford Bronco?	___

Table 8.9 Summary of Levels of Measurement

Provides:	Nominal	Ordinal	Interval	Ratio
Known order of variables		☑	☑	☑
Measureable difference between variables			☑	☑
Addition and subtraction of variables			☑	☑
Multiplication and division of variables				☑
Absolute zero				☑

Net Promoter Score

The Likert scale and semantic differential scale are traditionally used in questionnaires as measurement scales that ask people to rate a feeling, degree of agreement or disagreement, product, organization, brand, or any other entity within the frame of a multi-point set of rating options. Both scales are popular and widely used in marketing and academic research. More recently, some researchers in strategic communication use a net promoter score (NPS), a measurement scale ranging from 1 to 10, to measure customer experience and predict future phenomena. The NPS is designed to help companies track the positive and negative experiences of customers, producing a clear measure of an organization's performance through its target audience's experiences. In an NPS question, the customer replies on a scale of 1–10, rating how likely they are to refer a product, service, brand, or organization to a friend. The most common type of question for the NPS is formatted as in the following example:

> Considering your complete experience with Apple Watch Series 7, how likely is it that you would recommend the watch to a friend or colleague?[5]

The NPS provides a core measurement for customer experience management since customers are asked to rate their chances of recommending an organization or business to their family, friends, or colleagues.[6] Many marketing companies view NPS analysis as essential to improve customer experience, enhance corporate reputation, and strengthen brand image. Based on the number chosen on the scale, customers are classified into one of three types: detractors, passives, or promoters.[7]

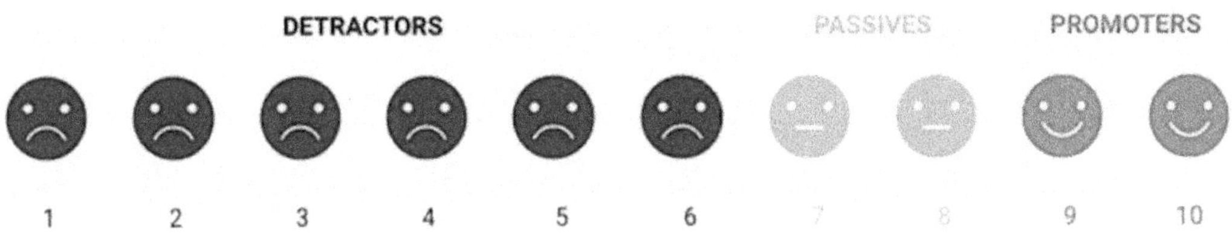

Source: QuestionPro Survey, 2023.

- 1–6: Detractors are unsatisfied customers who are unlikely to recommend the product while damaging the reputation of the product and impeding growth through negative word of mouth. They account for more than 80% of negative word of mouth.
- 7–8: Passives are quite content but less enthusiastic customers who may or may not recommend the product, considering competitive offerings from competitors. Their repurchase and referral rates are as much as 50% lower than those of promoters.
- 9–10: Promoters are loyal enthusiasts who will keep buying and recommending the product, fueling growth. Moreover, they account for more than 80% of referrals in most businesses.[8]

After collecting the respondents' NPS surveys, the calculation of the percentage range is made based on the following formula:

$$NPS = (\text{number of promoters} - \text{number of detractors}) / (\text{number of respondents}) \times 100$$

The range can be from a low of –100 (if all customers are detractors) to a high of 100 (if all customers are promoters). For example, suppose you did a survey for a new Apple Watch using the NPS, and 500 respondents who had purchased and used the Apple watch answered. The survey results might show:

- 20 responses were in the 1–6 range (detractors).
- 100 responses were in the 7–8 range (passives).
- 380 responses were in the 9–10 range (promoters).

Using the NPS calculation formula: $(380 - 20) / 500 \times 100 = 72$. The score of 72 advises the Apple company to promote future marketing and product strategies to turn passives into promoters.

Data Types: Categorical and Continuous Variables

In statistics, the data type is an important concept that allows researchers to apply appropriate statistical procedures to the analysis of quantitative data. As we understand the

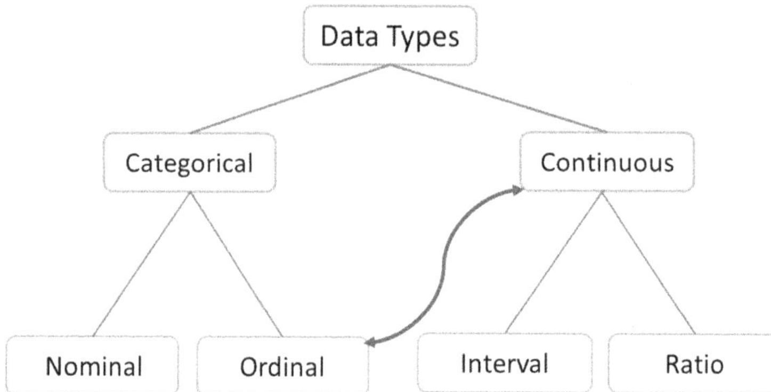

Figure 8.1 Visualization of data type
Source: Created by author

four measurement scales, it is important to look at higher-order concepts of statistical data types. There exist two types of data in statistics. One is categorical data, and the other is continuous data. The former includes the nominal and ordinal scales, while the latter includes the interval and ratio scales. Categorical data separate units into label variables (nominal scale) and measure nonmathematical variables (ordinal scale). Continuous data represent numerical variables that have an infinite number of possible values, either being measured with a true zero point (ratio scale) or no zero point (interval scale). See figure 8.1.

However, some researchers argue that the ordinal scale should be considered continuous data because some ordinal variables can be numerically ranked and ordered with accurate difference measurements. For example, a measurement of happiness in five categories is considered to be on the ordinal scale, so it belongs to categorical data. If a Likert scale gives the statement "I am happy" and asks the respondent to select the answer from "1 = strongly disagree," "2 = disagree," "3 = neutral," "4 = agree," and "5 = strongly agree," the answer is typically considered to be categorical data. However, some researchers recommend that ordinal variables be treated as continuous data if a question has more than five categories, like seven or nine.[9] For example, a question that can be considered continuous data might state, "Tell us how satisfied you are with our customer service," and the options are "1 = completely dissatisfied," "2 = mostly dissatisfied," "3 = somewhat dissatisfied," "4 = neither dissatisfied nor satisfied," "5 = somewhat satisfied," "6 = mostly satisfied," and "7 = completely satisfied." Figure 8.1 visualizes the relationships of the ordinal scale.

The reason data types are important is that specific statistical tests can only be applied to certain data types. You need to apply specific statistical tests differently to continuous data or categorical data. If you do not, your statistical results could be wrong. Therefore, identifying and differentiating the exact type of data you are analyzing enables you to choose the correct statistical tests of analysis. As we study the applications of different statistical tests relevant to data types in Chapters 10 and 11, brief information about data and tests is helpful to understand variables and data application. Common statistical tests that quantitative researchers in strategic communication use are chi-square, *t* test, ANOVA, correlation, and regression. Such tests are selected based on the measurement levels of scales and variables.

Validity and Reliability in Quantitative Research

The quantitative research method in comparison with the qualitative research method aims for statistical generalization, involving an act of reasoning to infer the results from a sample and apply them to a population. Generalization, regarded as a quality standard in quantitative research, is scientifically evaluated when the sample is selected randomly and is representative of the population. Generalization is achieved through the measurement of validity and reliability, which both indicate how well a method, technique, or test measures and analyzes the data.[10] When conducting research, quantitative researchers prioritize reliability and validity as the foundation for data collection. These factors are highly valued in the initial stages of planning the data collection process.

Reliability

Reliability is about the consistency of your results. It relates to the robustness of the measurement as being free from unstable errors. In other words, if the same result can be consistently achieved from the same method in similar circumstances, the measurement is considered reliable. Hence reliability refers to the ability of research findings to be repeatable. For example, a PR practitioner working for Estée Lauder Companies Inc. uses a skin care survey questionnaire to find customers' preferences for foam cleansers. Different PR practitioners working for other cosmetic companies use the same questionnaire with similar customers and get almost the same results. This indicates the high reliability of the survey. In a similar vein, if a group of housewives completed the skin care questionnaire and they repeated the same questionnaire a few months later with the same answers, your survey results would indicate high reliability.

Validity

Validity is the extent to which a method accurately measures what it is supposed to measure in quantitative research. If you want to claim that your research is valid, your method of collecting data must be valid. Suppose, for example, a survey is designed to explore corporate reputation on YouTube but what is actually measured is corporate image. This would not be considered a valid measurement, as image is not identical to reputation. There are three major types of validity:

- Content validity: The extent to which the measurement covers all the content that it should with respect to the variable. For example, a test that aims to measure levels of emotion among a group of soldiers contains items for depression, anxiety, and anger, but not happiness, which is essential in emotional tests. The test lacks content validity in measuring overall levels of emotion.

- Construct validity: The degree to which inferences can be made from the correspondence of a measure with theoretical constructs and the operationalizations of your research. For example, a digital marketing questionnaire can measure customers' desire to buy new products, and you can relate the questionnaire to the theory of cognitive dissonance. If strong associations between desire and the theory are computed, that would indicate high construct validity.
- Criterion validity: The extent to which the result of a measure predicts an outcome for another valid measure. A survey can have criterion validity if it is useful for predicting performance or behavior in another situation. For example, a survey is conducted in 2024 to measure voters' opinions of the governor in Nevada. If the results accurately predict the later outcome of the 2026 gubernatorial election in Nevada, this indicates that the survey has high criterion validity.[11]

In a nutshell, reliability refers to the consistency of a measure, where a participant is expected to have approximately the same responses each time the test or survey is repeated. Validity, on the other hand, refers to the accuracy of a measure, where researchers use questions that truly measure the issues of importance. The validity of quantitative research is considered to be the degree to which it measures what it intends to measure. As the quantitative research method has the advantages of objectivity, generalizability, and accuracy in terms of its results, a fundamental way of ensuring such advantages is to consider validity and reliability while designing your research from the earliest stage.

Application of an AI-Powered Tool

Box 8.1
ChatGPT Suggestions for Studying Quantitative Research

Using an AI-Powered Tool (ChatGPT) for the Study of Quantitative Research
Command syntax: Offer some suggestions about how to use ChatGPT for college students who are afraid of studying quantitative research methods because of numbers and statistics.

Answer: If you're a college student who's intimidated by quantitative research methods, don't worry, you're not alone! Here are some suggestions for how you can use ChatGPT to help you overcome your fear of numbers and statistics:

1. Start with the basics: You don't need to dive straight into complex statistical analyses right away. Start by asking ChatGPT to explain some of the basic concepts and terminology associated with quantitative research methods. This could include things like means, standard deviations, correlation coefficients, and *p* values. Understanding these foundational concepts can go a long way in demystifying the more complex statistical analyses.
2. Ask ChatGPT to walk you through an example: Sometimes, seeing a real-world example of how a statistical analysis is conducted can be incredibly helpful in understanding the process. You can ask ChatGPT to walk you through a hypothetical research scenario, explaining each step along the way. This will give you a better sense of how the numbers and statistics are used to draw conclusions.
3. Ask ChatGPT for additional resources: If you're really struggling with a particular concept or statistical analysis, ChatGPT can help point you in the direction of additional resources that might be helpful. This could include textbooks, online courses, or even YouTube videos that explain the concept in a different way.
4. YouTube may have free video tutorials on statistics and other quantitative research methods for students to access and watch on their own time. To find these resources, simply search for "free statistics tutorials" or "quantitative research methods tutorials" on YouTube.
5. Don't be afraid to make mistakes: Finally, remember that it's okay to make mistakes when you're learning something new. Don't be afraid to ask ChatGPT to clarify something or to help you work through a problem. The more you practice, the more comfortable you'll become with the numbers and statistics involved in quantitative research methods.

Overall, ChatGPT can be a useful tool for college students who are struggling with quantitative research methods. By utilizing ChatGPT and social media tutoring sites, students can gain a better understanding of the subject and improve their grades.

Summary

✓ Quantitative research is a deductive process.

✓ Quantitative research aims to generalize a particular phenomenon across groups of people.

- ✓ The researcher has a clearly defined hypothesis for which objectively analyzed answers are sought in numbers.
- ✓ Data obtained via quantitative methods are demonstrated in the form of numbers.
- ✓ A variable is any condition that can vary or change in quantity or quality.
- ✓ A variable in quantitative research simply refers to a phenomenon that is measured.
- ✓ The independent variable is the force that may influence or affect the other variable, the dependent variable.
- ✓ The independent variable can be manipulated or changed.
- ✓ A hypothesis is an educated guess or prediction regarding what is expected to happen in a particular situation.
- ✓ The alternative hypothesis can be either one tailed (directional) or two tailed (nondirectional).
- ✓ The two types of errors in hypothesis testing are Type I and Type II.
- ✓ There are four different levels of measurement scales: nominal, ordinal, interval, and ratio.
- ✓ Net promoter score (NPS) is a measurement scale ranging from 1 to 10 to measure customer experience and predict future phenomena.
- ✓ In statistics, data types are an important concept in order for researchers to apply correct statistical measurements to quantitative data.
- ✓ Researchers consider validity and reliability as data collection objectives when conducting research because validity and reliability are valued in the early stage of deciding how they will collect data.
- ✓ Reliability is about the consistency of results.
- ✓ Validity is the extent to which a method accurately measures what it is supposed to measure.

Key Terms

1. Quantitative research
2. Independent variable
3. Hypothesis
4. Directional/nondirectional
5. Reliability

6. Validity
7. Categorical data
8. Continuous data
9. Measurement
10. Generalization

Chapter 9

Statistical Analysis

Chapter Learning Outcomes

- Identify descriptive statistics.
- Explain central tendency and dispersion.
- Perform the computations for the mean, median, and mode.
- Recognize the relationship between variance and standard deviation.
- Differentiate between sample variance and population variance.
- Discuss how the normal distribution works.
- Apply the standard deviation to a normal curve.
- Apply the formulas to the calculations of *z* scores.
- Explain the concepts of confidence level and interval.
- Recognize the characteristics of the margin of error.
- Identify symbols of statistics.
- Learn how to use AI tools for statistics.

Statistics, a branch of applied mathematics, involves the collection, description, and analysis of numerical data, along with resulting inferences from those data. In strategic communication, statistics is an interdisciplinary science that provides insights into the characteristics of a population by studying a sample. Since it is often nearly impossible to gather data for an entire population, statistics uses sample data to describe, interpret, and generalize the characteristics of a specific sample to a population. As a result, statistics is widely used in various fields and professions, including corporations, government agencies, medical teams, investment companies, and academic research institutions. Researchers who use statistics as their primary method for data analysis apply their quantitative skills to design the data collection process, analyze the data, and interpret the results based on the aim of their research.

Using statistical analyses, researchers can quantitatively explain certain characteristics of a group of items or people. Statistics is divided into two major areas: descriptive statistics and inferential statistics. Descriptive statistics summarize the characteristics of sample and population data, while inferential statistics use those characteristics to test hypotheses, make interpretations, and draw conclusions. Researchers focus on descriptive statistics first to understand the fundamental elements of statistics before applying them to inferential statistics. Descriptive statistics summarize data with certain numbers such as frequency, mean, median, mode, range, variance, and standard deviation. These numbers can be categorized as measures of central tendency and dispersion.

MEASURES OF CENTRAL TENDENCY

Central tendency refers to the measures used to determine the center of a distribution of data. A measure of central tendency is a single summary of the data that typically describes the center of the data. It identifies a single score that is most representative of an entire data set. The concepts of mean, median, and mode are essential to understanding central tendency.

- Mean: The term *average* is frequently used in everyday language, but in statistics the arithmetic mean, or simply the mean, is the most common replacement for the average. In simple terms, the mean is the average. The mean can be calculated using the equations in Table 9.1. (The symbol Σ, the uppercase Greek letter sigma, is used as a summation notation.)
- Median: The median is the middle value when the numbers are arranged in an ascending or descending ordered list of scores. It is used in many real-life situations such as the median housing price or the median income. Revealing the center position of a set of values, the median is considered a superior index of central tendency. With an odd-numbered list, the median is identified as the middle value. However, for an even numbered list, there is no middle value, and the median is identified by finding the point halfway between the two values on either side of the center. Note that the steps for identifying the median are slightly different depending on whether you have an odd- or even-numbered list.

Table 9.1

Formula for mean	Exercise
$\bar{X} = \frac{\sum_{t-1}^{n} x_t}{n}$	A researcher wants to determine the mean age of 6 students where the ages of the students are 18, 19, 20, 21, 22, and 25. What is the mean? Mean age = (18+19 + 20+21 + 22+25) / 6=20.83

Table 9.2

Formula for median	Exercise
Odd-numbered list = [(*n* + 1) / 2]th *n* is the number of items in the set, and "th" just means the (*n*)th number.	An odd-numbered list is given to find the median: 32, 10, 12, 16, 28, 22, 18, 19, 21, 55, 23. To calculate the median, we arrange the data in ascending order: 10, 12, 16, 18, 19, 21, 22, 23, 28, 33, 55 Median = [(11+1) / 2]th = 6th. Therefore, 21 is the median.
Even-numbered list = add the two middle numbers and divide by two.	An even-numbered list is given to find the median: 10, 12, 16, 18, 19, 21, 22, 23, 28, 33. To identify the median, the fifth and sixth values are 19 and 21. Therefore, median = (19+21) / 2=20.

Table 9.3

Answers to mode	Examples
The most frequently given value is 54, the mode.	A list of numbers is given below to find the mode: 55, 78, 54, 22, 36, 65, 70, 54, 11, 27, 54
No repeated number is given, so there is no mode.	A list of numbers is given below to find the mode: 55, 78, 54, 22, 36, 65, 70, 98, 11, 27, 41

- Mode: Defined as the value that occurs most frequently in the data, the mode identifies the most repeated value. It is not hard to identify the mode in the data set, but some data sets do not have a mode when there is no repeated value.

A measure of central tendency identifies the central position within a set of data or locates the central value. The mean, median, and mode are used as measures of central tendency.

Frequency Distribution Table

Suppose you as a researcher ask your 30 participants: "How many hours did you spend in the past week watching Netflix?" You gathered their responses and organized them into Table 9.4. Such a table is called a frequency distribution table that shows the frequencies of the various responses. The frequency distribution table is designed to arrange data values in ascending order, offering information about the number of times a particular observation occurs in the data. Frequency tables can show frequencies of variables and percentages. For example, Table 9.4 shows the frequency of responses with their percentage, and Table 9.5 shows how one variable (hours spent watching Netflix) changes with another (gender).

Table 9.4 Frequency Distribution with Percentage

Hours per week Netflix viewing	Number of people	%
0–9	2	6.6
10–19	8	26.8
20–29	12	40.0
30–39	6	20.0
40 or more	2	6.6
	$N = 30$	100%

Table 9.5 Frequency Distribution by Gender

Hours per week Netflix viewing	Male	Female
0–9	1	2
10–19	5	6
20–29	2	5
30–39	4	1
40 or more	3	1
	$n = 15$	$n = 15$

A frequency table can be useful for identifying trends and comparing variables within a data set since it gives the number of particular observations. The advantage of using frequency tables is that you incorporate raw data into an easy-to-read format.

Measures of Dispersion

Dispersion refers to the degree to which data are spread around the center of a distribution, identified by the mean, median, and mode. Measures of dispersion illustrate the spread of the data around the central tendency. Both measures of central tendency and dispersion summarize quantitative data. Measures of dispersion include range, deviation, variance, standard deviation, and standard error.

- Range: The range is the difference between the highest and lowest values in the data set, computed simply by subtraction. The range is easily understood in descriptive statistics.
- Deviation: Deviation, sometimes also called the average deviation, describes the variation between observed scores and the mean score. It tells the absolute distance, ignoring the plus or minus sign. Hence, the difference takes on a positive value. Calculating the deviation involves the mean and a number of scores, as shown in Table 9.7.

Table 9.6

Formula for range	Exercise
Range = X highest – X lowest	A list of numbers is given below to find the range: 55, 78, 54, 22, 36, 65, 78, 54, 11, 27, 54 Range = 78 – 11 = 67

Table 9.7

Formula for deviation	Exercise
$\frac{\sum\lvert x-\mu\rvert}{n}$	Suppose test scores for 5 students were 90, 85, 80, 75, 60.
	Find the deviation.
Average = deviation	1. First, find the mean: (90 + 85 + 80 + 75 + 60) / 5 = 78
x = given value	2. Find the deviation from the mean: 90 – 78 = 12; 85 – 78 = 7; 80 – 78 = 2; 75 – 78 = –3; 60 – 78 = –18
μ = the mean	3. Find the sum of absolute values: 12 + 7 + 2 + 3 + 18 = 42
n = number of scores	4. Divide the sum by n: 42 / 5 = 8.4 (the average deviation)

Among the measures of dispersion, standard deviation is the most important and commonly used measure in statistics. Variance is usually computed before computing standard deviation because standard deviation is calculated as the square root of variance. To understand variance and standard deviation, we must understand when to use sample and population standard deviation. For example, if a professor gives an exam for his advertising students and wants to summarize the exam scores with the mean and standard deviation, *population standard deviation* should be used because the professor is only interested in the class of advertising students' scores. However, if the professor has randomly recruited 100 male students aged 18–22 years for a media effect study to investigate the emotional issues of male college students, *sample standard deviation* should be used because the results are to be generalized to the whole population of male college students within the age range. More importantly, there is a slight difference between sample and population standard deviation in terms of computational formulas.

- Variance: Variance measures the average of the squared differences from the mean. It indicates how far the data set spreads out from the mean. A large variance suggests that data points are spread widely, and a small variance suggests that the data points are closer to the mean. To calculate the variance, follow these steps: (1) compute the mean, (2) subtract each value from the mean, and (3) square each result. The formulas for sample and population variance are given in Table 9.8.

- Standard deviation: The square root of the variance is called the standard deviation (SD). SD measures the average spread of individual samples from the mean, demonstrating how valid that mean value actually is. A low number for SD indicates that most of the values are close to the average, while a high number for SD indicates that the values are more spread out. Simply put, SD is the dispersion of a data set relative to its mean. The formula for SD is given in Table 9.9.

The process of calculating SD is simple if you have the value of the variance. All you need is to place the square root over the number for variance. However, when a list of many and larger numbers is given and you are asked to calculate the SD, the computing process by hand is not pleasant. Consider that you plan to survey how many jobs college graduates apply for before graduation. You sampled 5 senior students ($n = 5$), and they answered 3, 5, 5, 7, and 10. Can you compute the SD of job applications? (Always find the mean first.) See Table 9.10 for the calculations.

Regarding measures of dispersion, especially for variance and standard deviation, we need to get familiar with the symbols used, especially for the sample statistic (from the sample drawn from the target population) and the population parameter (unknown numerical value). For researchers in strategic communication, sample statistics are mostly used. Table 9.10 illustrates these.

Table 9.8

Formulas for variance	Exercise
$\sigma^2 = \frac{\sum(x-\mu)^2}{N}$ Population variance	The given numbers are 1, 2, and 3. Calculate the population variance. The mean of 1, 2, and 3 is 2. $\sigma^2 = (1-2)^2 + (2-2)^2 + (3-2)^2 / 3 = 0.667$
$s^2 = \frac{\sum(x-\bar{x})^2}{n-1}$ Sample variance	The given numbers are 1, 2, and 3. Calculate the population variance. The mean of 1, 2, and 3 is 2. $s^2 = (1-2)^2 + (2-2)^2 + (3-2)^2 / 2 = 1$

Table 9.9

Formula for population *SD*	Formula for sample *SD*
$\sigma = \sqrt{\frac{\sum(X_i-\mu)^2}{N}}$	$s = \sqrt{\frac{\sum(x_i-\bar{x})^2}{(n-1)}}$

Table 9.10 Calculation of SD

x (value)	$\bar{x}$ (mean)	$x - \bar{x}$	$(x - \bar{x})^2$
3	6	3–6	9
5	6	5–6	1
5	6	5–6	1
7	6	7–6	1
10	6	10–6	16
$n = 5$			$\Sigma = 28$

Sample variance: $s^2 = \Sigma(x - \bar{x})^2 / (n - 1) = 28 / 4 = 7$. Therefore, sample *SD*: $s = \sqrt{7} = 2.64$.

Table 9.11 Symbols for Statistics

Description	Population parameter	Sample statistic
Number of values	N	n
Mean	μ "mu"	$\bar{x}$ "x-bar"
Variance	σ^2 "sigma squared"	s^2
SD	σ "sigma"	s

- Standard error: Very similar to SD, standard error (SE) measures the precision of the estimate of the sample mean. To put it simply, the two terms are almost equivalent, but SE indicates how much sample means vary from the standard deviation of the sampling distribution, which we call the SE of the sample mean. The SE is an estimate of how far the sample mean is likely to be from the population mean as a type of standard deviation. The SE is always smaller than the SD. The SE is strictly dependent on sample size. As the sample size increases, the SE gets closer to the true population mean with greater precision. Thus, the SE decreases if the sample size increases because the estimate of the population mean becomes more precise. See Table 9.12 for the calculation of SE.

Using Excel to Compute Measures of Dispersion

The calculation of dispersion does not need to be unpleasant with the complicated steps we have to go through, such as (1) calculating the mean, (2) subtracting the mean from each number, (3) squaring the results, (4) working out the mean of those squared differences, and (5) taking the square root of that sum. Two popular software packages make the process easy: Excel and SPSS. Since most PCs and laptops come with Excel, we practice the calculation of dispersion with Excel. Once you place your data into an Excel spreadsheet, click on Formulas from the Tools menu. Then select the drop-down menu

Table 9.12

Formula for standard error	Exercise
Standard error (SE) $= \frac{SD}{\sqrt{n}}$	You sampled 5 senior students about how many times they applied for jobs, and each of them answered: 3, 5, 5, 7, 10. What is the standard error? $n = 5$; $\bar{x} = 6$; $SD = 2.64$ $SE = 2.64 / \sqrt{5} = 1.18$

from the More Functions icon and select Statistical. You can choose VAR.S (sample variance) and highlight the values or numbers. For example, we can use the numbers for the job application example. You will get a variance of 7. The same process for SD could be applied if you choose STDEV.S for the sample standard deviation. You will get an SD of 2.645751311. Figures 9.1 and 9.2 illustrate the steps.

Data Distributions

Most data in strategic communication are likely to have a bell-shaped distribution. This refers to the bell-curved shape of the probability distribution, meaning that most data points are located close to the mean, with only a few lying far from the mean. For instance, if the mean score for a midterm exam in your research class is 80 out of 100 points, most students might score between 73 and 87 points, with a few scoring below 70 or above 90, and very few scoring below 50 or above 97. When data are normally distributed and plotted on a distribution curve, the data distribution shows the normal density of the values in the shape of a bell curve. Most researchers in strategic communication assume that their data are normally distributed. A normal distribution of data is characterized as follows:

- The data are symmetric around their mean.
- The mean, median, and mode are equal.
- The data are denser in the center and less dense in the tails.
- The data are defined by two parameters: the mean and standard deviation.
- 68.23% of the area is within one standard deviation of the mean (±1).
- Approximately 95% of the area is within two standard deviations of the mean (±2).
- 99.72% of the area is within 3 standard deviations of the mean (±3).[1]

Visualizing the characteristics of a normal distribution helps us understand the concept and practice of data distribution, as shown in Figure 9.3.

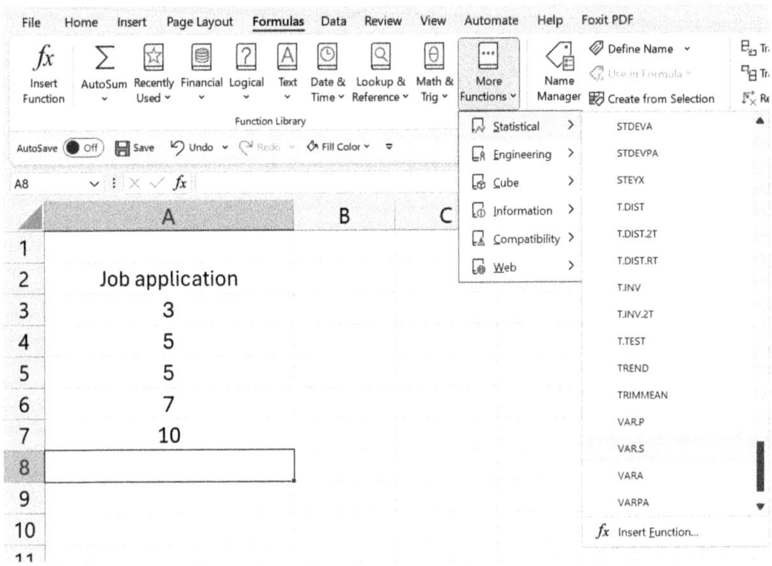

Figure 9.1 Excel for variance and standard deviation (part 1)

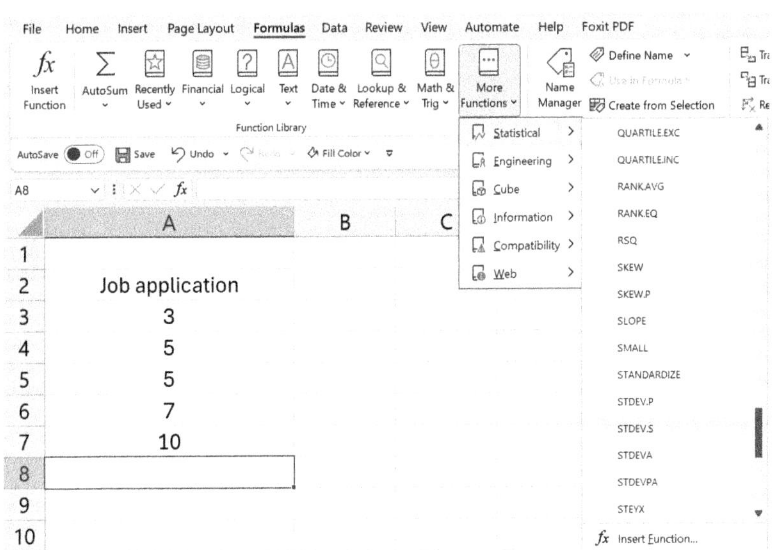

Figure 9.2 Excel for variance and standard deviation (part 2)

Source: Created by author.

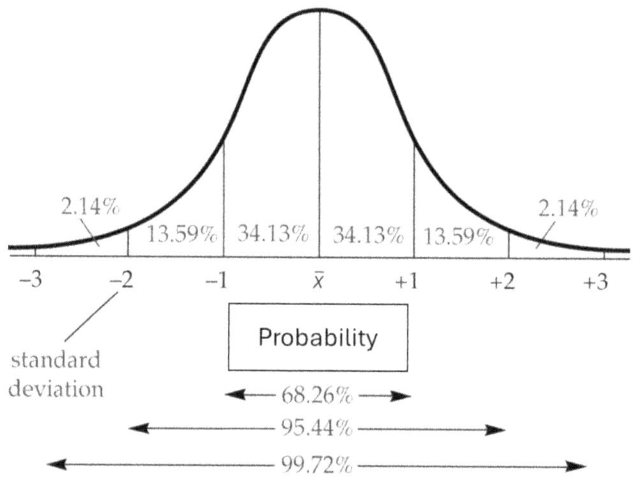

Figure 9.3 Normal distribution curve

Source: Created by author.

A normal distribution shows the patterns of a statistical data distribution: 50% of the distribution is on the left side of the mean, and 50% is on the right side of the mean. When we say that the data are normally distributed, the mean, median, and mode are the same. With the normal distribution curve, we gain a better understanding of how to apply standard deviation and other statistical functions to the practice of statistics. The following example should help us with the application of standard deviation and the normal distribution curve.

Suppose most students at your university watch YouTube between 10 and 24 hours a week, and the mean is 17 hours. Assume the data are normally distributed and the SD is 2. Based on the information, we can conclude: (1) one SD to the right of the mean is 19 hours, and 34.13% of students at your university watch YouTube between 17 hours and 19 hours a week; (2) over 68% of the students watch YouTube between 15 and 19 hours a week; and (3) almost all students at your university (99.72%) watch YouTube between 11 hours and 23 hours per week. See figure 9.4.

It is important to note that the empirical rule or the 3 SD rule (–3 to +3) tells us that almost all data fall into the range of three SDs from the mean: 99.72% is almost 100% on the curve. Another important point is that the curve never meets or touches the *x*-axis in either direction, regardless of how far the curve extends. While the normal distribution curve indicates that the data are symmetrically distributed with a bell-shaped curve, not all data are normally distributed. This is where the concepts of skewness and kurtosis come into play.

Skewness is the degree of asymmetry from the normal distribution. A perfectly symmetrical data set has a skewness of 0, so the normal distribution has zero skewness. When the bell curve is asymmetrical, two types of skewness exist: positive and negative. Positive

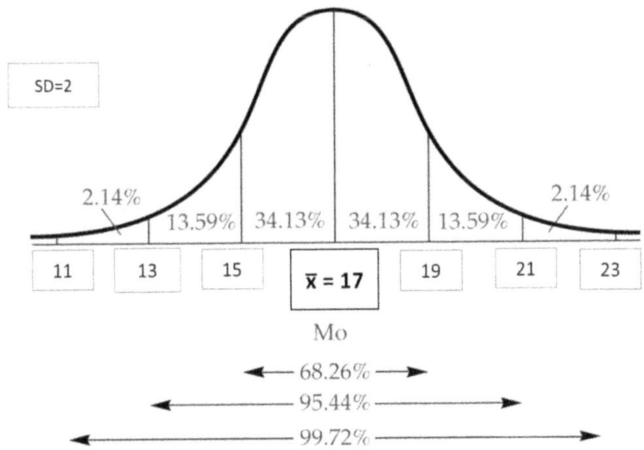

Figure. 9.4 Example of SD on the curve
Source: Created by author.

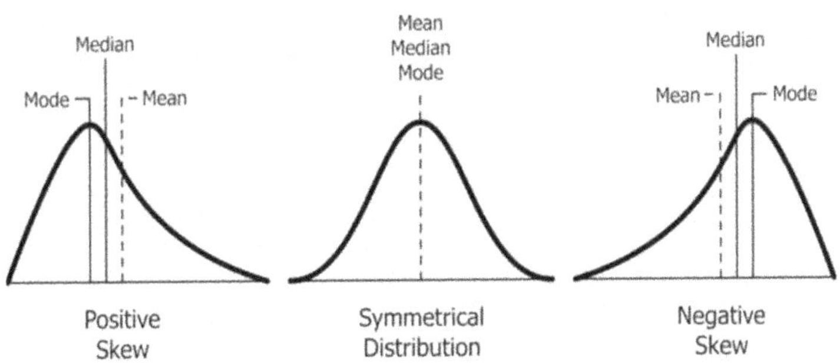

Figure. 9.5 Skewness of distribution
Source: Created by author.

skewness means that most values are gathered around the left tail of the distribution while the tail on the right side of the distribution is longer. The distribution is said to be right skewed or skewed to the right, and the mean is greater than the mode (mean > median > mode). Negative skewness occurs when the tail on the left side of the curve is longer than the tail on the right side. It is also said to be left skewed or skewed to the left, and the mean is smaller than the mode (mean < median < mode). See figure 9.5.

When all measures of central tendency (mean, median, and mode) are equal to each other, the data are normally distributed with a skewness of 0. Highly skewed data can be observed when the skewness is less than –1 (negatively skewed) or greater than 1 (positively skewed).

Kurtosis describes the tails of the data distribution as being light tailed or heavy tailed, measuring outliers in the distribution. There are three kinds of kurtosis: (1) mesokurtic—the kurtosis is zero, the normal distribution; (2) leptokurtic—the tail of the distribution is heavy with outliers, and kurtosis is higher than that of the normal distribution; and (3) platykurtic—the tail of the distribution is light without outliers, and kurtosis is less than that of the normal distribution. See figure 9.6.

z Scores

A normal distribution of data implies that the mean, mode, and median are identical. The normal distribution curve illustrates how values or data are symmetrically and normally distributed. A normal distribution, sometimes referred to as a bell curve, can be standardized by converting its values into *z* scores. This allows us to make comparisons between dissimilar samples on the same standard normal curve. For interpreting *z* scores, we use the *z* distribution, where the mean is always 0 and the standard deviation is 1. The *z* distribution is a specific type of normal distribution, also known as the standard normal distribution, where the mean is 0.[2] When the normal distribution is standardized (resulting in the standard normal distribution), the mean becomes 0, and the standard deviation becomes 1, facilitating statistical comparisons.

We use a *z* score in the process of standardizing a normal distribution for dissimilar measurements. The best way to understand a *z* score is to look at the standard normal distribution curve (see Figure 9.7). Instead of placing the mean in the middle of the curve, the standard normal distribution curve places 0 in the middle. By placing a *z* score on a normal distribution curve, we can interpret the difference in individual values. For instance, a positive *z* score indicates that the value is greater than the mean, while a negative *z* score suggests that the value is less than the mean. A *z* score of 0 corresponds to the mean value. Because converting a normal distribution into the standard normal

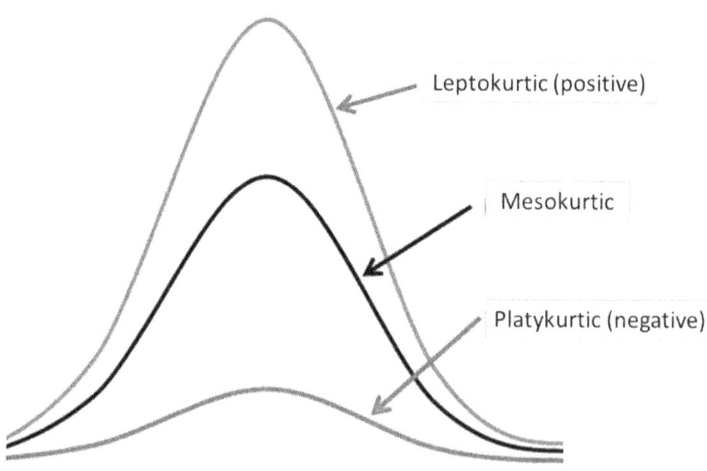

Figure. 9.6 Kurtosis of distribution

Source: Created by author.

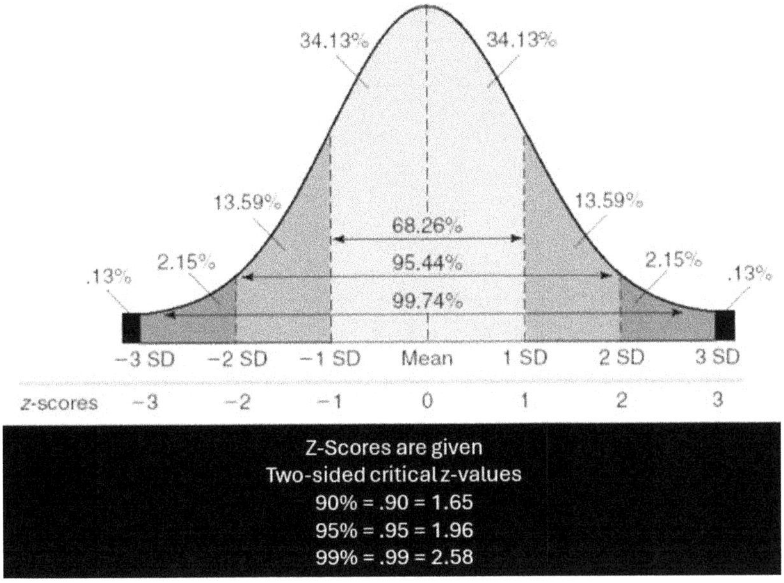

Figure 9.7 Z-score curve or the standard normal distribution curve
Source: Created by author.

distribution allows us to compare scores on different kinds of variables, we need to learn how to calculate the *z* score.

In practice, it is almost impossible for strategic communication researchers to know the value of the population standard deviation (σ). However, if the sample size is larger than 30, the sample standard deviation can be used to estimate the population standard deviation with a 95% confidence level. We notice from the distribution curve that it includes 95% of the probability between –1.96 and +1.96 standard deviations, and the *z* score at a 95% confidence interval is given as 1.96. The *z* score formulas also have two types—population and sample—but they don't differ significantly, as both formulas show that the *z* score is calculated by subtracting the mean score from the individual value and dividing the difference by the standard deviation. See Table 9.13 for the formulas for these calculations.

For example, suppose the mean is 50, the SD is 5, and a value is 55. With calculation, the *z* score is (55 – 50) / 5 = 1. This means the score of 55 has a *z* score of 1. What about the value of 35? The *z* score for the value of 35 is (35 – 50) / 5 = –3. Another example of using *z* scores is when you, as a researcher, find that college students follow influencers on Instagram 2 hours per day, and the standard deviation is 0.5. You are curious about the proportion of the population that follows Instagram influencers between 2 and 2.5 hours. To calculate the proportion, you find the *z* score for each hour: (1) 2 hours: (2 – 2) / 0.5 = 0, and (2) 2.5 hours: (2.5 – 2) / 0.5 = 1. The *z* scores are between 0 and 1. As the *z* scores of 0 and 1 on the distribution curve represent 34.13%, you can conclude that 34.13% of college students follow Instagram influencers between 2 and 2.5 hours daily.

Table 9.13

Formula for population *z* score	Formula for sample *z* score
$Z = \frac{X - \mu}{\sigma}$	$Z = \frac{X - \bar{X}}{s}$
x = individual value	x = individual value
μ = mean	$\bar{x}$ = mean
σ = standard deviation	s = standard deviation

One more complex example of a *z* score is given when you have 100 research participants who tend to watch YouTube 100 hours a month on average, and the SD is 15. Jennifer, one of the participants, answers that she watches 121 hours a month. You are curious about her *z* score: (121 – 100) / 15 = 1.4. The *z* score of 1.4 means that if you place the number 1.4 on the distribution curve, it matches 41.92% of the proportion on the right side. (To find the proportion of the distribution curve corresponding to this *z* score, you would typically refer to a *z* table.) If you add 50% from the left side of the curve, the total proportion is 91.92%, meaning that Jennifer's 121 hours of YouTube watching is in the top 8.08% of the YouTube viewing hours among the research participants (higher than 91.92% of other participants' YouTube-viewing hours).

What if you neither knew the population standard deviation (σ) nor had a sample size larger than 30? In such a case, you use a t-score instead of a *z* score. Regarding data distribution, the *t* score has a mean of 0 like the *z* score on a normal distribution curve. The *t* score is more accurate to use than the *z* score when you have small sample sizes (< 30) with an unknown population standard deviation. (See table 9.14.)

CONFIDENCE INTERVAL AND CONFIDENCE LEVEL

A confidence interval provides an estimated range of values, which is likely to include the true value of an unknown population parameter. The range is calculated from a given set of sample data. Confidence intervals measure the degree of certainty or confidence in a sampling method. The most commonly used confidence levels are 90%, 95%, and 99%. For strategic communication researchers, the 95% confidence level is most popular. A confidence interval shows the range within which the true population parameter is likely to fall, while a confidence level indicates the frequency with which the estimated interval would contain the population parameter if the experiment were repeated many times. For example, when news outlets such as CNN and Fox News broadcast poll results, they often include a confidence level, such as a 95% confidence level. This means that if the poll were conducted 100 times, the same result would be expected 95 times. What does that mean? A 100% confidence level indicates that the same result is guaranteed if the poll is repeated later.

Table 9.14

Formula for *t* score	Exercise
$t = \frac{\bar{x} - \mu}{S/\sqrt{n}}$	What is the *t* score if you have the following information?
	• population mean = 245
$\bar{x}$ = sample mean	• sample standard deviation = 35
μ = population mean	• size of the sample = 20
s = sample standard deviation	• sample mean = 210
n = number in the sample	$t = (210 - 245) / (35 \times \sqrt{20}) = -4.47$

To understand the concepts of confidence interval and confidence level, consider a simple example. Suppose you, as a researcher, measured the weights of 50 randomly chosen college freshmen and computed a mean weight of 180 pounds with a standard deviation of 15 pounds. You want to calculate the confidence interval, but you do not know the standard deviation of the entire population. However, if your sample size is larger than 30, you can use the sample standard deviation as an estimate of the population standard deviation. See Table 9.15 for the calculations.

There are two important rules of confidence intervals that we need to learn from this example. First, the *z* value is given: for a 90% confidence level, the *z* value is 1.65; for a 95% confidence level, the *z* value is 1.96; and for a 99% confidence level, the *z* value is 2.58. If the 99% *z* value were used in the example, the confidence interval would be 180 ± 5.47, meaning that 99% of all freshmen may weigh between 174.53 pounds and 185.47 pounds. Second, the value after 180 pounds ± is also called the margin of error, 4.16 at the 95% confidence level. The width of the confidence interval, ±4.16 at the 95% confidence level, indicates how certain we are about the true value in the population. Hence, the formula for the margin of error is $z \times (S / \sqrt{n})$. See figure 9.8.

A margin of error used with the confidence level is a statistical measurement of the difference between survey results and the population value. We can improve our understanding of the concepts of confidence level and margin of error if we consider the practice of election polls. Media or polling agencies such as CBS News and the Pew Research Center often report a margin of error of plus or minus 3.5 percentage points at the 95% confidence level with predictions for presidential elections.[3] These numbers indicate that if the agency conducted the same poll 100 times, it would expect the result to be within 3.5 points of the true population value 95 times out of 100. The calculation of the margin of error without knowing the standard deviation uses a different formula when the sample proportion is known. See Table 9.16.

It is important to understand that a confidence level is expressed as a percentage, and a 95% confidence level is what most researchers use in the field of strategic communication.

Table 9.15

Formula for confidence interval	Exercise
$\bar{x} \pm z\frac{s}{\sqrt{n}}$	You have the following information:
CI = confidence interval	50 freshmen, mean weight = 180, s = 15,
$\bar{x}$ = sample mean	z value for 95% CI = 1.96
z = z value	CI = $180 \pm 1.96 \times 15 / \sqrt{50} = 180 \pm 4.16$
s = sample standard deviation n = number of observations	The confidence interval = 180 pounds ±4.16 pounds = from 175.84 to 184.16 pounds

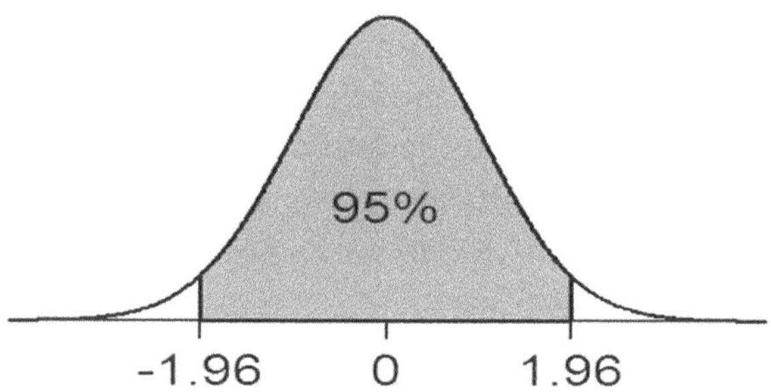

Figure 9.8 Z-score at 95% confidence level.
Source: Created by author.

Table 9.16

Formula for margin of error	Exercise
$z*\sqrt{\frac{\hat{p}(1-\hat{p})}{n}}$ MOE = margin of error $\hat{p}$ = sample proportion z = z value n = number of observations	Suppose that an ABC News poll sampled 1,000 Americans, and the results show that 560 people (56%) support how the president is handling his job and 440 people (44%) disapprove of him. What is the margin of error (MOE) at a 95% confidence level (z = 1.96)? $MOE = 1.96 \times \sqrt{}\ (0.56)\ (0.44)\ /\ 1{,}000 = 0.030$ Based on the MOE, the pollsters conclude that 56% of Americans approve of the president ± 3% (from 53% to 59%) with 95% confidence.

Suppose, for example, you conduct a survey asking a group of LGBTQ+ college students how many times per year they attend support group meetings. You test your statistics at the 95% confidence level and calculate a confidence interval of 10–14 times. This means they attend meetings between 10 and 14 times a year, and your findings are statistically valid at the high level of 95%. In sum, the three concepts of confidence level, confidence interval, and margin of error should be understood together in the pursuit of knowledge of fundamental statistics.

Learning Statistics With AI: A Friendly Guide for Research Rookies

Statistics often gets a bad rap—a complex language spoken only by number wizards—leaving many research students feeling lost and intimidated. However, AI technology has made significant strides in recent years, and its applications in the field of statistics are numerous. AI can help simplify complex statistical concepts, perform calculations, and even interpret results. Here is some guidance for students on how to leverage AI tools to navigate statistics with confidence:

- Interactive learning platforms: Platforms like Khan Academy and Coursera offer interactive courses that combine AI-driven simulations and explanations.[4] These platforms provide a hands-on approach to learning statistics, allowing students to visualize concepts and gain practical insights.
- AI-based tutoring: AI-driven tutoring systems, such as Carnegie Learning and Knewton, provide personalized assistance to students struggling with statistics.[5] These platforms adapt to individual learning styles, offering targeted explanations and practice problems.
- Statistical simulations: AI can generate simulations to help you understand statistical concepts better.[6] For example, you can use simulations to understand the central limit theorem, hypothesis testing, and confidence intervals.
- Data analysis tools: AI-powered data analysis tools can perform complex statistical analyses with just a few clicks. These tools can calculate measures of central tendency, dispersion, correlation, regression, and more.[7] They also provide visualizations, making it easier to understand and interpret the results.

Statistics transcends mere formula memorization and intricate calculations. At its core, it revolves around comprehending data and facilitating informed decision making. It is crucial for research students to recognize that integrating AI into statistical endeavors is not an act of capitulation to machines; rather, it is a strategic empowerment. The aim is to provide students with the right tools to conquer their apprehension of statistics, unlocking the vast potential of data in the realm of strategic communication research. By incorporating AI technologies into their statistical journeys, students embark on a transformative experience. This integration allows them to demystify intricate statistical concepts, fostering a deeper understanding. Consequently, students not only build confidence in their analytical capabilities but also cultivate a positive and enthusiastic attitude toward statistical research. This synergy of human intellect and AI prowess becomes a catalyst for meaningful exploration and discovery in the dynamic field of research.

Application of an AI-Powered Tool

Box 9.1
Explanation from Google Gemini about How to Compute a Poll

Using an AI-Powered Tool (Google Gemini) for a Poll
Command syntax: An ABC News/Washington Post poll in May 2024 found that 68% of Americans say the president is too old for another term, with a margin of sampling error of 3.5 percentage points and a sample size of 1,006 people. Explain how the poll was computed, including every step of the calculations with equations and formulas for college students who have a weak statistical background.

Answer: Sure. Here are the steps on how the poll was computed, including the equations and formulas used, for college students who have a weak statistical background:

1. A random sample of 1,006 people was selected from the population of the United States. This means that each person in the population had an equal chance of being selected.
2. The respondents were asked the question "Do you think the president is too old for another term?"
3. The number of respondents who answered "yes" to this question was counted.
4. The margin of sampling error was calculated. The margin of sampling error is a measure of how accurate the poll results are likely to be. It is calculated using the following formula: margin of sampling error = z * sqrt(p(1 – p) / n).

where:

- z is the z score for the desired confidence level (typically 95%).
- p is the proportion of the population that is expected to answer "yes" to the question.
- n is the sample size.

In this case, the z score is 1.96, the proportion of the population that is expected to answer "yes" to the question is 0.68, and the sample size is 1,006. Therefore, the margin of sampling error is 3.5 percentage points. MoSE = 1.96 × sqrt(0.68 × (1 – 0.68) / 1006) = 3.5.

5. The poll results were reported with the margin of sampling error. In this case, the poll results would be reported as "68% of Americans say the president is too old for another term, with a margin of sampling error of 3.5 percentage points."

It is important to note that the margin of sampling error does not mean that the poll results are wrong. It simply means that the results could be off by as much as 3.5 percentage points in either direction. The true percentage of Americans who think the president is too old for another term could be anywhere between 64.5% and 71.5%.

It is also important to note that sampling error is not the only source of error in polls. Other sources of error include the wording of the questions, the way the poll is conducted, and the demographics of the sample.

Here is a simplified explanation of the margin of sampling error: The margin of sampling error is a measure of how accurate the poll results are likely to be. The larger the margin of sampling error, the less accurate the poll results are likely to be. The smaller the margin of sampling error, the more accurate the poll results are likely to be.

Here is an example of how the margin of sampling error can be used: A poll finds that 68% of Americans say the president is too old for another term. The poll has a margin of sampling error of 3.5 percentage points. This means that the true percentage of Americans who think the president is too old for another term could be anywhere between 64.5% and 71.5%.

I hope this helps!

Summary

- ✓ There are two major areas of statistics, known as descriptive statistics and inferential statistics.
- ✓ Descriptive statistics describe the characteristics of sample and population data.
- ✓ Central tendency refers to the measures used to determine the center of distribution data.
- ✓ In statistics, the arithmetic mean, or simply the mean, is most commonly used to replace the average.
- ✓ The median is the middle value when the numbers are arranged in an ascending- or descending-order list of scores.

- ✓ The mode identifies the most repeated value.
- ✓ Frequency tables can be useful for identifying trends and comparing variables within a data set while describing the number of particular observations.
- ✓ The difference between the highest value and the lowest value in the data set is called the range.
- ✓ The variation between an observed score and the mean score is described by deviation.
- ✓ The average of the squared differences from the mean is measured by variance.
- ✓ Standard deviation measures the average spread of individual samples from the mean.
- ✓ Standard error (SE) measures the precision of the estimate of the sample mean.
- ✓ Skewness is the degree of asymmetry from the normal distribution.
- ✓ Kurtosis describes the tails of the data distribution as being light tailed or heavy tailed, indicating outliers in the distribution.
- ✓ A *z* score is used in the process of standardization of a normal distribution for dissimilar measurements.
- ✓ The standard normal distribution (*z*-score distribution) places 0 in the middle of the normal distribution curve.
- ✓ A confidence interval indicates an estimated range of values, measuring the degree of probability in a sampling method with three popular limits of 90%, 95%, or 99% confidence levels.
- ✓ A margin of error used with the confidence interval is a statistical measurement of the difference between survey results and the population value.
- ✓ A confidence level is expressed as a percentage, and a 95% confidence level is what most researchers use in the field of strategic communication.
- ✓ AI tools can calculate measures of central tendency, dispersion, correlation, regression, and more.

Key Terms

1. Descriptive statistics
2. Central tendency
3. Frequency
4. Variance

5. Standard deviation
6. Normal distribution
7. *z* score
8. Skewness
9. Confidence interval
10. Confidence level

CHAPTER 10

Inferential Statistics

CHAPTER LEARNING OUTCOMES

- Identify the characteristics of inferential statistics.
- Explain probability and odds.
- Recognize the *p* value of .05.
- Apply the *p* value to determine significance.
- Differentiate between the *t* test and ANOVA.
- Discuss how hypothesis testing is performed.
- Explain the process of comparisons between critical and calculated values.
- Perform a *t* test and an ANOVA in Excel.
- Explain the concepts of ANCOVA and MANCOVA.
- Become familiar with distribution tables.
- Understand rejection or failure to reject the null hypothesis.
- Incorporate AI technology into the study of inferential statistics.

Inferential statistics is a subset of statistics that allows us to make educated guesses about a population based on a sample. This branch of statistics is used to estimate population characteristics from a sample of data. To apply inferential statistics, one must collect a sample of data from the population of interest. The sample should accurately represent the population, meaning it should reflect the population as a whole. Once the sample data are collected, inferential statistics can be used to make inferences about the population. There are various inferential statistical techniques, each serving a different purpose. Some of the most common techniques include:

- Hypothesis testing: This technique is used to test whether there is a statistically significant difference between two groups.

- Confidence intervals: These are used to estimate the range of values within which the true population parameter is likely to fall.
- Regression analysis: This technique is used to predict the value of one variable based on the value of another variable.

Inferential statistics is a powerful tool for making inferences about populations from samples. However, it is crucial to remember that inferential statistics is not an exact science. There is always some degree of uncertainty associated with inferential statistics, and the results of an inferential statistical test should always be interpreted with caution.

CONCEPTS USED IN INFERENTIAL STATISTICS

Analyzing results from sample data requires an understanding of the main concepts of inferential statistics, including probability, odds, p values, significance, and hypothesis testing.

Probability and Odds

Probability is a measure of the likelihood of an event occurring, expressed as a fraction of the number of desired outcomes to the total number of possible outcomes. For instance, the probability of rolling a 1 on a single six-sided die is calculated as 1 / 6 = .167, or a 16.7% chance. If the probability of an event occurring is X, then the probability of the event not occurring is $1 - X$. In the dice example, the probability of the event is .167, so the probability that the event will not occur is 1 – .167 = .833 or 83.3%. In essence, in the example of rolling a 1 on a six-sided die, the probability is 1/6 and the odds are 1 to 5. This means that for every time you roll a 1, you will not roll a 1 five times.

Odds, on the other hand, are defined as the ratio of the probability that an event will happen to the probability that the event will not happen. The formula to calculate odds is $Y = X / (1 - X)$. For example, the odds of flipping a coin to tails (with a probability of .5 or 50%) are 1 to 1, or even. If the probability is .75 or 75%, then the odds are 3 to 1. This represents three units won for every one unit bet.

In real-world scenarios, understanding probability and odds can be useful. For instance, when playing roulette in Las Vegas, knowing the probability and odds of placing bets on the numbers of the roulette wheel can be beneficial. An American roulette wheel has the numbers 1 to 36, 18 red spaces, 18 black spaces, and 2 green spaces (0 and 00). If you bet on red, your probability of winning is calculated as .4737 or 47.37% (18 / 38 = .4737). The odds of winning are a bit different. Odds compare the number of ways you can win to the number of ways you can lose. This is calculated by dividing the probability of winning (.4737 or 47.37%) by the probability of losing (.5263 or 52.63%). When you divide .4737 by .5263, you get approximately .9, which is expressed as 9 to 10 in terms of odds. This means that, for every 10 times you play, you can expect to win about 9 times. However, the odds of winning are always in favor of the casino, meaning that over time, you will lose money if you consistently bet on red in American roulette. Hence, knowing the probability and odds of winning a game of chance can help you make informed decisions about whether or not to play.

p *Value and Significance*

In inferential statistics, a p value is a product of hypothesis testing. It represents the probability of obtaining results from the test of the null hypothesis. Conventionally, a p value of .05 or less is considered statistically significant. This means that if the p value is .05 or less, the statistical test is deemed significant. Researchers often state $p < .05$ or $p > .05$ to indicate the significance of their results. The lower the p value (i.e., $p < .05$), the greater the statistical significance of the results. However, it is important to note that the p value does not indicate the effectiveness of the sample size or the likely effect size on the total population.[1]

A p value is used solely to determine whether there is evidence to reject or fail to reject (accept) the null hypothesis. In practice, most quantitative researchers conventionally use the combination of $p < .05$ and statistical significance to demonstrate the scientific outcomes of their research. When the p value is less than .05, the researcher claims that there is a significant relationship or difference between variables. In other words, the results are declared statistically significant.

As a quantitative researcher, you do not need to worry about calculating the p value since computer software packages such as Excel and SPSS will compute it for you. Your role is to form null and alternative hypotheses, gather data, input the data into the software package, run statistical tests, read the p value provided by the software program, and draw a conclusion on whether there is statistical significance. This process is called *hypothesis testing*. For example, if the software provides a p value of .09, which is greater than .05, you would accept your null hypothesis. If the p value given by the software is .03, less than .05, your null hypothesis is rejected. However, many statistics experts currently warn against heavy dependence on the p value and statistical significance. According to the American Statistical Association (ASA), researchers should not base their conclusions solely on the p value of .05, nor should they believe that a difference or relationship exists just because it was statistically significant.[2] Despite this, the combination of the p value and significance is still dominantly used by most quantitative researchers in the fields of social science and strategic communication. Therefore, we should understand how to use them and apply them to hypothesis testing.

Hypothesis Testing

Hypothesis testing is a process used by researchers to evaluate assumptions about a population based on a sample. It involves comparing two mutually exclusive assumptions about a population to determine which is better supported by the sample data. Hypothesis testing leads to a decision about statistical significance. The common steps for hypothesis testing are:

- Formulate a null and an alternative hypothesis.
- Identify a statistical test that can be used to assess the truth of the null hypothesis.
- Analyze the sample data using specific tests.
- Either reject or fail to reject (accept) the null hypothesis.

The null hypothesis always states that there is no difference, relationship, or association between variables. In contrast, the alternative hypothesis states that there is a difference, relationship, or association. These hypotheses are mutually exclusive. For example, if an alternative hypothesis states that there is a relationship between stress levels and binge-watching habits, the null hypothesis would state that there is no relationship between the variables.

Null hypotheses (H_0): There is no relationship between stress levels and binge-watching habits among college students.

Alternative hypotheses (H_a): There is a relationship between stress levels and binge-watching habits among college students.

Based on these hypotheses, you would conduct a hypothesis test by analyzing your sample data. Suppose your data analysis yields a p value of .02, which is less than .05. This means that there is a 2% chance of finding a relationship larger than the one in your study assuming that the null hypothesis is true. If the probability is low ($p = .02$), this suggests that the data are inconsistent with the null hypothesis, and there is evidence to support the alternative hypothesis. If there is a chance of less than 5% ($p < .05$), you would regard the results as statistically significant. When the p value is less than .05, you reject the null hypothesis and accept the alternative hypothesis. Your conclusion is that there exists a relationship or association between stress levels and binge-watching habits among college students. However, you do not yet identify the direction of the relationship (i.e., whether stress levels increase or decrease with binge-watching).

Some researchers argue that we should never say we "accept" the null hypothesis when the p value is larger than .05. Instead, they recommend saying that we "fail to reject" the null hypothesis. This phrasing indicates that the data are insufficient to choose the alternative hypothesis over the null hypothesis. Therefore, some statisticians and researchers prefer to say they "fail to reject" the null hypothesis rather than "accept" the null hypothesis, declaring the results statistically nonsignificant. Conversely, when the p

value is less than the significance level ($p < .05$ for researchers in strategic communication), they say to reject the null hypothesis and accept the alternative hypothesis.

FINDING THE RIGHT STATISTICAL TEST

After formulating the null and alternative hypotheses and collecting data, it is time to select the appropriate statistical test(s) to correctly analyze the data. Statistical tests are used in hypothesis testing to determine whether an independent variable has a statistically significant relationship with a dependent variable. They are also designed to estimate the difference or relationship between variables. Depending on the data types (levels of measurement scales), you choose the appropriate statistical test(s). As discussed in Chapter 8, there are four scale types of data that can be gathered and measured in quantitative research: nominal, ordinal, interval, and ratio. Broadly, nominal and ordinal scales of data are considered nonparametric or categorical, while interval and ratio scales of data are regarded as parametric or continuous. Inferential statistics generally classify such data into two categories: parametric (continuous) and nonparametric (categorical), and statistical tests for parametric data rely on the assumption that the data are normally distributed in a bell-shaped distribution.

Categorical data might not have a logical order since they tend to include categorical variables such as gender, political affiliation, marital status, and ethnicity. Continuous data have a clear logical order with numeric values (e.g., speed, weight, height, age, time). A general statistical rule of thumb suggests that a nonparametric test be selected when the dependent variable's level of measurement scale is nominal or ordinal. In contrast, if the dependent variable's scale is considered continuous, then a parametric test should be selected. Generally, researchers feel more comfortable with parametric tests than nonparametric tests regarding hypothesis testing with the assumption of a normal data distribution. Popular tests for parametric data are the *t* test and analysis of variance (ANOVA), whereas the chi-square test is mostly used for nonparametric data analysis. We study the popular tests for parametric or continuous data on the measurement scales of interval and ratio in this chapter.

t TEST

A *t* test is used to determine if there is a significant difference or relationship between the means of two groups. It is one of the hypothesis-testing tools, which tests an assumption to make an application to a population. An important concept of a *t* test is that researchers use it to compare the average values of two data sets from two different groups. In other words, when you seek a difference between two groups of people or units, you use a *t* test to declare statistical significance. Statistically, a *t* test takes sample data from each of the two groups with a null hypothesis stating that there is no difference between the means of the two groups (they are equal). Thus, the alternative hypothesis for a *t* test states that there is a difference between the two means of the groups. The results from the *t* test will inform you if there is or is not a difference, so you decide to accept or reject the null hypothesis. Before running a *t* test, you assume that your data sets belong to:

- the measurement of dependent variables on continuous scales such as interval or ratio
- a randomly selected portion of the population
- the bell-shaped curve of a normal distribution
- homogeneity of variance with approximately equal standard deviations

Again, as an assumption about the population from which the sample was randomly drawn, continuous (parametric) data from two different groups with a normal distribution are required for a *t* test. There are three types of *t* tests we can perform:

1. A two-sample *t* test: This test compares the means for two different sample groups. For example, if you compare the means of driving miles between male and female college students, a two-sample *t* test should be used. The measurement scale of driving miles is on a ratio scale that has an absolute 0, and the dependent variable is driving miles that may be altered by the independent variable of gender.
2. A paired-sample *t* test: This test compares the means from the same group at two different times. You collect the mean of a data set from a sample at one time and then collect another mean of the same sample at a later time, maybe a week or a month later. A paired samples *t* test is usually used when you compare a pretest result with a posttest result after a particular intervention is given by you between the two time points (e.g., before and after the intervention). For example, you ask your participants to take a public relations history test after reading a PR history text, and then maybe a week later you ask them to take another PR history test after watching a YouTube PR history video. You compare the two test scores and decide if the video did something to increase or decrease the test scores.
3. A one-sample *t* test: This test examines whether an unknown population mean is different from a specific or known value. In a one-sample *t* test, you seek whether your sample mean is different from the population mean. For example, you have an official government statistic on the national average of male longevity, 79 years, and you want to compare the average longevity of a sample of female Americans to this value. In this case, a one-sample *t* test is used.

The two-sample *t* test among the three types of *t* test tends to be most commonly used for college students as a *t*-test exercise, and it is also known as a Student's *t* test or two-sample *t* test.[3]

The Two-Sample* t *Test (Independent Samples* t *Test or Student's* t *Test)

When you want to know if there is a statistically significant difference between the means of two different groups, you perform the two-sample *t* test. For example, you can examine if the means of home workout hours a week while watching YouTube fitness channels differ between freshman and senior college students. You collect a sample of each group of students and record their home workout hours as they follow along with YouTube training coaches. For the *t* test, your hypotheses are formulated as follows:

H_0: The mean of freshmen equals the mean of seniors ($\mu_1 = \mu_2$).

H_a: The mean of freshmen is different from the mean of seniors, or there is a difference between the two groups ($\mu_1 \neq \mu_2$).

Suppose you randomly selected 10 participants from each group and collect the data shown in Table 10.1:

Based on the data, you compare the two groups and find if there is a statistically significant difference. For the comparison, you run the independent *t* test, meaning that you calculate the test by hand with the *t*-test formula in order to get the *t* score, as shown in Table 10.2:

Calculating the Two-Sample* t *Test by Hand and in Excel

We follow standardized steps to compute the *t* score. First, we need to get the means, such as the mean of freshman students, 90 / 10 = 9, and the mean of senior students,

Table 10.1

	Hours of home workout a week while following and emulating YouTube trainers									
10 freshman students	6	10	7	12	8	9	9	5	11	13
10 senior students	3	2	5	4	7	4	6	9	4	6

Table 10.2

Independent samples *t*-test formula	
$t = \frac{(\bar{X}_1 - \bar{X}_2)}{\sqrt{\left(\frac{s_1^2}{n_1} + \frac{s_2^2}{n_2}\right)}}$	$\bar{x}_1$ and $\bar{x}_2$ = the mean of each group s_1^2 and s_2^2 = the variance of each group n_1 and n_2 = the sample size of each group

Table 10.3

$t = \dfrac{(\bar{X}_1 - \bar{X}_2)}{\sqrt{\left(\dfrac{s_1^2}{n_1} + \dfrac{s_2^2}{n_2}\right)}}$	$t = \dfrac{(9-5)}{\sqrt{\left(\dfrac{6.66}{10} + \dfrac{4.22}{10}\right)}} = 3.83$

50 / 10 = 5. After arriving at the means of 5 and 9, we compute each group's standard deviation. Finally, we place all numbers into the formula as shown in Table 10.3:

Now that we have the *t* score of 3.83, we need to find the degrees of freedom (*df*) for the score. The *df* refers to the maximum number of independent values that are free to vary. It sounds confusing, but the simplest way to understand or use the *df* is that it equals the sample size minus the number of parameters you need to calculate. For a *t* test, the *df* is calculated by subtracting 1 from the number of items: $df = n - 1$. When there are two samples, such as the independent *t* test, we get the *df* as $(n_1 + n_2) - 2$. Hence, the *df* for the YouTube workout case is $df = (10 + 10) - 2 = 18$. With the *df* and *t* score we calculated, we find the *t* table critical value, which is given in the *t* distribution tables. In the tables, we locate the critical value of $df = 18$ with a two-tailed *p* value of .05. We find the number of 2.101, which is the critical value for *t*-test interpretation. See figure 10.1.

The next step is to do hypothesis testing with the calculated *t* value of 3.83 and the critical value of 2.101. If the calculated *t* value is larger than the critical value, you can reject the null hypothesis. In contrast, if the calculated *t* value is smaller than the critical value, you accept the null hypothesis. In this case of comparing YouTube workout hours between freshmen and seniors, your calculated value (3.83) is larger than the critical value (2.101). Hence, you reject the null hypothesis and accept the alternative hypothesis, meaning that you found a significant difference between the two groups in terms of home workout hours a week with YouTube coaches. In comparing the difference between means of 9 and 5 hours, you interpret that college freshman students do more home workouts while following along with YouTube gym coaches than senior students do. More important, you find the results statistically significant. In sum, to do hypothesis testing with a *t* test, you need to go through the following steps:

1. Calculate the *t* score value (number).
2. Find the *df* and *t* critical value (number).
3. Compare the calculated *t* score with the given critical score.
4. Reject the null hypothesis if the calculated number is larger than the critical number, or accept the null hypothesis if the calculated number is smaller than the critical number.

t Table

cum. prob	$t_{.50}$	$t_{.75}$	$t_{.80}$	$t_{.85}$	$t_{.90}$	$t_{.95}$	$t_{.975}$	$t_{.99}$	$t_{.995}$	$t_{.999}$	$t_{.9995}$
one-tail	**0.50**	**0.25**	**0.20**	**0.15**	**0.10**	**0.05**	**0.025**	**0.01**	**0.005**	**0.001**	**0.0005**
two-tails	**1.00**	**0.50**	**0.40**	**0.30**	**0.20**	**0.10**	**0.05**	**0.02**	**0.01**	**0.002**	**0.001**
df											
1	0.000	1.000	1.376	1.963	3.078	6.314	12.71	31.82	63.66	318.31	636.62
2	0.000	0.816	1.061	1.386	1.886	2.920	4.303	6.965	9.925	22.327	31.599
3	0.000	0.765	0.978	1.250	1.638	2.353	3.182	4.541	5.841	10.215	12.924
4	0.000	0.741	0.941	1.190	1.533	2.132	2.776	3.747	4.604	7.173	8.610
5	0.000	0.727	0.920	1.156	1.476	2.015	2.571	3.365	4.032	5.893	6.869
6	0.000	0.718	0.906	1.134	1.440	1.943	2.447	3.143	3.707	5.208	5.959
7	0.000	0.711	0.896	1.119	1.415	1.895	2.365	2.998	3.499	4.785	5.408
8	0.000	0.706	0.889	1.108	1.397	1.860	2.306	2.896	3.355	4.501	5.041
9	0.000	0.703	0.883	1.100	1.383	1.833	2.262	2.821	3.250	4.297	4.781
10	0.000	0.700	0.879	1.093	1.372	1.812	2.228	2.764	3.169	4.144	4.587
11	0.000	0.697	0.876	1.088	1.363	1.796	2.201	2.718	3.106	4.025	4.437
12	0.000	0.695	0.873	1.083	1.356	1.782	2.179	2.681	3.055	3.930	4.318
13	0.000	0.694	0.870	1.079	1.350	1.771	2.160	2.650	3.012	3.852	4.221
14	0.000	0.692	0.868	1.076	1.345	1.761	2.145	2.624	2.977	3.787	4.140
15	0.000	0.691	0.866	1.074	1.341	1.753	2.131	2.602	2.947	3.733	4.073
16	0.000	0.690	0.865	1.071	1.337	1.746	2.120	2.583	2.921	3.686	4.015
17	0.000	0.689	0.863	1.069	1.333	1.740	2.110	2.567	2.898	3.646	3.965
18	0.000	0.688	0.862	1.067	1.330	1.734	2.101	2.552	2.878	3.610	3.922
19	0.000	0.688	0.861	1.066	1.328	1.729	2.093	2.539	2.861	3.579	3.883
20	0.000	0.687	0.860	1.064	1.325	1.725	2.086	2.528	2.845	3.552	3.850
21	0.000	0.686	0.859	1.063	1.323	1.721	2.080	2.518	2.831	3.527	3.819
22	0.000	0.686	0.858	1.061	1.321	1.717	2.074	2.508	2.819	3.505	3.792
23	0.000	0.685	0.858	1.060	1.319	1.714	2.069	2.500	2.807	3.485	3.768
24	0.000	0.685	0.857	1.059	1.318	1.711	2.064	2.492	2.797	3.467	3.745

Figure 10.1 t-distribution tables

Source: Created by author.

5. Make the conclusion whether there is a statistically significant difference between the groups.

It takes too much time and energy to do the calculation and hypothesis testing by hand. We can use Excel for a quick and convenient solution, performing the steps shown in Table 10.4.

1. Place the numbers in Excel.
2. Click the Data tab and then the Data Analysis tab.
3. Select "t-Test: Two-Sample Assuming Equal Variances." (The basic assumptions are that the distributions are normal and that the variances of the two distributions are the same.)
4. Select the two groups' values in the Variable 1 and Variable 2 Range boxes.
5. Click OK.
6. Look at the results and do hypothesis testing.

As the results in Excel show (see Table 10.4), "t Stat" represents the *t* score of 3.83, "t Critical two-tail" represents the critical value of 2.101, and "df" shows the degrees of freedom of 18. Based on the results shown in Excel, you can conclude that there is a difference between the groups, as the calculated *t* score of 3.83 is larger than the critical value of 2.101. It is convenient to perform the Excel test to skip all the arduous "by-hand" steps. There is a better and faster way of doing hypothesis testing with the results in

Table 10.4 Independent Samples *t* Test in Excel

Performing independent samples *t* test in Excel	Results

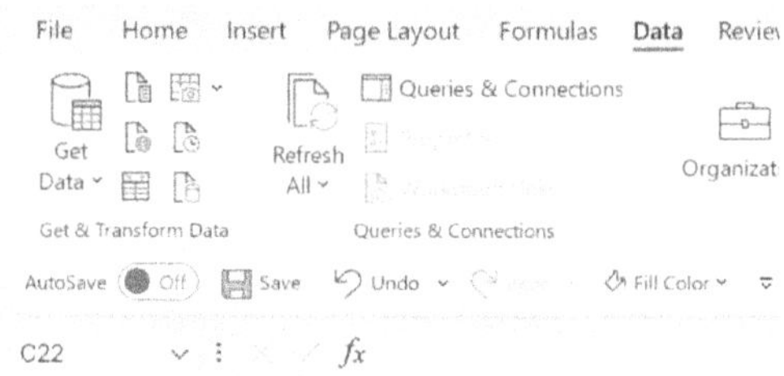

	A	B	C
1	t-Test: Two-Sample Assuming Equal Variances		
2			
3		*Variable 1*	*Variable 2*
4	Mean	9	5
5	Variance	6.666667	4.222222
6	Observations	10	10
7	Pooled Variance	5.444444	
8	Hypothesized Mean Difference	0	
9	df	18	
10	t Stat	3.833259	
11	P(T<=t) one-tail	0.000609	
12	t Critical one-tail	1.734064	
13	P(T<=t) two-tail	0.001218	
14	t Critical two-tail	2.100922	

Source: Created by author.

Excel. In the "P (T<=t) two-tail" box, you see the number, 0.001217706. It represents the *p* value, which is less than .05 (<.05). When the *p* value is less than .05, you find the results statistically significant and conclude that there is a difference between the groups. You reject the null hypothesis and accept the alternative hypothesis. Hence, all you need is the *p* value to do hypothesis testing and make a conclusion while skipping the calculation and comparison steps.

Calculating a Paired Samples *t* Test in Excel

Now that we are familiar with *t*-test procedures and hypothesis testing, a paired samples *t* test should be easily understood. Suppose that you are studying the influence of Black Friday ads on one's desire to buy the advertised products. You select $n = 10$ students and ask them to choose a number rating for Black Friday shopping desire on a scale of 1–10. After they choose the number, you expose them to Black Friday television commercials for 2 minutes, and you again ask the numbers rating their shopping desire on the same scale. The dependent variable is change in the number rating shopping desire after the 2-minute exposure. You are testing a nondirectional hypothesis to know if there is any effect of television commercials. For your paired *t* test, your hypotheses are formulated as follows:

H_0: The mean before exposure equals the mean after exposure ($\mu_1 = \mu_2$).

H_a: There is a difference between the means before and after TV commercial exposure ($\mu_1 \neq \mu_2$).

Suppose your randomly selected 10 participants provide the data shown in Table 10.5.

Table 10.5

	Desire for Black Friday shopping before and after exposure to TV commercials									
Pretest: before commercial exposure	1	5	7	2	8	3	4	5	1	3
Posttest: after commercial exposure	1	5	8	2	10	1	5	6	1	5

Based on the data, we use Excel to perform a paired *t* test using the following steps:

1. Place the numbers in Excel.
2. Click the Data tab and then the Data Analysis tab.
3. Select "t-Test: Paired Two Sample for Means."
4. Select the two groups' values in the Variable 1 and Variable 2 Range boxes.
5. Click OK.
6. Look at the results and do hypothesis testing (see Table 10.6).

Instead of making numerical comparisons between the calculated t-value and the critical value, you only focus on the *p* value for the hypothesis testing as shown in Figure 10.8. The result at "P (T<=t) two-tail" provides the value of 0.212. This means that the *p* value is larger than .05 (>.05), and you accept the null hypothesis, concluding that there is no difference between the pretest and posttest. In the case of television commercials, you could interpret that Black Friday television ads are not effective in terms of changing the shopping desires of college students based on the statistical test, which says there is no statistical significance to the results.

ANALYSIS OF VARIANCE (ANOVA)

When researchers need to compare more than two groups or means, they often turn to analysis of variance. Unlike a *t* test, which is used for comparing two groups, ANOVA

Table 10.6 Paired Samples *t* Test in Excel

Performing a paired samples *t* test in Excel	**Results**

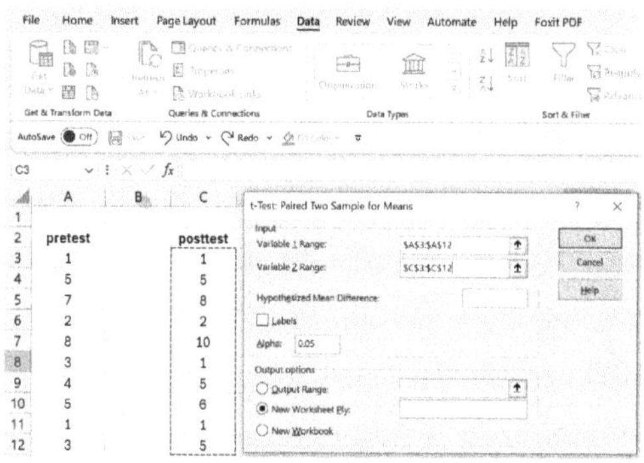

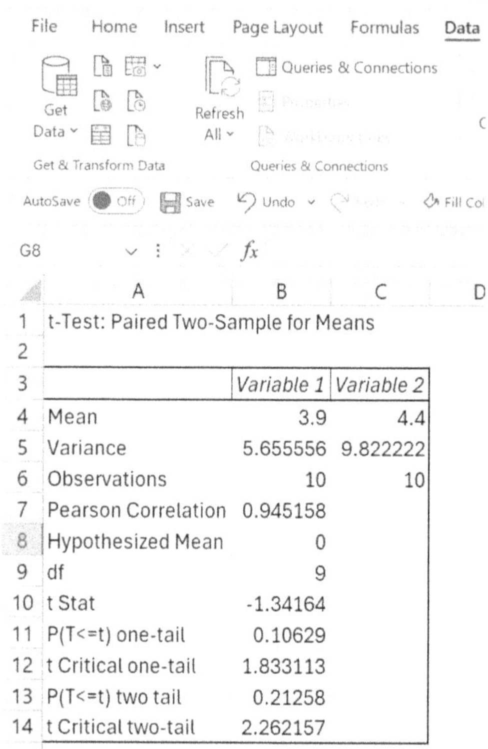

t-Test: Paired Two-Sample for Means

	Variable 1	Variable 2
Mean	3.9	4.4
Variance	5.655556	9.822222
Observations	10	10
Pearson Correlation	0.945158	
Hypothesized Mean	0	
df	9	
t Stat	-1.34164	
P(T<=t) one-tail	0.10629	
t Critical one-tail	1.833113	
P(T<=t) two tail	0.21258	
t Critical two-tail	2.262157	

Source: Created by author.

allows for the analysis of more than two groups. For instance, if there are three groups to compare, the differences among group means can be analyzed using ANOVA. There are two main types of ANOVA: one-way and two-way. The terms *one-way* and *two-way* refer to the number of independent variables in the ANOVA test. A one-way ANOVA has one independent variable, while a two-way ANOVA has two. In a typical case, a one-way ANOVA is what college students encounter and practice in the general ANOVA test. A one-way ANOVA is used to determine whether there are any statistically significant differences between the means of three or more independent groups. To perform a one-way ANOVA, we usually follow these steps:

1. State the null and alternative hypotheses.
2. Calculate the mean for all three groups along with the overall mean.

3. Calculate the regression sum of squares (SSR):

   $SSR = \Sigma n_i(\bar{x}_i - \bar{x})^2$, where $\bar{x}_i$ is the mean of group i, $\bar{x}$ is the overall mean of the three groups, and n is the sample size of group i.

4. Calculate the error sum of squares (SSE):

   $SSE = \Sigma(x_{hi} - \bar{x}_i)^2$, where x_{hi} is the hth observation in group i and $\bar{x}_i$ is the mean of group i.

5. Calculate the total sum of squares (SST):

   $SST = SSR + SSE$.

6. Calculate the F-test score (F symbolizes ANOVA).

   F = variance between groups / variance within groups

7. Find the F critical value in the F distribution table (given value).

8. Compare the two scores (F calculated and F critical).

9. Do hypothesis testing (accept or reject the null hypothesis).

One-Way ANOVA

A one-way ANOVA is typically what college students use to practice the general ANOVA test. It is used to determine if there is a significant difference between the means of three or more groups. To perform a one-way ANOVA, we usually follow these steps:

1. State the null and alternative hypotheses.

2. Calculate the mean for all groups and the overall mean.

For example, if you want to test the statistical significance of the difference between the means of three different groups, a one-way ANOVA is used. This is particularly useful when you have collected data about one categorical independent variable (with at least three different groups) and one continuous dependent variable. The null hypothesis (H_0) of ANOVA is that there is no difference between group means, and the alternative hypothesis (H_a) is that at least one group is different from the overall mean of the dependent variable. The hypotheses are formulated as follows:

H_0: $\mu_1 = \mu_2 = \mu_3$

H_a: The means are not all equal.

Let's suppose that we randomly selected 18 participants from a larger population and assigned them to one of three Covid vaccine groups. Within each group of 6 people, participants received a different shot of the vaccines. In Group 1, participants received Pfizer; in Group 2, participants received Moderna; and in Group 3, participants received Johnson & Johnson. After 3 weeks, we measured the antibody levels (0% to 100%) of each subject. The results for all 18 participants appear in Table 10.7.

Table 10.7

	Vaccines	
Pfizer	**Moderna**	**Johnson**
95	92	90
99	93	79
96	92	84
90	95	65
95	94	86
96	96	77

If you want to calculate the ANOVA F-value, you need to use the ANOVA table to make comparisons among the three groups in pursuit of the F calculated value and F critical value (see Table 10.8). After you have the values or numbers, you compare them and finalize your hypothesis testing in the same method of t test: if the calculated value is larger than the critical value, you reject the null hypothesis.

Table 10.8 ANOVA Table

Source of variance	**Degrees of freedom (*df*)**	**Sums of squares (*SS*)**	**Mean squares (*MS*)**	***F***
Between (columns)	$k - 1$	$\text{SSB} = \sum n_j(\bar{X}_j - \bar{X})^2$	$\text{MSB} = \frac{SSB}{k-1}$	$F = \frac{\text{MSB}}{\text{MSE}}$
Within (error)	$n - k$	$\text{SSE} = \sum\sum(X - \bar{X}_j)^2$	$\text{MSE} = \frac{\text{SSE}}{N-k}$	
Total	$n - 1$	$\text{SST} = \sum\sum(X - \bar{X})^2$		

As you may have noticed, it takes enormous time and effort to calculate the *F* value. If you did the calculation by hand, you would fill in Table 10.8 as shown in Table 10.9.

Table 10.9 ANOVA Table Practice

Source of variance	Degrees of freedom (*df*)	Sums of squares (*SS*)	Mean squares (*MS*)	*F*
Between (columns)	2	819	409.5	13.86
Within (error)	15	443	29.53	
Total	17	1,262		

Your calculated *F* value is 13.86. The value of 13.86 means nothing unless you find the critical value to compare it to. Like the *t* distribution table, AVOVA has its own *F* distribution table. As you have *df* = 2 (between) and *df* = 15 (within), you find where *df* = 2 (horizontal) and *df* = 15 (vertical) meet in the distribution table in Figure 10.2. In this case, the critical value is 3.6823.

In the case of the vaccine comparison, you find the difference in vaccine effectiveness to be statistically significant because the calculated *F* value, 13.86, is larger than the critical value, 3.68. Hence, you conclude that at least one of the vaccines has a better effect in terms of antibody levels because their means show some difference. Not surprisingly, rather than going through such a hard calculation process, you can use Excel to make the process more convenient and faster. Based on the data, you perform a one-way ANOVA with the following steps:

	DF1	α = 0.05																	
DF2	1	2	3	4	5	6	7	8	9	10	12	15	20	24	30	40	60	120	Inf
1	161.45	199.5	215.71	224.58	230.16	233.99	236.77	238.88	240.54	241.88	243.91	245.95	248.01	249.05	250.1	251.14	252.2	253.25	254.3
2	18.513	19	19.164	19.247	19.296	19.33	19.353	19.371	19.385	19.396	19.413	19.429	19.446	19.454	19.462	19.471	19.479	19.487	19.49
3	10.128	9.5521	9.2766	9.1172	9.0135	8.9406	8.8867	8.8452	8.8123	8.7855	8.7446	8.7029	8.6602	8.6385	8.6166	8.5944	8.572	8.5494	8.526
4	7.7086	6.9443	6.5914	6.3882	6.2561	6.1631	6.0942	6.041	5.9988	5.9644	5.9117	5.8578	5.8025	5.7744	5.7459	5.717	5.6877	5.6581	5.628
5	6.6079	5.7861	5.4095	5.1922	5.0503	4.9503	4.8759	4.8183	4.7725	4.7351	4.6777	4.6188	4.5581	4.5272	4.4957	4.4638	4.4314	4.3985	4.36
6	5.9874	5.1433	4.7571	4.5337	4.3874	4.2839	4.2067	4.1468	4.099	4.06	3.9999	3.9381	3.8742	3.8415	3.8082	3.7743	3.7398	3.7047	3.668
7	5.5914	4.7374	4.3468	4.1203	3.9715	3.866	3.787	3.7257	3.6767	3.6365	3.5747	3.5107	3.4445	3.4105	3.3758	3.3404	3.3043	3.2674	3.229
8	5.3177	4.459	4.0662	3.8379	3.6875	3.5806	3.5005	3.4381	3.3881	3.3472	3.2839	3.2184	3.1503	3.1152	3.0794	3.0428	3.0053	2.9669	2.927
9	5.1174	4.2565	3.8625	3.6331	3.4817	3.3738	3.2927	3.2296	3.1789	3.1373	3.0729	3.0061	2.9365	2.9005	2.8637	2.8259	2.7872	2.7475	2.706
10	4.9646	4.1028	3.7083	3.478	3.3258	3.2172	3.1355	3.0717	3.0204	2.9782	2.913	2.845	2.774	2.7372	2.6996	2.6609	2.6211	2.5801	2.537
11	4.8443	3.9823	3.5874	3.3567	3.2039	3.0946	3.0123	2.948	2.8962	2.8536	2.7876	2.7186	2.6464	2.609	2.5705	2.5309	2.4901	2.448	2.404
12	4.7472	3.8853	3.4903	3.2592	3.1059	2.9961	2.9134	2.8486	2.7964	2.7534	2.6866	2.6169	2.5436	2.5055	2.4663	2.4259	2.3842	2.341	2.296
13	4.6672	3.8056	3.4105	3.1791	3.0254	2.9153	2.8321	2.7669	2.7144	2.671	2.6037	2.5331	2.4589	2.4202	2.3803	2.3392	2.2966	2.2524	2.206
14	4.6001	3.7389	3.3439	3.1122	2.9582	2.8477	2.7642	2.6987	2.6458	2.6022	2.5342	2.463	2.3879	2.3487	2.3082	2.2664	2.2229	2.1778	2.130
15	4.5431	3.6823	3.2874	3.0556	2.9013	2.7905	2.7066	2.6408	2.5876	2.5437	2.4753	2.4034	2.3275	2.2878	2.2468	2.2043	2.1601	2.1141	2.065
16	4.494	3.6337	3.2389	3.0069	2.8524	2.7413	2.6572	2.5911	2.5377	2.4935	2.4247	2.3522	2.2756	2.2354	2.1938	2.1507	2.1058	2.0589	2.009
17	4.4513	3.5915	3.1968	2.9647	2.81	2.6987	2.6143	2.548	2.4943	2.4499	2.3807	2.3077	2.2304	2.1898	2.1477	2.104	2.0584	2.0107	1.960
18	4.4139	3.5546	3.1599	2.9277	2.7729	2.6613	2.5767	2.5102	2.4563	2.4117	2.3421	2.2686	2.1906	2.1497	2.1071	2.0629	2.0166	1.9681	1.916
19	4.3807	3.5219	3.1274	2.8951	2.7401	2.6283	2.5435	2.4768	2.4227	2.3779	2.308	2.2341	2.1555	2.1141	2.0712	2.0264	1.9795	1.9302	1.87
20	4.3512	3.4928	3.0984	2.8661	2.7109	2.599	2.514	2.4471	2.3928	2.3479	2.2776	2.2033	2.1242	2.0825	2.0391	1.9938	1.9464	1.8963	1.843
21	4.3248	3.4668	3.0725	2.8401	2.6848	2.5727	2.4876	2.4205	2.366	2.321	2.2504	2.1757	2.096	2.054	2.0102	1.9645	1.9165	1.8657	1.811
22	4.3009	3.4434	3.0491	2.8167	2.6613	2.5491	2.4638	2.3965	2.3419	2.2967	2.2258	2.1508	2.0707	2.0283	1.9842	1.938	1.8894	1.838	1.783
23	4.2793	3.4221	3.028	2.7955	2.64	2.5277	2.4422	2.3748	2.3201	2.2747	2.2036	2.1282	2.0476	2.005	1.9605	1.9139	1.8648	1.8128	1.75
24	4.2597	3.4028	3.0088	2.7763	2.6207	2.5082	2.4226	2.3551	2.3002	2.2547	2.1834	2.1077	2.0267	1.9838	1.939	1.892	1.8424	1.7896	1.73
25	4.2417	3.3852	2.9912	2.7587	2.603	2.4904	2.4047	2.3371	2.2821	2.2365	2.1649	2.0889	2.0075	1.9643	1.9192	1.8718	1.8217	1.7684	1.71

Figure 10.2 ANOVA F table distribution

Source: Created by author.

1. Place the numbers in Excel.
2. Click the Data tab and then the Data Analysis tab.
3. Select "ANOVA: Single Factor."
4. Select all group numbers at once in the Input Range box.
5. Click OK.
6. Look at the results and do hypothesis testing.

There are two ways to use the results in Excel. As Excel provides the calculated (13.86) and critical (3.68) values, you can compare them and conclude to reject the null hypothesis. The other way is to look at the *p* value. The one-way ANOVA in Excel (see Table 10.10) offers a *p* value of 0.0004, which is less than .05 (<.05). Based on the *p* value, you reject the null hypothesis and accept the alternative hypothesis, arguing that there is a significant difference among the three vaccines. If you mention the means of each of the vaccines, you see a significant difference between Pfizer (95.167) and Johnson & Johnson (80.167) or between Moderna (93.667) and Johnson & Johnson (80.167). Thus, your alternative hypothesis is supported by the statement that at least one group of the independent variable (vaccine brand) is statistically different from the overall mean of the dependent variable (antibody levels).

Table 10.10 One-Way ANOVA Test in Excel

Performing one-way ANOVA in Excel

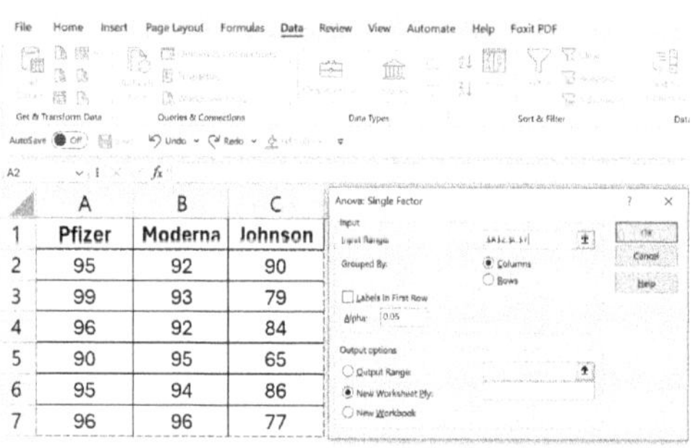

	A	B	C
1	Pfizer	Moderna	Johnson
2	95	92	90
3	99	93	79
4	96	92	84
5	90	95	65
6	95	94	86
7	96	96	77

Results

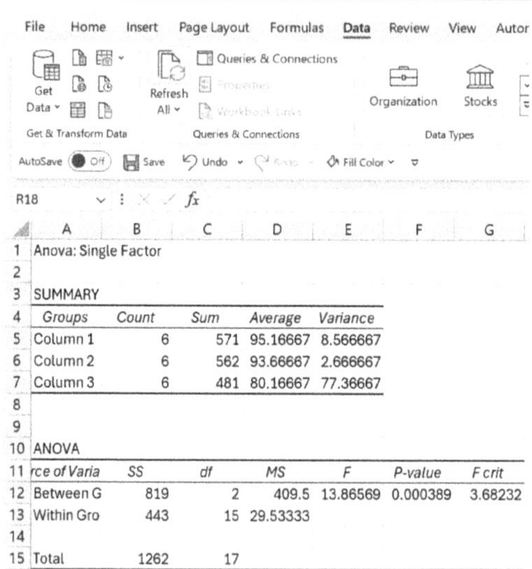

	A	B	C	D	E	F	G
1	Anova: Single Factor						
2							
3	SUMMARY						
4	*Groups*	*Count*	*Sum*	*Average*	*Variance*		
5	Column 1	6	571	95.16667	8.566667		
6	Column 2	6	562	93.66667	2.666667		
7	Column 3	6	481	80.16667	77.36667		
8							
9							
10	ANOVA						
11	*rce of Varia*	*SS*	*df*	*MS*	*F*	*P-value*	*F crit*
12	Between G	819	2	409.5	13.86569	0.000389	3.68232
13	Within Gro	443	15	29.53333			
14							
15	Total	1262	17				

Source: Created by author.

Two-Way ANOVA

A two-way ANOVA (an extension of the one-way ANOVA) is used to determine whether there is a significant difference between the means of two or more groups that are classified by two factors. The two factors can be either categorical or continuous variables. Researchers use a two-way ANOVA to learn how two independent variables in combination influence the dependent variable. In other words, one-way or two-way refers to the number of independent variables in the ANOVA test. For example, a two-way ANOVA allows a researcher to compare social media habits based on two independent variables, such as the gender of college students and the race of college students, while a one-way ANOVA limits the independent variable to one, either gender (male, female) or race (White, Black, Hispanic). A two-way ANOVA also explores the interactive effect between the two variables or factors (e.g., gender and race). For example, a researcher may want to test the effects of two different treatments (Factor 1) and two different age groups (Factor 2) on a particular outcome variable. In this case, a two-way ANOVA test would be appropriate to determine whether there are significant differences in the outcome variable based on the two independent variables (treatment and age group). However, before conducting a two-way ANOVA, you need to make sure that your data meet the following assumptions:

1. Normality: The data should be normally distributed within each group and for each combination of the two independent variables.
2. Homogeneity of variances: The variances of the dependent variable should be equal across all groups and for each combination of the two independent variables.
3. Independence: The observations within each group and for each combination of the two independent variables should be independent of each other.
4. Interaction: There should be no significant interaction between the two independent variables.

It is important to note that a two-way ANOVA requires three sets of hypotheses. The null and alternative hypotheses for each of the sets are given in Table 10.11.

Researchers commonly use a two-way ANOVA when trying to analyze the impact on a dependent variable of a combined effect of gender, education level, and race. For example, you are interested in exploring whether college students' involvement in political conversation on X is influenced by their gender and race. Based on your research interest, you recruit participants and ask them about their frequency of use of X to tweet about politics per month. You then divide the participants by gender (male and female) and then again by race (White, Black, and Hispanic). The dependent variable is "the number of tweets about politics per month," and the two independent variables are gender and

Table 10.11 Two-Way ANOVA Hypotheses

Null hypotheses	Alternative hypotheses
The means of the first variable (factor) are the same.	There is a difference between the means of the first independent variable.
The means of the second variable (factor) are the same.	There is a difference between the means of the second independent variable.
There is no interaction between the two variables (factors).	There is an interaction effect between the first independent variable and the second independent variable.

race. When performing a two-way ANOVA, you will find Excel useful since doing it by hand is almost impossible in a complicated process. Performing a two-way ANOVA in Excel is similar to the process for *t* tests and one-way ANOVAs. You choose "Anova: Two-Factor With Replication" instead of "Anova: Two-Factor Without Replication" from the Data Analysis tool; when you have two factors, not one factor, you choose the "With Replication" option. For example, your data set with the X example can be organized in Excel as shown in Table 10.12, and you perform a two-way ANOVA test to do the hypothesis testing.

Table 10.12 Example of Number of Tweets on X by Gender and Race

Race	Male	Female
Whites	2	4
	12	9
	19	1
	22	35
	8	2
Blacks	2	14
	7	11
	1	3
	8	2
	5	7
Hispanics	3	11
	11	8
	8	3
	4	2
	19	9

Analysis of Covariance (ANCOVA) and Multivariate Analysis of Variance (MANOVA)
ANOVA has its siblings that are used for more complicated and difficult analyses, including analysis of covariance (ANCOVA) and multivariate analysis of variance (MANOVA).

- ANCOVA: Like ANOVA, ANCOVA has a single continuous dependent variable. However, ANCOVA allows the researcher to compare a dependent variable by both a factor and an extraneous variable (e.g., comparing test scores by both levels of income and the number of hours spent on social media). The term for the extraneous variable used in ANCOVA is called a covariate, or control variable. The covariate is a continuous independent variable. For example, if female and male students who are about to graduate from college show a difference in English proficiency scores, this could stem from the fact that female students take more literature courses in college. ANCOVA allows the researcher to adjust the English proficiency scores based on the relationship between the number of English courses taken and proficiency achievement. The researcher can then determine if male and female students still have different English proficiency scores after making the adjustment.[4] Figure 10.3 illustrates an example of ANCOVA.

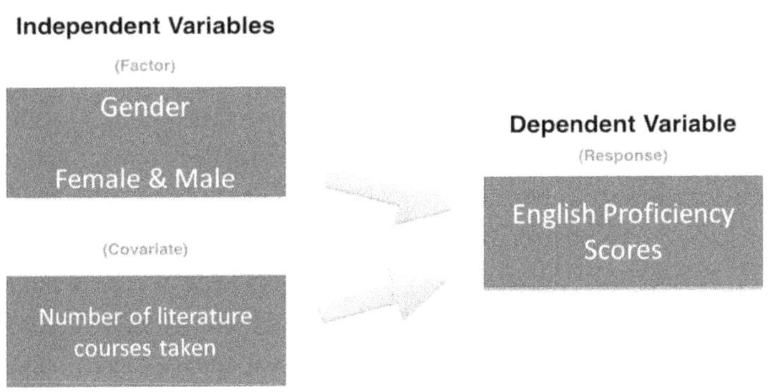

Figure 10.3 ANCOVA illustration
Source: Created by author.

- MANOVA: MANOVA is a procedure for comparing multivariate sample means. It is an extension of ANOVA with two or more continuous dependent variables. There are one-way and two-way MANOVAs, similar to ANOVA. A one-way MANOVA is used to determine whether there is a difference between different groups on more than one continuous dependent variable, while a one-way ANOVA determines the difference on one continuous dependent variable. For example, if you want to study the impact of different use levels of social media platforms on annual income and on the number of books read a year, you would use MANOVA. You would randomly select 30 participants for each group of Facebook users, Instagram users, and Snapchat users. Their annual incomes and the number of books read are measured as

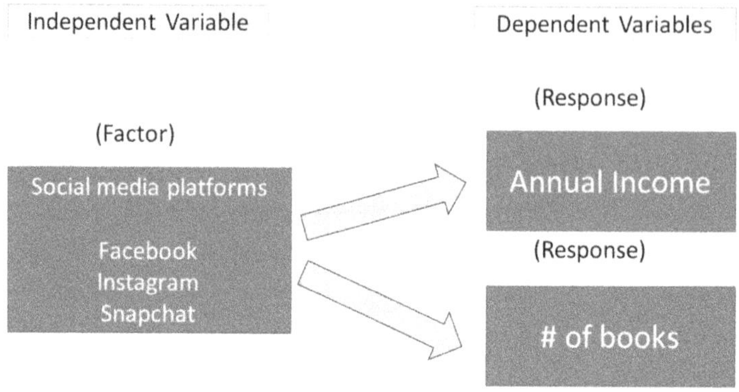

Figure 10.4 MANOVA illustration
Source: Created by author.

two dependent variables. The independent variable has three social media platforms. Figure 10.4 illustrates this example of MANOVA.

Descriptive statistics are used to summarize and present straightforward statistical information, while inferential statistics involve making inferences or generalizations about the population based on hypothesis testing using data from a sample. As inferential tests allow researchers to draw conclusions, researchers commonly use *t* tests and ANOVA to determine whether their results are statistically significant. It is worth noting that researchers should be familiar with all quantitative research concepts and practices to perform inferential tests, including hypothesis testing, independent and dependent variables, *p* values, different levels of measurement scales, and data distributions. While Excel allows you to perform all kinds of *t* tests and ANOVA tests, it does not provide more sophisticated features such as graphics that have more analytical features and post hoc analyses. Therefore, it is recommended that you learn how to use other statistical software packages, including SPSS, R, SAS, and Stata. For researchers in strategic communication, SPSS is the most popular.

How AI Technology Empowers Research Students in Inferential Statistics

Many college students dread inferential statistics due to its perceived complexity and mathematical nature. However, AI is emerging as a powerful tool to demystify this field and empower students to confidently analyze data and draw meaningful conclusions. AI can empower students in understanding and applying inferential statistics in the following ways:

1. Automated statistical analysis: AI technology can assist students in conducting complex statistical analyses by automating the process of selecting and applying the appropriate statistical tests.[5] AI algorithms can help in identifying patterns, correlations, and relationships within data sets, simplifying the interpretation of results for students.

2. Automatic data cleaning and exploration: Data cleaning and exploration are often tedious tasks. AI tools can automate these processes by identifying missing values, outliers, and potential errors.[6] They can also visually represent data through interactive charts and graphs, helping students grasp trends and identify potential relationships. This frees up time for students to focus on interpreting the data and formulating research questions.
3. Interactive learning platforms: AI-powered interactive learning platforms can offer personalized support and resources to students struggling with inferential statistics concepts. These platforms can provide real-time feedback, practice exercises, and tutorials tailored to individual learning needs, fostering a deeper understanding of statistical analysis methods.
4. Hypothesis testing: AI can assist in formulating and testing hypotheses. It can suggest appropriate statistical tests based on the nature of the data and the research questions, making the process of hypothesis testing more straightforward and less prone to errors.[7]

Although AI is not a replacement for understanding the fundamental concepts of inferential statistics, it is a powerful tool that can augment learning, save time, and boost confidence. By automating complex procedures, providing personalized instruction, and assisting with the interpretation of results, AI can make the subject of inferential statistics more accessible and less intimidating. In essence, college research students can overcome their apprehensions, focus on the practical applications of statistical methods, and develop a nuanced understanding of how data shapes strategic communication research. This approach aligns with the evolving landscape of data-driven decision making in the field of strategic communication.

APPLICATION OF AN AI-POWERED TOOL

BOX 10.1
MICROSOFT COPILOT'S SUGGESTIONS FOR COLLEGE STUDENTS TO GET HELP WITH INFERENTIAL STATISTICS

Using an AI-Powered Tool (Microsoft Copilot) to Get Help with Inferential Statistics

Command syntax: Provide lots of practical suggestions about how to use Microsoft Copilot for college students who struggle with inferential statistics.

BOX 10.1 (CONT.)

Answer: Sure! Inferential statistics can seem intimidating at first, but it's important to remember that it's just a tool to help us understand information and make decisions. There are many resources available to help college students learn about inferential statistics, including textbooks, online tutorials, and even AI tools!

Microsoft Copilot can be a great resource for college students who are afraid of statistics. You can ask me questions about inferential statistics and I'll do my best to provide clear and concise explanations. I can also provide examples and suggest resources to help you learn more.

Here are some examples of how I can help college students with inferential statistics in terms of *t* tests and ANOVA:

- I can provide explanations of what *t* tests and ANOVA are and when to use them. For example, a *t* test is used to compare the means of two groups to see if they are different, while an ANOVA is used to compare the means of more than two groups.
- I can provide step-by-step instructions on how to perform a *t* test or ANOVA by hand or using statistical software.
- I can help students interpret the results of a *t* test or ANOVA and understand what the *p* value and other statistics mean.
- I can provide examples of real-life scenarios where *t* tests and ANOVA are used and explain how the results can be used to make decisions.

Here are some tutorial sites that may be helpful:

- Khan Academy has a unit on Analysis of Variance (ANOVA) that includes lessons on calculating SST (total sum of squares), SSW and SSB (total sum of squares within and between), and hypothesis testing with the *F* statistic.
- Stat Trek has an ANOVA tutorial that explains how to use analysis of variance to assess the effect of one or more factors on a single interval- or ratio-scale variable. The tutorial focuses on four classic experimental designs: single-factor independent groups design, full factorial independent groups design, randomized block design with independent groups, and repeated measures design.

These sites provide examples and explanations to help students understand *t* tests and ANOVA. Additionally, practicing with sample problems and solutions can be a great way to reinforce understanding.

My advice for college students who are afraid of statistics is to take it one step at a time. Start by learning the basics and then build on that foundation. Don't be afraid to ask questions and seek help when you need it. And remember, Microsoft Copilot is always here to help!

Summary

- ✓ Statistical analyses in comparing samples with each other and finding any significant difference or relationship between variables are exclusively used for inferential statistics.
- ✓ Inferential statistics is a set of statistical techniques used to estimate the characteristics of a population to be drawn from a sample of data.
- ✓ Probability can be defined as a measurement of how likely it is that an event will occur in a specified unit of time.
- ✓ Odds are defined as the probability that an event will happen divided by the probability that the event will not happen.
- ✓ A p value is the product of hypothesis testing, concerning the probability of obtaining results from the test of the null hypothesis.
- ✓ A p value is only used to determine whether there is evidence to accept or refuse to accept (reject) the null hypothesis.
- ✓ Hypothesis testing is the process used by researchers to evaluate an assumption from a sample regarding a population.
- ✓ The null hypothesis always states that nothing is going on between variables: no difference, no relationship, or no effect.
- ✓ Commonly, if there is a chance less than 5% ($p < .05$), you regard the results as statistically significant.
- ✓ When it comes to the significance level, there are three popular ones: $p < .01$, $p < .05$, and $p < .10$.
- ✓ Inferential statistics generally classify data into two possible categorizations: parametric (continuous) and nonparametric (categorical).
- ✓ A t test is used to determine if there is a significant difference or relationship between the means of two groups.
- ✓ Statistically, a t test takes sample data from each of two groups, with a null hypothesis stating that there is no difference between the means of the two groups.
- ✓ The degrees of freedom (*df*) refers to the maximum number of logically independent values that are free to vary.
- ✓ Whereas a t test is used to compare the means of two groups, the use of analysis of variance (ANOVA) is for analyzing more than two groups.
- ✓ A two-way ANOVA, an extension of the one-way ANOVA, is used to examine how the mean of a dependent variable changes according to the levels of two or more independent variables.

- ✓ ANCOVA allows the researcher to compare a dependent variable with both a factor and an extraneous variable.
- ✓ A one-way MANOVA is used to determine whether there is a difference between different groups on more than one continuous dependent variable.
- ✓ AI can assist in formulating and testing hypotheses.

Key Terms

1. Inferential statistics
2. Probability
3. Odds
4. *p* value
5. Two-sample *t* test
6. Hypothesis testing
7. ANOVA
8. Two-way ANOVA
9. ANCOVA
10. MANOVA

Chapter 11

Advanced Data Analysis Techniques

Chapter Learning Outcomes

- Recognize the chi-square test for categorical data.
- Apply a two-sample chi-square test to hypothesis testing.
- Explain the characteristics of correlations.
- Apply Pearson's *r* and Spearman's rho to correlation tests.
- Differentiate between simple linear regression and multiple linear regression.
- Discuss how coefficients are interpreted.
- Explain the assumptions of a linear relationship between variables.
- Perform linear regression in Excel.
- Be familiar with each representation of the regression equation.
- Identify the strength, direction, and causation of regression analysis.
- Apply AI technology to advanced statistics.

While the *t* test and ANOVA are commonly used statistical tests for college students, these tests require at least one continuous or parametric data set and are best suited for data of interval and ratio scales of measurements. However, when a data set consists of nonparametric or categorical data (i.e., nominal or ordinal measurement scales), researchers need to make different assumptions and use different statistical tests for hypothesis testing.

Nonparametric Statistics

Nonparametric statistical tests are based on fewer assumptions, making them easier to explain. They do not assume that data are drawn from a normal distribution, nor do they assume equal variances. As a result, nonparametric statistics are suitable for data that belong to the nominal and ordinal scales of measurement. Nonparametric statistics rely on the analysis of data frequency and rankings. In particular, nonparametric statistics include the following elements regarding variables and characteristics:

1. The dependent variable contains data that count the frequency.
2. The dependent variable contains data that show a ranking or ordering of sorts.
3. Population characteristics cannot be generalized, as normal distributions and equal variances are not assumed.
4. No assumption about the sample size is made since the data can be far from normally distributed.

The most important fact about nonparametric statistics is that the level of measurement of all the variables is nominal or ordinal.

CHI-SQUARE TEST

Among the nonparametric statistical tests, the chi-square test is the most popular and useful statistical test for hypothesis testing when the variables are nominal or ordinal. The chi-square (χ^2) test determines whether there is an association or a difference between categorical variables, providing information about whether the variables are independent or related to each other. As the chi-square test is commonly used to test the association between two or more categorical variables, it is not used to compare continuous variables. If you as a researcher decide to use the chi-square test as the main statistical test for your data, you must ensure that the data meet the following assumptions:

- The data in the cells should be frequencies or counts of cases rather than percentages or some other transformation of the data.
- The variables' levels (or categories) are mutually exclusive; a particular subject fits into one and only one level of each variable.
- Each subject may contribute data to only one cell in the χ^2 table.
- There are two variables, and both are measured as categories, usually at the nominal level.
- Data also can be measured at the ordinal level.
- The dependent variables in the comparisons are simple counts of events.
- The value of the expected cell should be 5 or more in at least 80% of the cells, and no cell should have an expected of less than 1.[1]

There are two popular types of the chi-square test: the one-sample test and the two-sample test.

- The one-sample chi-square test is used to test whether a single categorical variable follows a hypothesized population distribution. For example, you could use a one-sample chi-square test to test whether the distribution of gender in your sample is the same as the distribution of gender in the general population.
- The two-sample chi-square test is used to test whether two categorical variables have any relationship or association. For example, you could use a two-sample chi-square test to test whether there is a relationship between gender and political party affiliation in your sample.

Both types of chi-square test embrace the core concepts of an expected frequency (E) and an observed frequency (O). We use hypothetical cases to better understand the different types and concepts of the test.

One-Sample Chi-Square Test

Suppose you want to know which news sources college students rely on when they check daily news. After formulating hypotheses, you surveyed 100 students (see Table 11.1). The null hypothesis (H_0) states that there is no difference between the news sources, while the alternative hypothesis (H_a) states that there is a difference between the news sources.

H_0: There is no difference between the news sources.

H_a: There is a difference between the news sources.

Table 11.1

	Facebook feed	CNN website	Fox News	TikTok
Observed frequency	28	30	22	20

To conduct the one-sample chi-square test, the chi-square formula should be used, shown in Table 11.2.

Table 11.2

Formula for chi-square test	Exercise
$x^2 = \sum \frac{(0-E)^2}{E}$	To compute, we place the frequency numbers into the formula.
	• Observed frequencies: 28, 30, 22, 20
O: observed frequency	• Expected frequencies: 100/4 = 25
E: expected frequency	$\chi^2 = [(28-25)^2/25] + [(30-25)^2/25] + [(22-25)^2/25]$ $+ [(20-25)^2/25]$
Σ: sum	$= 0.36 + 1 + 0.36 + 1 = 2.72$

To compute the chi-square value, you need the observed and expected frequencies. The surveyed numbers represent the observed frequencies. You can calculate the expected frequencies from an equal probability hypothesis that assumes each news source is equally represented. The expected frequency is calculated as follows:

100 (number of students) / 4 (number of sources) = 25 (the expected frequency)

Based on the chi-square value of 2.72, you need to do hypothesis testing that requires degrees of freedom (*df*) to find the critical value and then form a conclusion. The *df* for a one-sample chi-square test is calculated as the number of groups (columns) – 1. In this case, the *df* is 4 – 1 = 3. With the values of chi-square and *df*, you find the critical value in the chi-square table given in Figure 11.1.

The critical value is found at the place where the alpha level of .05 and the *df* of 3 meet: 7.815. Upon comparison, you accept or fail to reject the null hypothesis because the calculated value, 2.72, is less than the critical value of 7.815. Hence, you claim that there is no statistically significant difference in the frequencies with which college students use the various news sources.

df	0.995	0.99	0.975	0.95	0.90	0.10	0.05	0.025	0.01	0.005
1	---	---	0.001	0.004	0.016	2.706	3.841	5.024	6.635	7.879
2	0.010	0.020	0.051	0.103	0.211	4.605	5.991	7.378	9.210	10.597
3	0.072	0.115	0.216	0.352	0.584	6.251	7.815	9.348	11.345	12.838
4	0.207	0.297	0.484	0.711	1.064	7.779	9.488	11.143	13.277	14.860
5	0.412	0.554	0.831	1.145	1.610	9.236	11.070	12.833	15.086	16.750
6	0.676	0.872	1.237	1.635	2.204	10.645	12.592	14.449	16.812	18.548
7	0.989	1.239	1.690	2.167	2.833	12.017	14.067	16.013	18.475	20.278
8	1.344	1.646	2.180	2.733	3.490	13.362	15.507	17.535	20.090	21.955
9	1.735	2.088	2.700	3.325	4.168	14.684	16.919	19.023	21.666	23.589
10	2.156	2.558	3.247	3.940	4.865	15.987	18.307	20.483	23.209	25.188
11	2.603	3.053	3.816	4.575	5.578	17.275	19.675	21.920	24.725	26.757
12	3.074	3.571	4.404	5.226	6.304	18.549	21.026	23.337	26.217	28.300
13	3.565	4.107	5.009	5.892	7.042	19.812	22.362	24.736	27.688	29.819
14	4.075	4.660	5.629	6.571	7.790	21.064	23.685	26.119	29.141	31.310
15	4.601	5.229	6.262	7.261	8.547	22.307	24.996	27.488	30.578	32.801
16	5.142	5.812	6.908	7.962	9.312	23.542	26.296	28.845	32.000	34.267
17	5.697	6.408	7.564	8.672	10.085	24.769	27.587	30.191	33.409	35.718
18	6.265	7.015	8.231	9.390	10.865	25.989	28.869	31.526	34.805	37.156

Figure 11.1 Chi-Square distribution table

Source: Created by author.

Two-Sample Chi-Square Test

The purpose of using a two-sample chi-square test is to find any association or relationship between two categorical variables. The null hypothesis (H_0) and alternative hypothesis (H_a) of the two-sample chi-square test can be expressed as follows:

H_0: There is no relationship between the two categorical variables.

H_a: There is a relationship between the two categorical variables.

When you classify your data into two categorical variables, you summarize them in the two-way contingency table, which represents the observed counts. Note that the variables in the table have to be exclusive of each other. Suppose you have data with two categorical variables of gender and participants' favorite between the two biggest bulk retailers: Costco Wholesale and Sam's Club. Table 11.3 shows how your 100 participants answered (or were observed) for their favorite retailer.

What makes a two-sample chi-square test different from a one-sample test is the calculation formulas for the degrees of freedom and the expected frequency (see Table 11.4).

You can simply calculate the *df* as equal to (2 – 1) × (2 –1) = 1, as two columns (Costco and Sam's Club) and two rows (male and female) exist. Calculating the expected frequency requires some work by hand. For example, the expected frequency for the male and Costco cell is computed as (60 × 50) / 100 = 30; for the female and Costco cell, (60 × 50) / 100 = 30; for the male and Sam's Club cell, (40 × 50) / 100 = 20; and for the female and Sam's Club cell, (40 × 50) / 100 = 20. Therefore, the expected frequencies are inserted in parentheses, as shown in Table 11.5.

Table 11.3

	Costco	Sam's Club	Total
Male	20	30	50
Female	40	10	50
Total	60	40	100

Table 11.4

Formula for degrees of freedom	Expected frequency formula
df = (number of rows − 1) × (number of columns − 1)	*E* = (total number in column × total number in row) / total sample size

Table 11.5

	Costco	Sam's Club	Total
Male	20 (30)	30 (20)	50
Female	40 (30)	10 (20)	50
Total	60	40	100

Note. Values in parentheses are expected values.

Table 11.6

Formula for two-sample χ^2	Exercise
$X^2 = \sum_{i=1}^{r}\sum_{j=1}^{c}\frac{(0_{ij} - E_{ij})^2}{E_{ij}}$ r = row c = column	To compute, we place the frequency numbers into the formula. • Observed frequencies: 20, 40, 30, 10 • Expected frequencies: 30, 30, 20, 20 $\chi^2 = [(20 - 30)^2 / 30] + [(40 - 30)^2 / 30] + [(30 - 20)^2 / 20] + [(10 - 20)^2 / 20]$ $= 3.33 + 3.33 + 5 + 5 = 16.66$

With the observed and expected frequencies, the calculation can proceed with the two-sample test formula given in Table 11.6.

To do hypothesis testing, you turn to the chi-square distribution table and find the critical value where $df = 1$ and the alpha level of .05 meet. The critical value is 3.841, and your calculated value, 16.66, is greater than that. Therefore, the null hypothesis is rejected, indicating that there is a significant relationship between gender and preferred bulk retailers. The frequency table clearly illustrates that female shoppers are more inclined to shop at Costco as compared to Sam's Club, unlike male shoppers.

The chi-square test is most useful when you analyze cross-tabulations of response data. For example, the two-sample chi-square test determines if the frequency of observations within multiple categories (e.g., gender, education level, income level, race) means there is a statistically significant relationship between the categorical variables. It is a useful statistical test for a question such as, "Is there a relationship between the race of college students and their selection of majors?" However, the chi-square test has two limitations: (1) it only uses frequency counts, though many data can be classified into ratio scales, and (2) it cannot analyze the cause-and-effect relationship between the variables. Chi-square tests can be performed in Excel, but more intuitive statistical software packages such as SPSS, R, and SAS are widely used in academic fields.

CORRELATIONS

Researchers often formulate research questions or hypotheses that seek to understand the relationship between variables. For example, you might be curious about the relationship between the use of Instagram by college students to follow influencers and the level of social jealousy they feel toward the influencers. You would want to know if there is any positive or negative relationship between the two variables, and if a relationship exists, how strongly they are related. The chi-square test does not provide these answers, but the test of correlations does.

A correlation is used to describe the linear relationship between variables by measuring the strength and direction of the relationship. It is a statistical measure of the extent to which two variables are related. Researchers see a correlation as an expressed number that identifies the strength and direction of a relationship between two variables. For example, if you found the phenomenon that college students tend to feel jealous about influencers' lavish lifestyles on Instagram, you could conclude that the two variables—following influencers on Instagram and the level of jealousy—are correlated. There are three results of correlational research: a positive correlation, a negative correlation, and no correlation.

- A positive correlation is a direct relationship between two variables, in which if one variable increases, the other one also increases. The two variables move in the same direction. An example of a positive correlation would be hours of advertising and customer traffic. The more time a restaurant owner advertises her business, the more customers she will have.
- A negative correlation, also known as an inverse correlation, is a relationship where two variables move in opposite directions. A well-known example can be found in the stock market. If international crude oil prices go up, airline stock prices go down as the oil prices will have a negative impact on airline companies' profits. If oil prices go down, stock prices can go up for airline companies. Hence, the two variables have a negative correlation.
- A zero correlation occurs when there is no relationship between two variables, suggesting that no indication of a positive or negative relationship is detected. In particular, a linear relationship does not exist between the two variables. For example, there is no linear relationship between the amount of milk sold in Tennessee and the number of car accidents in the same state.

When a correlation is used to analyze a linear relationship of data, researchers often present correlation graphs to illustrate a scatterplot that displays plotted numbers as a point in x and y coordinates. A scatterplot demonstrates the values of one variable, which appear on the x-axis, and the values of the other variable, which appear on the y-axis of the graph. When the points make a straight line, the correlation tends to get higher between the two variables.

Three common correlation graphs are illustrated in Figure 11.2.

One of the advantages of using a correlation is that it can be used to measure the strength and direction of the linear relationship between two variables. This can be statistically computed and numerically expressed by a correlation coefficient. The coefficient shows the number or value of a correlation, allowing researchers to measure how strong a relationship is and in what direction. The value of the coefficient ranges between –1.0 and 1.0. A perfect positive correlation means that the correlation coefficient is exactly 1, while –1.0 demonstrates a perfect negative correlation. If the coefficient gets closer to 0 or is 0, there exists no relationship. To compute a correlation coefficient, we need to recognize

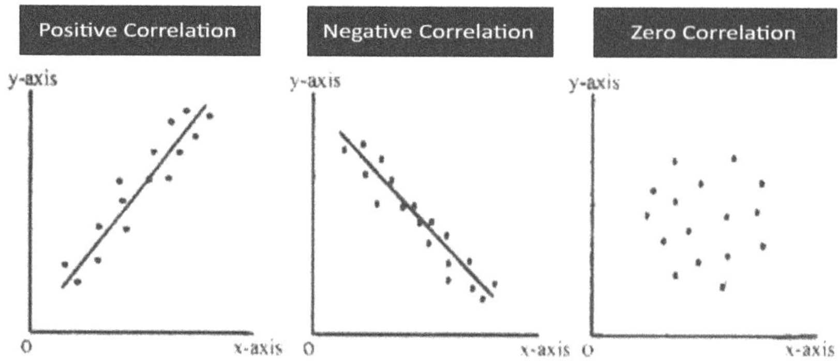

Figure 11.2 Correlation graphs
Source: Created by author.

two different types of correlation coefficients, as they apply different formulas: Pearson's *r* correlation and Spearman's rho correlation.

Pearson's r *Correlation*

Pearson's *r* correlation is the most widely used correlation test. When researchers refer to the correlation coefficient, they are usually talking about Pearson's *r*. It focuses on measuring the strength of a linear association between two variables and is denoted by *r*. For Pearson's *r* to be performed, two assumptions should be met: (1) each variable should be continuous (interval or ratio scales), and (2) linearity should be formed, meaning that a straight line, not a curved one, should be formed between all scattered points drawn from left to right.

The stronger the relationship between the two variables, the closer the Pearson's *r* will be to either +1 or –1 depending on whether the relationship is positive or negative, respectively.[2] For example, if there are two continuous variables, (1) Zoom class days and (2) sick days, Pearson's *r* will tell us about their positive or negative, or zero, relationship and how strong it is. If Pearson's *r* is .9, a strong positive correlation between Zoom class days and sick days is found. The common rule of thumb for interpreting the strength of a relationship is based on its *r* value: $r < .3$ (none or very weak), $.3 < r < .5$ (weak), $.5 < r < .7$ (moderate), and $r > .7$ (strong). Researchers commonly agree that if the *r* value is greater than .7, the relationship between two variables is considered strong.[3]

The formula and process to calculate Pearson's *r* seem complicated, as shown in Table 11.7.

Table 11.7

$r_{xy} = \frac{n\sum x_i y_j - \sum x_i \sum y_j}{\sqrt{n\sum x_i^2 - (\sum x_i)^2}\sqrt{n\sum y_i^2 - (\sum y_i)^2}}$	r_{xy} = Pearson *r* coefficient between *x* and *y* n = number of observations x_i = value of *x* (for *i*th observation) y_i = value of *y* (for *i*th observation)

Table 11.8

Participant	Age (x)	Social media addiction (y)
1	20	9
2	25	7
3	30	7
4	35	5
5	40	3
6	45	1

To practice, suppose you formulate a hypothesis: There is a negative correlation between age and social media addiction measured by the Social Media Addiction Scale (1–10). The data gathered by you are given in Table 11.8.

Based on the data set, you perform Pearson's r test. Since it takes too much work by hand, you use Excel with the following steps:

1. Place the numbers in Excel.
2. Click the Data tab and then the Data Analysis tab.
3. Select "Correlation."
4. Select all numbers of columns (X) and (Y) into the Input Range box.
5. Click OK.
6. Look at the results and do hypothesis testing (see Table 11.9).

The value of Pearson's r is –.98, which indicates a strong negative correlation between age and social media addiction. Based on the correlation coefficient, you conclude that older people tend to have less addiction to social media, and those who are younger tend to be more addicted to social media. However, when you report your r, the p value should be included because academic research papers in the field of strategic communication require the results of statistical tests in APA format. For the results of Pearson's r correlation, the values of r and p are required to be reported in the format $r(df) = .XX$, $p < .05$ or $p > .05$.

The df for correlations is $n - 2$ (the number of data points minus 2). Although you have the r value of –.98, your statistical test is not done yet without the p value. The fastest way to get the p value in Excel is to use the regression function. Instead of selecting "Correlation," during the Excel procedures, you select "Regression." Other steps are the same. The Excel test will offer a summary of outputs, and you find the number in the box

Table 11.9 Pearson's *r* Test in Excel

Performing Pearson's *r* in Excel	**Results**
	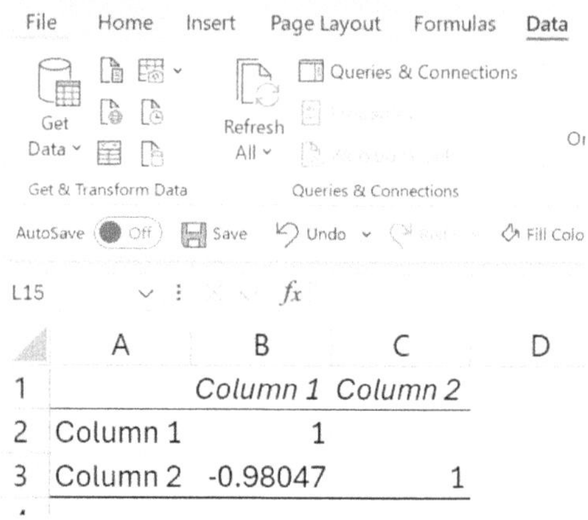

under the "Significance F," which represents the p value—in this case, .000568. Finally, you report in your paper that there is a significant negative correlation between age and social media addiction, $r(4) = -.98, p < .05$. See figure 11.3.

It is important to note that the correlation coefficient does not imply causation. In other words, seeing two variables positively or negatively moving together does not mean that you can tell if they are in an independent or dependent relationship. In a correlation, there are simply two variables without a necessary impact on each other. The two variables are not distinguished as an independent variable and dependent variable, in which the independent variable causes changes in the dependent variable. Hence, a correlation provides evidence of a relationship, not an underlying causal effect.

Spearman's Rho Correlation

Spearman's rho correlation, symbolized with ρ, is a nonparametric statistical version of Pearson's *r* correlation. It allows researchers to measure the strength and direction of a relationship between two categorical variables, mostly ordinal or ranked scales of data. Researchers use Spearman's ρ correlation when the assumptions of Pearson's *r* correlation are violated. We need to acknowledge the difference between Pearson's *r* and Spearman's ρ: the former determines the strength and direction of a linear relationship between two continuous variables, whereas the latter determines the strength and direction of a monotonic relationship between two categorical variables. A monotonic relationship refers to the condition where the variables tend to change together, but not necessarily at a constant rate. This means that if the x variable increases, the y variable never decreases (monotonically increasing), or if the x variable increases, the y variable never increases

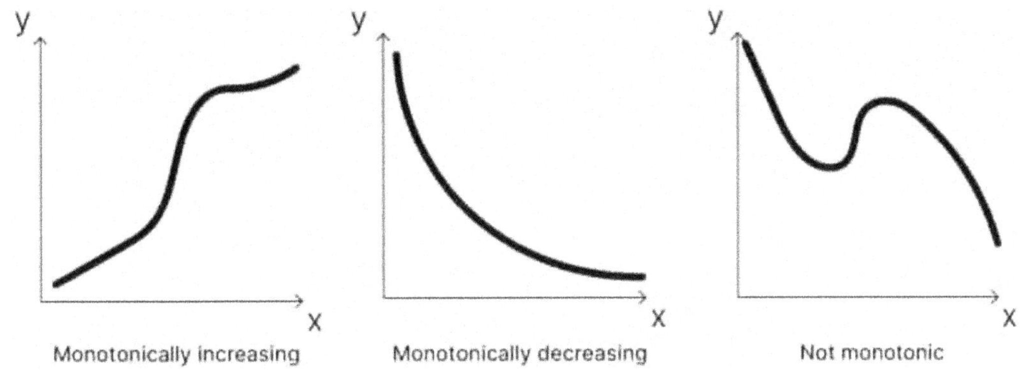

Figure 11.3 Spearman's *rho* (ρ) correlation graphs
Source: From Statstutor.

(monotonically decreasing); but if the *y* variable sometimes decreases and sometimes increases when the *x* variable increases, the relationship is not monotonic.[4] In a nutshell, Spearman's ρ is used when the data do not meet the assumptions of normality or when the relationship between the variables is nonlinear.

Spearman's rho correlation coefficient, ρ, ranges between –1 and 1, like Pearson's *r*, and its interpretation is also similar to that of *r*, based on its ρ value: $\rho < .3$ (none or very weak), $.3 < \rho < .5$ (weak), $.5 < \rho < .7$ (moderate), and $\rho > .7$ (strong). The formula to calculate Spearman's rho (ρ) is expressed as shown in Table 11.10.

In the application of Spearman's ρ, suppose you formulate a hypothesis: H_a: There is a positive relationship between the performance of customer relations representatives ranked on Yelp and the representatives' public relations training. The seven representatives are ranked from 1 = "Best" to 7 = "Worst" in terms of dealing with customer complaints. For the PR training variable, the best representative with the highest PR training score is ranked number 1, and the one with the lowest training score is ranked number 7. The data appear in Table 11.11.

The calculation for Spearman's ρ can be done by hand with $\Sigma D^2 = 20$: $\rho = 1 - [(6 \times 20) / 7(49 - 1)] = 1 - [0.357] = .643$. Hence, you conclude that the correlation shows a moderately positive relationship between the two variables. In particular, the value of $\rho = .643$ indicates a positive relationship (moderate) between the rank of representatives who were evaluated on Yelp and their PR training scores. However, keep in mind that both Pearson's *r* and Spearman's ρ only measure the strength and direction of a relationship between two variables rather than the causal effect of two variables on each other.

In the Yelp case, the ρ value does not indicate that a certain level of PR training led to or caused better performance of customer relations among the representatives. Correlation coefficients, such as Pearson's and Spearman's, only measure the strength

Table 11.10

$\rho = 1 - \frac{6\sum D^2}{n(n^2-1)}$	D = difference between ranks n = number of events Σ = sum

Table 11.11

Representative	Rank on Yelp	Rank by scores	*D*	*D*²
Mike	1	1	0	0
David	2	4	−2	4
Jake	3	5	−2	4
Steve	4	3	1	1
Bill	5	2	3	9
Joe	6	7	−1	1
Greg	7	6	1	1

of the linear or monotonic relationship between two variables, X and Y, which always lies between −1.0 and 1.0. However, they do not provide information on which variable influences the other. To investigate causality, researchers use regression analysis as a statistical method. Regression analysis helps researchers understand how one variable affects another or what changes it causes in the other.

REGRESSION ANALYSIS

Regression analysis is a set of statistical methods used to describe the relationships between a dependent variable and one or more independent variables. The key advantage of regression analysis is its ability to formulate predictive models, with regression equations serving as the cornerstone for making statistical predictions. Regression analysis predicts how changes in each independent variable affect changes in the dependent variable. When performing a regression analysis, you are expected to produce a regression equation with coefficients that represent the relationship between each independent variable and the dependent variable. This means that regression analysis has the capacity to statistically control every variable in the equation.

For instance, consider a marketing expert for surfboards who wants to predict the sale price of surfboards based on selected physical characteristics, such as distance to the beach and local tax rates. The expert visits dozens of surfboard shops in California and Hawaii and investigates the distance and tax rates related to the price of surfboards. The relationship among all characteristics of price, distance, and tax rate is expressed in the form of a regression equation that identifies the dependent (response) variable and the independent (predictor) variable. In this case, the dependent variable is the price of surfboards, and the predictor variables are the distance and tax rates.

There are two types of regression analysis that researchers in strategic communication commonly use: simple linear regression and multiple linear regression. Both types are based on six fundamental assumptions:

- The dependent and predictor variables show a linear relationship indicated by the slope and the intercept.
- The independent variable is not random.
- The value of the residual (error) is zero.
- The value of the residual is constant across all observations.
- The value of the residual is not correlated across all observations.
- The residual values follow a normal distribution.[5]

Most terms such as *slope*, *intercept*, and *residual* (error) may seem strange to many students, but these terms can be understood through the application of the two types of regression equations.

Simple Linear Regression

In simple linear regression, each equation consists of two values: the dependent variable and the predictor variable. The two variables involved in simple linear regression analysis are designated x and y. One variable, denoted x, is regarded as the predictor, and the other variable, denoted y, is regarded as the dependent variable. Simple linear regression focuses on the analysis of one predictor variable that affects the outcome of the dependent variable. If we let y represent the dependent variable and x represent the predictor variable, then the equation of simple linear regression is represented by:

$$y = \beta_0 + \beta_1 x$$

where β_0 is the y intercept of the regression line and β_1 is the slope. β_0 and β_1 are the parameters of the model of the population, and they are usually called regression coefficients. It should be mentioned that the difference between the dependent value of y and the straight line ($\beta_0 + \beta_1 x$) can be conceptualized as an error, ε, a random variable. Thus, a more correct model for linear regression is written:

$$y = \beta_0 + \beta_1 x + \varepsilon$$

The error term ε in the equation represents the variability in y that cannot be explained by the linear relationship between x and y. It accounts for the fact that data points do not lie perfectly on a straight line. Simply put, the error term ε indicates the uncertainty in the model. A regression equation usually includes the error term because, in real life, predictor variables alone cannot perfectly predict the dependent variable. However, we can use the equation without the ε when x provides enough information to determine the value of y. In this case, the error term ε equals 0, and there is no other factor that influences y other than x. Hence, the form of simple linear regression, after we take out the error term, has a straight line in the sample. As we predict the sample value of y from the sample value of x, simple regression analysis is most used with the equation:

$$\hat{y} \ (y \text{ hat}) = a + bx$$

where $\hat{y}$ (y hat) = predicted value of y for a given value of x, a = the y intercept (also known as the *constant*), and b = the slope (measure of the direction either positive or negative and the steepness of the line). Hence, the equation describes this relationship for the sample.

To understand the equation better, suppose you have the equation of salary (x) and donation ($\hat{y}$): $\hat{y} = 0.11 + 0.18(x)$. It indicates that the salary coefficient (b) is 0.18 and the y intercept (a) is 0.11. When the salary is \$1, the donation is predicted to be 0.29 cents. When the salary is \$2, the donation is predicted as .47 cents. (The y intercept, 0.11, represents the predicted donation when the salary is zero; however, in real-world scenarios, a salary of zero might not make sense, so this point might not have practical significance but is valid mathematically.) The variables have a positive relationship, and the salary is the predictor variable, meaning that it positively affects the outcome of donation, the dependent variable. However, we need the p value, the df, and the R^2 value (the indication of total variation) to complete the test and the report. Like other statistical tests, we had better practice a simple regression analysis with an example. The process of calculating a simple linear regression can be done by hand with the formula, which guides us in computing the constant and the slope to complete the equation. The best way is to follow the three steps for the creation of a table, as described in Table 11.12.

Suppose your hypothesis states that there is a relationship between age and hours using TikTok per week. You have sampled 6 participants and created a data table. Based on the predictor variable of age (x) and the dependent variable of hours of TikTok use (y), you add three more columns to calculate the simple linear regression, as shown in Table 11.13.

From Table 11.13, $\Sigma x = 195$, $\Sigma y = 46$, $\Sigma xy = 1{,}955$, $\Sigma x^2 = 6{,}775$, and $\Sigma y^2 = 258$. The sample size (n) is 6. Now you use the equations of a and b to form the simple linear equation.

$$a = ([46 \times 6{,}775] - [195 \times 1{,}995]) \ / \ (6 \ [6{,}775] - 195^2) = -0.695$$

$$b = (6 \ [1{,}995] - [195 \times 46]) \ / \ (6 \ [6{,}775] - 195^2) = 0.385$$

Table 11.12

Formulas for simple regression	Calculation steps
$a = \frac{[(\sum y)(\sum x^2) - (\sum x)(\sum xy)]}{[n(\sum x^2) - (\sum x)^2]}$ $b = \frac{[n(\sum xy) - (\sum x)(\sum y)]}{[n(\sum x^2) - (\sum x^2)]}$	1. Create a table using the data that you have gathered from an observation. Label the independent variable *x* and the dependent variable *y*. 2. Add 3 more columns to your table. The first column should be labeled *xy* and should reflect the product of the *x* and *y* values in your first two columns. 3. Label the next column x^2. It should reflect the square of the *x* value. The final column should be labeled y^2 and reflect the square of the *y* value.[1]

[1]Christopher Wanamaker. (2020). How to create your own simple linear regression equation. https://owlcation.com/stem/How-to-Create-a-Simple-Linear-Regression-Equation.

Table 11.13

Participant	Age (*x*)	Hours of TikTok (*y*)	*xy*	x^2	y^2
1	20	5	100	400	25
2	25	7	175	625	49
3	30	9	270	900	81
4	35	10	350	1,225	100
5	40	13	520	1,600	169
6	45	12	540	2,025	144
Σ	195	46	1,955	6,775	258

The equation is $\hat{y} = -0.695 + .385x$. The *y* intercept or the constant is −0.695, and the slope is .385. The process of calculating the equation by hand is doable but arduous. We use Excel to get it done faster and obtain more accurate statistical information.

Based on the data set in Table 11.14, you can perform a regression test. Since it takes too much work by hand, you use Excel with the following steps:

1. Place the data into two columns in Excel.
2. Click the Data tab and then the Data Analysis tab.
3. Select "Regression."
4. Select the data for *y* into the "Input Y Range" box.
5. Select the data for *x* into the "Input X Range" box.

6. Click OK.
7. Look at the results and do hypothesis testing (see Table 11.15).

The results in Excel provide detailed information on the statistical test. You need to pay attention to several important outputs for accurate regression interpretation.

- Multiple R: This is the correlation coefficient, telling you how strong the linear relationship is. Your multiple *R* is .958, meaning that the two variables have a strong positive relationship, as a value of 1 means a perfect positive relationship.

Table 11.14

Participant	Age (*x*)	Hours of TikTok (*y*)
1	20	5
2	25	7
3	30	9
4	35	10
5	40	13
6	45	12

Table 11.15 Simple Linear Regression Test in Excel

Performing regression in Excel	Results
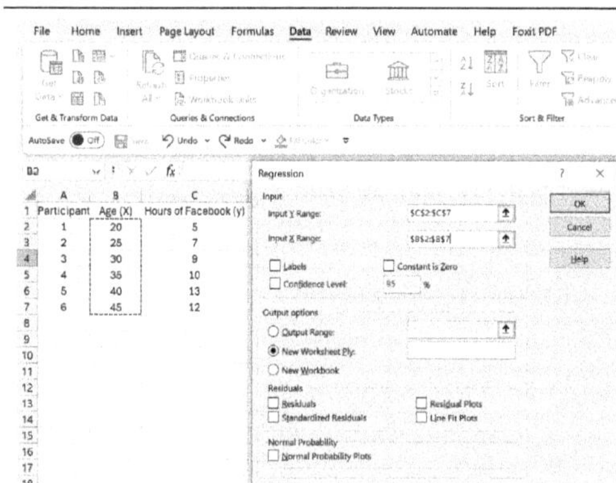	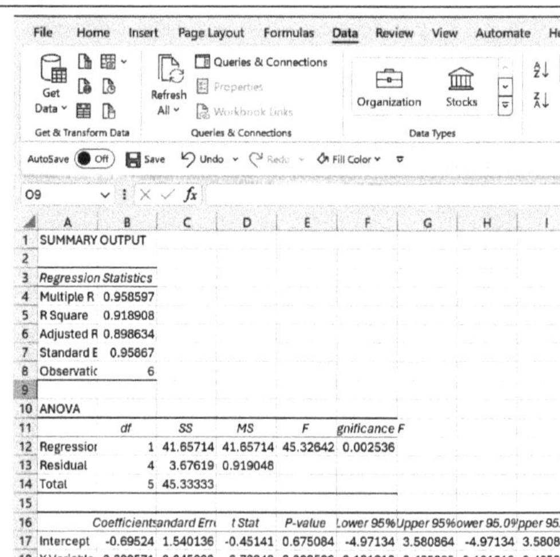

- R Square: R^2 equals .919, which is a very good fit. About 92% of the variation in hours of using TikTok is explained by the predictor variable, age.
- Significance F: In Excel, "Significance F" represents the p value, allowing you to see if your results are statistically significant. The linear regression test's p value shown in the box right below "Significance F" is 0.0025, which is < .05. Hence, you can conclude that the impact of age on the hours of using TikTok is statistically significant.
- Coefficients: The regression equation is $\hat{y}$ (TikTok hours) $= -0.695 + 0.308x$ (age), since the "Intercept" row is a (the y intercept) and the "X variable" row is b (the slope). The equation is interpreted that with a one-year increase in age, using TikTok increases by 0.308 hours.

Multiple Linear Regression

Multiple linear regression, often simply referred to as multiple regression, is used to predict the outcome of a dependent variable based on more than one predictor variable. It is an extension of simple linear regression that includes at least two predictor variables thought to influence the dependent variable. Multiple regression typically involves continuous scales of predictor variables and one dependent variable. However, the predictor variables can be either continuous (i.e., interval or ratio variables) or categorical (i.e., nominal or ordinal variables), while the dependent variable must be continuous. Since multiple regression commonly estimates the relationship between two or more predictor variables and one dependent variable on an interval or ratio scale, it requires the following assumptions:

1. Normality: Residuals (errors) should be normally distributed with a mean of 0.
2. No multicollinearity: Collinearity is a linear association between two predictors, and multicollinearity occurs when two or more predictor variables are highly correlated with each other. If two predictors are too highly correlated, then only one of them should be used in the multiple regression model.
3. Linearity: There is a linear relationship between the dependent variable and each of the independent variables; there is also a linear relationship between the dependent variable and the independent variables combined together.
4. Homogeneity of variance (homoscedasticity): The variance of the residuals (errors) is constant across all levels of the predictor variables, meaning that the spread of residuals is roughly the same for all fitted values of the dependent variable.[6]

Multiple regression enables researchers to determine the relative contribution of each of the predictor variables to the total variance explained. In particular, the coefficient of determination (R^2) measures how much of the variation in the dependent variable can be explained by variation in the predictor variables. R^2 is numbered between 0 and 1, where 0 indicates no explanation by any of the predictor variables and 1 indicates perfect prediction of the outcome, without error, by the independent variables. The equation for multiple regression of a population model is as follows:

$$y = \beta_0 + \beta_1 x_1 + \beta_2 x_2 + \ldots + \beta_n x_n + \varepsilon$$

where we assume that ε has a normal distribution with a mean of 0. Similar to simple linear regression, multiple regression has the equation based on sample data for a predicted value written as:

$$\hat{y} = b_0 + b_1 x_1 + b_2 x_2 + \ldots + b_n x_n$$

where $\hat{y}$ is the predicted value of the dependent variable; x_1 through x_n are distinct predictor variables; b_0 is the y intercept, or the value of y when all of the predictor variables are equal to zero; and b_1 to b_n are the regression coefficients. Simply put, multiple regression constructs a regression equation with multiple predictor variables instead of one.

To practice multiple regression, suppose you add one more predictor variable to the age and TikTok case. The new variable is the monetary value of cars participants drive, as you assume that people driving fancy cars tend to post videos of their car activities on TikTok. Your data are shown in Table 11.16.

Use Excel with the following steps:

1. Place the data into three columns in Excel.
2. Click the Data tab and then the Data Analysis tab.
3. Select "Regression."
4. Select the data for y into the "Input Y Range" box.
5. Select the data for both x_1 and x_2 into the "Input X Range" box.

Table 11.16

Participant	Age (x_1)	Car value (x_2)	Hours of TikTok (y)
1	20	\$11,000	5
2	25	\$38,000	7
3	30	\$27,000	9
4	35	\$5,500	10
5	40	\$22,000	13
6	45	\$76,000	12

The results are shown in Figure 11.5, and you can interpret what the numbers mean.

- Multiple R is 0.97, meaning that the two predictors and the one dependent variable have a strong positive relationship.
- R Square is 0.948, which means that 94.8% of the variation of y around its mean is explained by the predictors x_1 and x_2.
- Significance F is 0.0116, which is < .05. Hence, you can conclude that the impact of age + car value on the hours of using TikTok is statistically significant.
- Coefficients lead to constructing the equation:

$$\hat{y}\text{ (TikTok hours)} = -1.12 + 0.344\text{ (age)} - 2.43\text{ (car value)}$$

The equation produces an estimate of hours of TikTok usage due to age and car value. The p value (Significance F) is .0116, which is less than .05. Hence, you can conclude that the effects of age and car value on the hours of using TikTok are statistically significant. However, in this example, if you look at the separate p values, age's p value is .0068, which reaches statistical significance (< .05), and the car value's p value is .279, which does not reach statistical significance in the multiple regression model. Some researchers argue that regardless of each predictor variable's statistical insignificance, all predictor variables should be included in the model to control for possible confounding and biased estimation. In contrast, other researchers insist on including only predictor variables that are statistically significant in the regression model. An important fact is that by performing regression analysis, researchers can determine whether or not predictor variables have an impact on the dependent variable in a causal relationship.

Table 11.17 Multiple Linear Regression Test in Excel

Performing regression in Excel

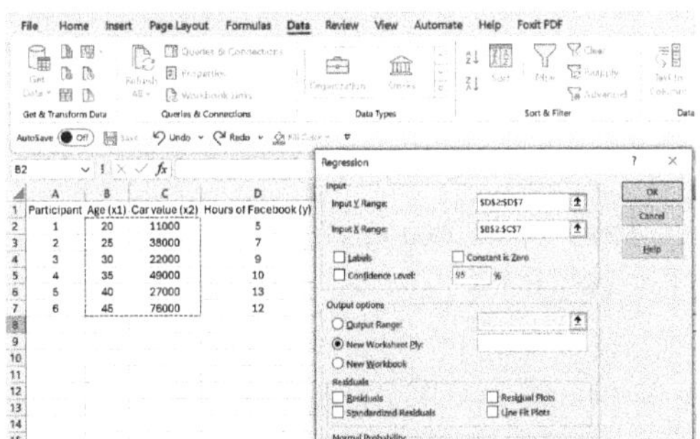

Results

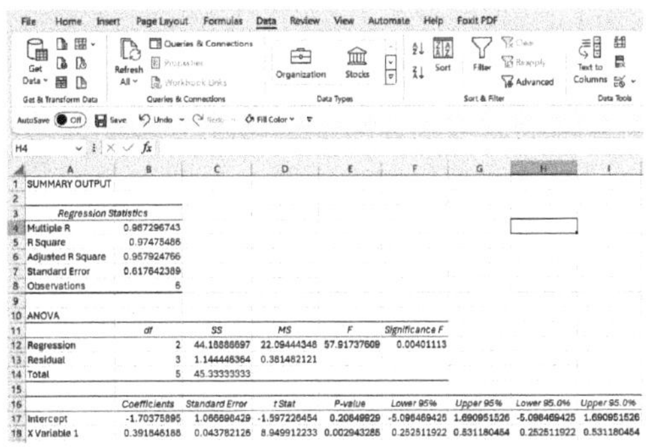

Source: Created by author.

LEVERAGING AI TECHNOLOGY FOR ADVANCED STATISTICS

The transformative potential of AI technology in the realm of advanced statistics becomes increasingly apparent, particularly with regression and correlation analyses. AI technology, with its capacity to handle vast data sets and detect patterns, serves as a valuable tool for students grappling with intricate statistical concepts. It not only demystifies these concepts but also offers practical, hands-on learning experiences.[7] For example, AI-powered tools can streamline the execution of regression analyses, aiding students in comprehending the relationships between variables. These tools can automatically generate regression equations, compute coefficients, and interpret results, providing students with instant feedback and enhancing their understanding.

Similarly, AI can simplify correlation analysis. By automatically calculating correlation coefficients and generating scatterplots, AI allows students to visualize and better understand the relationships between variables.[8] This can be particularly useful when dealing with multiple variables, as AI can quickly compute and display multiple correlations. Furthermore, AI can assist students in grasping the assumptions underlying these statistical methods and in verifying that their data meet these criteria. For instance, in regression analysis, AI can check for linearity, homoscedasticity, and normality, while in correlation analysis, it can assess if the variables are normally distributed. Ultimately, AI makes advanced statistics more approachable and less daunting for students. By automating complex calculations and providing clear outputs, AI enables students to focus on interpreting and applying results rather than being bogged down in computations.

The integration of AI technology holds immense promise for advancing our comprehension and application of advanced statistics. By leveraging these tools, students not only gain a profound and intuitive grasp of regression and correlation analysis but also confidently apply these methodologies in their research endeavors. As the evolution of AI technology continues, its integral role in statistics education and practice is poised to become even more significant.

APPLICATION OF AN AI-POWERED TOOL

BOX 11.1
APPLICATIONS OF STATISTICAL TESTS TO COMPANIES, ACCORDING TO CHATGPT

Using an AI-Powered Tool (ChatGPT) for Applications of Statistical Tests

Command syntax: Tell us which statistical tests are popular for companies with examples and offer us a specific example with regression.

Answer: Statistical tests such as chi-square, *t* test, ANOVA, correlations, and regression are commonly used by companies to gain insights into various aspects of their business. The choice of test depends on the specific questions being asked and the type of data being analyzed.

For example, a company may use a chi-square test to determine if the observed frequencies of a particular variable are significantly different from the expected frequencies. This test can be used in market research to determine if there is a significant difference in the product preferences of different demographics.

Similarly, an ANOVA test can be used when comparing the means of more than two groups. This test can be used by a company to determine if there is a significant difference in the performance of different versions of a product. For example, a company that sells a software product can conduct an ANOVA test to determine if there is a significant difference in the user satisfaction ratings of different versions of the software.

Another commonly used statistical test is the *t* test. A company may use an independent samples *t* test to compare the means of two groups. For instance, a company that sells a skincare product may conduct an independent samples *t* test to determine if there is a significant difference in the effectiveness of the product on two different skin types. More examples are:

1. *t* test: A *t* test is used to compare the means of two independent groups. For example, a company may want to compare the salaries of male and female employees to see if there is a significant difference in pay.
2. ANOVA: ANOVA (analysis of variance) is used when comparing the means of more than two groups. For instance, a company may want to compare the effectiveness of three different marketing strategies on increasing sales.
3. Correlations: Correlation analysis is used to determine the strength and direction of the relationship between two variables. For example, a company may want to investigate if there is a relationship between customer satisfaction and repeat purchases.
4. Chi-square test: The chi-square test is used to compare observed frequencies with expected frequencies to determine whether there is a significant association between two variables. For instance, a company may want to test whether there is a significant difference in the number of male and female employees in different departments.
5. Regression: Regression analysis is used to identify the relationship between one dependent variable and one or more independent variables. For example, a

company may want to predict the number of sales for a new product based on the price, advertising, and promotions.

Imagine a company wants to predict sales of their new fitness tracker. They believe price (X_1) and advertising spending (X_2) might affect sales (Y). The linear regression equation would look like this: $Y = b_0 + b_1X_1 + b_2X_2$ (where b_0, b_1, and b_2 are coefficients).

Here's a breakdown:

- Y: Sales (predicted number of fitness trackers sold)
- X_1: Price (of the fitness tracker)
- X_2: Advertising spending (amount spent on advertising)
- b_0: Y-intercept (predicted sales when price and advertising spending are zero)
- b_1: Price coefficient (how much sales change for every $1 price increase)
- b_2: Advertising spending coefficient (how much sales change for every $1 increase in advertising spending)

Let's say we get some data and run the analysis. We end up with this equation:

$$Y = 100 + 5X_1 + 2X_2$$

Interpreting the equation:

- Even with no advertising or price set (X_1 and $X_2 = 0$), the predicted sales are 100 units (b_0). This could represent baseline sales due to brand recognition or other factors.
- For every $1 increase in price ($X_1$), sales are predicted to increase by 5 units (b_1). This suggests a positive relationship between price and sales, which might be surprising! It could be because the higher price positions the product as more premium.
- Every $1 increase in advertising spending (X_2) is predicted to increase sales by 2 units (b_2). This is a positive relationship, as expected.

Important to note:

- This is a simplified example. Real-world regression models may include more variables and may not always have a perfectly linear relationship.
- Correlation doesn't equal causation. Just because price and sales are related in this model doesn't necessarily mean a higher price causes more sales. There could be other factors at play.

Summary

- ✓ Nonparametric statistics rely on the analysis of data frequencies and rankings.
- ✓ The chi-square (χ^2) test determines whether there is an association or relationship between categorical variables.
- ✓ There are two popular types of the chi-square test: the one-sample test and the two-sample test.
- ✓ To compute the chi-square value, the observed and expected frequencies are needed.
- ✓ The degrees of freedom for a one-sample chi-square test is the number of groups (columns) – 1, and for a two-sample chi-square test it is (number of rows – 1) × (number of columns – 1).
- ✓ A correlation is used to describe the linear relationship between variables.
- ✓ There are three possible results of correlational research: a positive correlation, a negative correlation, and no correlation.
- ✓ When a correlation is used to analyze a liner relationship of data, researchers often present correlation graphs in the form of a scatterplot.
- ✓ The value of the correlation coefficient ranges between –1.0 and 1.0.
- ✓ Pearson's *r* correlation focuses on measuring the strength of a linear association between two variables and is denoted by *r*.
- ✓ The degrees of freedom for correlations is $n - 2$ (the number of participants in your sample minus 2).
- ✓ Spearman's rho correlation, signified by ρ, is a nonparametric statistical version of Pearson's *r* correlation.
- ✓ The degrees of freedom (*df*) refers to the maximum number of logically independent values that are free to vary.
- ✓ Regression analysis is a set of statistical methods used for the description of the relationships between the independent or predictor variable(s) and the dependent variable.
- ✓ One advantage of regression analysis is its ability to predict dependent variables.
- ✓ When performing a regression analysis, researchers are expected to provide a regression equation that contains the coefficients.
- ✓ There are two types of regression analysis that researchers in strategic communication commonly use: simple linear regression and multiple linear regression.
- ✓ In simple linear regression, each equation consists of two values: the dependent variable and the predictor variable.
- ✓ The simple linear regression formula is written as $\hat{y}$ (*y* hat) = $a + bx$.

- ✓ Multiple linear regression is used to predict the outcome of a dependent variable from more than one predictor variable.
- ✓ The formula for multiple regression is $\hat{y} = b_0 + b_1x_1 + b_2x_2 + \ldots + b_nx_n$.
- ✓ AI-powered tools can streamline the execution of regression analyses.

Key Terms

1. Chi-square test
2. Nonparametric data
3. Degrees of freedom
4. Correlations
5. Pearson's *r*
6. Simple linear regression
7. Multiple regression
8. Predictor variable
9. Significance F
10. Coefficients

Chapter 12

Experimental Research

Chapter Learning Outcomes

- Identify fundamentals of experimental research.
- Explore the cause-and-effect relationship in experiments.
- Explain the concepts of treatments and manipulation checks.
- Discuss how to reduce the Hawthorne effect.
- Apply true experimental designs in experimental research.
- Differentiate between extraneous variables and confounding variables.
- Discuss how internal and external validity can be assured.
- Explain the characteristics of the Solomon four-group design.
- Describe the components of the experimental research checklist.
- Acknowledge the weaknesses of the quasi-experimental design.
- Apply field experiments to the real world.
- Leverage AI tools for experimental research.

When it comes to research, there are numerous methods available, each falling under either the qualitative or quantitative approach. Each approach has its own principles and characteristics that govern its execution and analysis. Experimental research stands out as a unique and scientific method that enforces strict research designs. Due to its increasing importance in strategic communication, understanding the standard requirements and rules for conducting experimental research is necessary. Researchers who engage in experimental research must adhere to rigorous rules in their research designs, including the fundamental framework of quantitative research.

Basic Concepts of Experimental Research

Experimental research is based on the premise that it should take place in a controlled environment to accurately measure the impact of the independent variable on the dependent variable. The goal of experimental research is to establish a causal relationship between these two variables. In this type of research, the variables are identified and defined, and a hypothesis is formulated. However, what sets experimental research apart is the process of manipulating or controlling variables within a regulated laboratory setting.[1] Researchers alter the variables and observe how these changes impact the results of the research.

While laboratory settings are preferred due to the ability to control variables, experimental research can also be conducted outside a lab. Some researchers have found ways to overcome difficulties in an open field setting. Research experiments involve the manipulation of one variable to observe whether it affects another variable. The process of manipulation and measurement relies on randomly assigning research participants to specific groups of manipulated and nonmanipulated variables. When researchers are conducting experimental research in strategic communication, lab settings are often used, particularly for media and advertising effects. This allows researchers to manipulate one or more independent variables as treatments and to randomly assign participants to different treatment levels. The results of the manipulation or treatment on the dependent variable can then be observed.

Researchers often prefer conducting experiments in a laboratory setting to avoid potential interference from extraneous variables that could affect the outcome of the study. For instance, suppose you are investigating whether following diet influencers on TikTok leads to eating disorders among college students. In this case, TikTok diet influencers would be the independent variable, and eating disorders would be the dependent variable. To ensure accurate results, you would only include college students who follow such diet influencers on TikTok while excluding other influencers from various media platforms that could be considered extraneous variables. If you allow such extraneous variables to interfere, your experimental research could lead to incorrect conclusions about the causal relationship between the independent and dependent variables.

Despite its challenging and complicated requirements, many researchers in strategic communication choose to use experimental research because of its ability to identify variables that have causal relationships. This method allows researchers to determine the direction and strength of these relationships, including whether they are statistically significant. Although it may seem similar to regression analysis, which is used to find cause-and-effect relationships between variables, experimental research is used to gather data that can be analyzed using regression analysis. Hence, experimental research is a methodological approach that allows researchers to investigate causal relationships between variables. The following are the main concepts involved in experimental research:

- Independent and dependent variables: In an experiment, the researcher seeks to establish a causal relationship between two variables, the independent and the dependent variable. The independent variable is manipulated to observe its effect on the dependent variable. By altering the level or amount of the independent variable, the researcher can measure the corresponding changes in the dependent variable.

- Treatment: A unique aspect of experimental research is the treatment, which is a specific level or condition of the independent variable manipulated by the researcher. The treatment is used to control the cause in a cause-and-effect relationship. For instance, a researcher who wants to study the impact of playing violent video games on mental health might ask participants to play these games for varying lengths of time each day for a month and then observe the effects on their mental health.
- Manipulation check: This is a way to make sure that when researchers change something in an experiment (like having people follow social media celebrities), it actually has the effect they want it to have. It's like a test within the study to see if the manipulation really works as planned. For example, if researchers want to see how following fancy celebrities on Instagram affects how well students do on a Marketing 101 test, they might ask the students to rate how fancy and luxurious the celebrities' posts are. By doing this, researchers can check if following the celebrities actually made students perceive things as more fancy and luxurious. If the students don't really see the posts as fancy and luxurious, then the manipulation (following celebrities) might not be working as intended. The manipulation check is important because it helps researchers make sure that the changes they make in the study (like following celebrities) are connected to the outcomes they expect (like performance on the Marketing 101 test).[2]
- Experimental group: Also known as the treatment group, this group of participants receives the treatment that the researcher is investigating. They are exposed to the manipulated independent variable, and the effect on the dependent variable is measured after the treatment is administered.
- Control group: This group of participants does not receive the experimental treatment. They should closely resemble the experimental group in all respects except for the treatment. The researcher compares the control group with the experimental group to determine if the treatment has caused any changes. This allows the researcher to isolate the effect of the independent variable.
- Extraneous variables: In the realm of strategic communication research, understanding extraneous variables is crucial. The independent variable (IV) wields the power to influence the dependent variable (DV) in a causal relationship. However, if the DV is swayed by unrelated factors, we encounter extraneous variables. These variables can lead to inaccurate outcomes, distorting the causal link between the IV and DV. Researchers meticulously plan experiments to eliminate the influence of extraneous variables in order to ensure that only the manipulation

of the independent variable impacts the dependent variable. For example, in a study assessing whether YouTube tutorials on Bitcoin investment enhance students' comprehension of finance, two groups can be formed: one that watches the tutorials and the other that does nothing on the topic. Extraneous variables, like prior Bitcoin knowledge, must be mitigated by selecting participants without such background knowledge.

- Confounding variables: Similar to extraneous variables, confounding variables can impact the relationship between causally linked variables. Unlike extraneous variables, confounding variables affect both the independent and dependent variables. Acknowledging the presence of these variables is vital, as they can jeopardize the validity of experiments aiming to establish cause-and-effect relationships. Consider a hypothesis suggesting that Facebook users experience higher happiness levels than nonusers. Confounding variables, such as users also utilizing platforms like Instagram, could skew the results. Researchers thus rigorously control these variables. For instance, age can be a confounding variable, with parents more likely to use Facebook compared to children, who favor newer platforms like TikTok. Figure 12.1 illustrates confounding variables.

Experimental research is a robust scientific approach, often conducted in controlled environments like laboratories. In strategic communication, laboratory experiments are prevalent for studying advertising and media effects related to marketing communication and media psychology. For instance, if you were a researcher studying the effects of social media advertising promoting unhealthy products like alcohol and tobacco on preschool-aged children, you would select a sample of children and then expose them to such ads in a laboratory. You would then measure their cognitive development and any interest they show in detecting persuasive intent in social media advertising. Despite the precision afforded by laboratories, researchers must navigate certain pitfalls, such as the Hawthorne effect, which can cause participants to alter their behavior due to their awareness of being observed. To minimize this effect, researchers need to ensure the

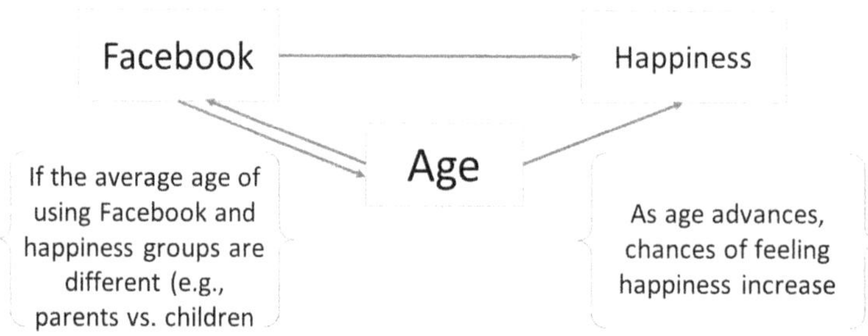

Figure 12.1 An example of confounding variables
Source: Created by author.

confidentiality and anonymity of the participants' responses. This will help to produce trustworthy results from the experiment.

Experimental Research Checklist

When planning an experiment, researchers must make critical decisions regarding participant selection, treatment administration, and validity checks. Laboratory experiments, in particular, require a high level of control for hypothesis testing compared to field experiments. In controlled environments or labs, researchers use random assignment and purposeful manipulations, allowing them to control experimental conditions. To guide this process, researchers often refer to an experimental research checklist, adapted from Professor John W. Creswell's list, which includes the following considerations:

1. Who are the participants in the experiment?
2. What population do they represent, and how will the results generalize to this population?
3. How will the participants be selected? Will a random selection method be used?
4. How will the participants be assigned to experimental and control groups?
5. How many participants will be in each group?
6. What is the dependent variable in the experiment, and how will it be measured?
7. What is the treatment, and how will it be administered to the experimental group?
8. How frequently will the treatment levels be manipulated?
9. What experimental design will be used?
10. What statistical analysis will be used to measure the experiment's outcome?
11. What steps will you take in the experiment, including random assignment of participants to groups, administration of treatment, and analysis of data?
12. How will you minimize the threat to internal and external validity in the experiment?
13. Will you perform a pilot test?
14. How will you ensure the ethical process of experimental research?[3]

This checklist provides practical guidance for researchers to plan and execute experiments in a methodical and scholarly manner. As experiments often involve human participants, it is crucial for researchers to prioritize ethical considerations and ensure that the research does not cause harm. The Milgram and Stanford prison experiments serve as stark reminders of the importance of ethics in experimental research (see Chapter 3). The checklist specifically addresses experimental design (No. 9) and internal and external validity (No. 12), which are crucial aspects to be discussed for a comprehensive understanding of experimental research.

DESIGN OF EXPERIMENTS (DOE)/EXPERIMENTAL DESIGN

Experimental research involves gathering data in accordance with the principles of experimental design or design of experiments (DOE). This approach allows researchers to test a hypothesis in a controlled environment, ensuring that the experiment is conducted under scientifically acceptable conditions. Experimental design aims to establish causal (internal) validity, which pertains to the cause-and-effect relationship between variables. Three classic criteria support causal validity:

1. Association (correlation): The cause-and-effect variables are distinctively identified in a systematic relationship.
2. Temporal order: The cause variable must precede the effect variable in time.
3. Nonspuriousness: Researchers must demonstrate that the effect variable is caused only by the cause variable and not by other variables.[4]

For example, in studying the relationship between smoking and lung cancer, nonspuriousness would require the researcher to prove that smoking is the only cause of lung cancer, even among coal miners and restaurant chefs who do not smoke but suffer from lung cancer. Because meeting the non-spuriousness criterion can be challenging in experimental research, researchers pay close attention to the early stages of experimental design to ensure the causal (internal) validity of their research.

Experimental research, particularly when conducted in a laboratory setting, often involves the collection of quantitative data. There are three primary types of experimental design:

- preexperimental design
- quasi-experimental design
- true experimental design

Each of these designs incorporates four key elements:

1. Independent variable (IV): This is the variable that researchers manipulate, often referred to as the treatment variable.

2. Dependent variable (DV): This is the variable that researchers measure, which is influenced by the manipulated IV.
3. Experimental group: This group of participants receives the treatment or manipulation.
4. Control group: This group of participants is used for comparison with the experimental group. The control group remains constant or receives no treatment.

Preexperimental Design

Preexperimental design involves observing a single group of participants or various dependent groups after applying a manipulative effect on the independent variable to presumably cause a change. The prefix *pre* indicates that this is the simplest form of experimental design, lacking a control or comparison group, or both. Researchers further categorize preexperimental designs into three types, with diagrams including symbols such as X = treatment, O_x = observation, NR = nonrandomized assignment, and R = randomized assignment.

- One-shot case study: This design involves only one dependent group or variable with no control group (see Table 12.1), resulting in no causal validity. For example, if you asked your participants to view Dwayne "The Rock" Johnson's Instagram photos and videos and measured their desire to go to the gym, you wouldn't be able to measure the change since there was no pretest about their gym-going desires before the treatment.
- One-group pretest-posttest: This design incorporates pretest and posttest structures by conducting an experiment on a single group. The treatment is administered to the group, and the effect is measured afterward (see Table 12.2). For instance, you could measure participants' desire to go to the gym before they view Johnson's photos and videos (pretest). After their exposure to the content (treatment), you could compare the desired scores to determine the results.

Table 12.1 One-Shot Case Study Design

Treatment	Posttest
X	O_1

Table 12.2 One-Group Pretest-Posttest Design

Pretest	Treatment	Posttest
O_1	X	O_2

- Static-group comparison: Also known as the posttest-only nonequivalent group design, this design involves two or more groups. Researchers administer treatment to only one of the groups while the other groups remain static (see Table 12.3). There is no pretest process, and the posttest comparison between the groups is assumed to be a result of the treatment. For example, only one group is asked to look at Johnson's Instagram photos and videos as treatment, and the other group does nothing. The desire to hit the gym between the two groups can be measured as a result of the treatment.

Quasi-Experimental Design

Quasi-experimental design is a type of nonrandomized experimental research. The prefix *quasi* implies a resemblance or partial similarity, reflecting the absence of one key component of a true experiment: random assignment. For instance, a marketing class section with 200 students might be selected as the treatment group, while a biology class section with 200 students serves as the control group. The lack of random assignments can potentially result in nonequivalent groups. Researchers often use quasi-experimental designs when enforcing randomization is challenging. Due to the absence of randomization, researchers often lack control over the treatment in quasi-experimental design, which can compromise the experiment's internal validity, or the ability to establish a cause-and-effect relationship.

However, quasi-experiments can effectively conduct retrospective studies of a single treatment over a specific period. For example, a social media researcher might want to examine whether college students who start following celebrities on Instagram experience better outcomes in terms of overcoming loneliness compared to those who already follow celebrities on TikTok. The latter group serves as the preexisting control group for studying the loneliness symptom in comparison with the participants who receive the new treatment of Instagram. Quasi-experimental research design can be classified into three types, namely, (1) nonequivalent group design, (2) interrupted time series design, and (3) regression-discontinuity design.

- Nonequivalent groups design: Researchers use this design to measure changes in an outcome after treatment. They select existing groups that appear similar, and two non-randomly assigned groups are compared. Only one group receives treatment, and data are gathered at two different time points, before and after the

Table 12.3 Posttest-Only Nonequivalent Groups Design

Treatment	**Posttest**
X	O_1
	O_2

treatment (see Table 12.4). However, since the groups are not selected randomly, there may be preexisting differences between them that can distort the posttest data. Therefore, researchers should choose groups of participants who are as similar as possible to avoid such extraneous variables.

- Interrupted time series (ITS) design: Researchers collect data over a long-term period (weekly, monthly, or yearly) before and after a point of treatment to evaluate the treatment's impact on the dependent variable (see Table 12.5). The main goal of the ITS design is to determine if there is a data pattern observed post-treatment compared with observed pre-treatment at multiple time points. This design is used to show changes caused by the treatment.
- Regression-discontinuity (RD) design: Researchers assign participants to the treatment and the control group based on an arbitrary cutoff score (see Table 12.6). This score serves as the threshold to offer the treatment for those who receive a score either above or below the cutoff score. The RD design is seen as a useful method for determining whether a treatment is effective, with the advantage of the cutoff threshold enabling researchers to target treatment for those in need. For example, a new drug can be tested for patients with stage IV pancreatic cancer as the cutoff score. However, this design can deprive the treatment of stage III patients because of the threshold.

Quasi-experiments are used to determine the causal relationship of treatment but are not regarded as true experimental research because of the absence of random assignment. Because participants are not randomly assigned, quasi-experiments fail to avoid the issue of extraneous or confounding variables.

Table 12.4 Nonequivalent Groups Design

Group	Pretest	Treatment	Posttest
Experimental group: NR	O_1	X	O_2
Control Group: NR	O_1		O_2

Table 12.5 Interrupted Time Series Design

O_1	O_2	O_3	O_4	X	O_5	O_6	O_7	O_8

Table 12.6 Regression-Discontinuity Design

Group	Pretest	Treatment	Posttest
Above cutoff	O_1	X	O_2
Below cutoff	O_1		O_2

True Experimental Research Design

True experimental research design differs from quasi-experimental design in one key aspect: random assignment. This design is considered the most accurate type of experimental design and includes four elements: treatment, control, random selection, and random assignment.

- Treatment: The purposeful manipulation or change of the independent variable by the researcher in the setting.
- Control: The prevention of outside variables that can affect the experimental outcome.
- Random selection: The process of choosing participants at random to create a sample that accurately represents a population.
- Random assignment: Involves assigning individuals by chance to control and treatment groups, ensuring that any differences between the groups can be attributed to the treatment.

When an experiment is thoroughly manipulated and systematically controlled, it allows confidence in the causal effect of the treatment as observed in the outcome. This design requires the researcher to manipulate the independent variable and randomly assign participants to different groups. True experimental research design requires at least two randomly assigned posttest groups, though the requirement for pretest groups depends on the type of the design. The four different types of true experimental design include the posttest-only control group design, the pretest-posttest control group design, the Solomon four-group design, and the factorial design.

- Posttest-only control group design: In this design, research groups are randomly assigned to the experimental and control groups. The researcher provides the experimental group with a treatment, and then both the experimental and control groups are observed (see Table 12.7). The process involves forming two or more groups, administering the treatment, collecting data after the treatment, and comparing data between groups to determine treatment effectiveness.[5] For example, you might randomly assign 30 students identified as at risk for failure in a quantitative research course into experimental and control groups. You administer the experimental group to read a book titled *The Cartoon Guide to Statistics* as the treatment, and the control group receives no treatment. You give both groups a test and compare the average scores to determine the effect of reading the additional cartoon book on the test scores. Although the posttest-only control design is quite simple to perform, you cannot be certain that a difference in test scores

Table 12.7 Posttest-Only Control Group Design

Group	Treatment	Posttest
Experimental group: R	X	O_1
Control group: R		O_2

Table 12.8 Pretest-Posttest Control Group Design

Group	Pretest	Treatment	Posttest
Experimental group: R	O_1	X	O_2
Control group: R	O_3		O_4

between the groups was caused by the manipulated independent variable because there was no pretest that could identify any difference between the groups at the beginning of the experiment.

- Pretest-posttest control group design: In this design, research participants are randomly assigned to experimental and control groups with a pretest measure (see Table 12.8). This design enables you to compare the final posttest results between the two groups, producing an idea of the overall effect of the treatment. One advantage of this design in comparison with the posttest-only control design is that you can measure how both groups changed from pretest to posttest. For instance, if you're interested in examining the impact of a protein powder that enhances the performance of your swim class students, you could randomly divide them into two groups. Prior to the experiment, you test both groups on their 100-meter freestyle swimming performance. The experimental group receives a daily protein shake for a month, while the control group is not given any. After a month, you retest both groups to compare their swimming performance. By analyzing the results, you can determine if there was a significant difference in swimming ability between the two groups due to the protein powder. However, some researchers are worried that regardless of the treatment, the pretest process consciously pressures participants to change their behavior for the posttest to make themselves appear advanced (the pretest influence).
- Solomon four-group design: In this design, participants are divided into two treatment groups and two control groups. One experimental group and one control group undergo a pretest, while the other two groups do not (see Table 12.9). This design combines elements of the posttest-only and pretest-posttest control group designs, focusing on evaluating the impact of pretesting on subsequent measurements. The Solomon four-group design is used to minimize the influence

of confounding and extraneous factors, as well as changes in the dependent variable due to effects of the pretest on the posttest. Despite its effectiveness in addressing internal validity issues and controlling variables, the Solomon four-group design is not widely used among researchers due to the significant time, resources, and effort required.

- Factorial design: While an experiment is commonly designed to determine the effect of one independent variable upon one dependent variable, a factorial design allows researchers to observe changes in the dependent variable caused by two or more independent variables, including interactions between the independent variables (factors). This design is specifically used when interactions between the factors are expected to occur, allowing researchers to avoid misleading conclusions. In a factorial design, a factor is considered a major independent variable. The main effect of a factor is defined as the change in the dependent variable that is caused by the treatment at a specific level of that factor. A 2×2 factorial design is the most basic design that administers two treatments, each with two levels (see Table 12.10). For example, suppose you want to compare the Bitcoin investment outcomes of two different types of social media platforms (X [Twitter] and YouTube lessons), and you also want to examine whether these effects vary with the time of taking lessons (5 or 10 hours per week). You identify two factors: social media platform and hours of taking lessons. Each factor consists of two levels, X and YouTube for the first factor and 5 and 10 hours for the second factor, as shown in Figure 12.2. As researchers often include multiple independent variables

Table 12.9 Solomon Four-Group Design

Group	Pretest	Treatment	Posttest
Pretested experimental group: R_1	O_1	X	O_3
Pretested control group: R_2	O_2		O_4
Non-pretested experimental group: R_3		X	O_5
Non-pretested control group: R_4			O_6

Table 12.10 Factorial Design

Group	Treatment	Posttest
R	X_{11}	O
R	X_{12}	O
R	X_{21}	O
R	X_{22}	O

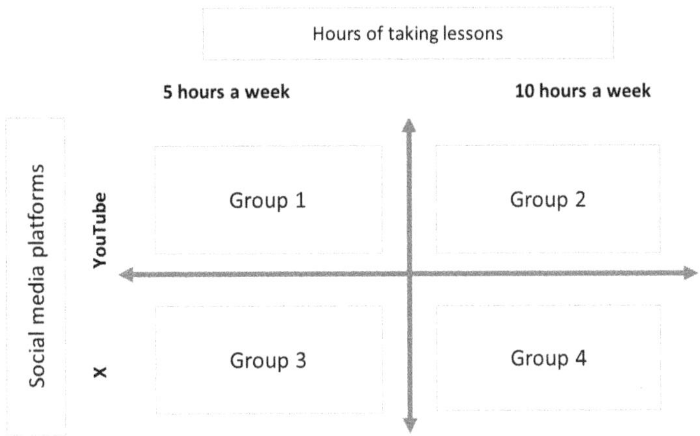

Figure 12.2 An example of a 2 } 2 factorial design
Source: Created by author.

in their experiments, a factorial design serves as their research guidance, in which each level of each independent variable is combined with each level of the other independent variables to create all possible conditions. In the Bitcoin case, two analyses will be conducted: (1) the dollar difference in investment outcomes between X and YouTube, and (2) the difference in dollar investment outcomes between 5 hours and 10 hours per week. Hence, a factorial design can be applied to an experiment with more than one independent variable, but the main effects may not be meaningful with a large interaction. In a 2×2 factorial design, there are four groups, one for each combination of the levels of the factors, and the groups are randomly assigned to a posttest-only design without a pretest process.

Reliability and Validity in Experiments

Experimental research comprises several key elements, including treatment, variables, designs, and groups. All these elements work together to meet the expectation of conducting scientific research that justifies its academic value with reliability and validity. Because experiments are characterized as a methodological branch of quantitative research, the outcomes of experiments should demonstrate reliability and validity.

Reliability

In experimental research, reliability refers to the level of consistency observed between repeated experiments and their corresponding results. To achieve reliability, it is necessary to perform an experiment multiple times, ensuring that any significant findings can be replicated and are not simply coincidental. For instance, if another researcher were to conduct the same experiment in a similar setting, they should obtain identical results to validate the initial findings from a reliability standpoint. Essentially, an experiment is considered highly reliable if it produces consistent results under consistent conditions across multiple trials. There are three different types of reliability in experimental research:

- Interrater reliability: The degree to which two or more different observers agree on what has been observed.
- Internal consistency: The degree to which different items in a survey that measure the same thing correlate with one another.
- Test-retest reliability: The degree to which the outcomes of a particular measure remain consistent over multiple administrations.[6]

Validity

In experimental research, validity holds greater significance than reliability as it encompasses the entire experimental concept. This includes following all procedures and rules of experiments to generate valid results derived from a scientific research method. Some researchers believe that reliability is one of the indicators of scientific research validity. High validity ensures that the research method accurately measures what it is supposed to measure, resulting in empirical results that correspond to real characteristics of populations. There are two major types of experimental validity:

1. Internal validity: The primary goal of experimental research is to explore the causal relationship between variables, and internal validity deals with this issue. The logic is based on the assumption that if you manipulate the independent variable and see any difference in the dependent variable, which must have been caused by the manipulation or treatment, your experiment demonstrates strong internal validity. In this case, the results support a direct cause-and-effect relationship between the variables. Under a tightly controlled laboratory setting, you strengthen internal validity by minimizing the possibility of extraneous and confounding variables. In short, strong internal validity means a clear link of cause to effect. In contrast, research involving correlations between variables has low internal validity since there is no causal relationship to be identified by correlations. One more requirement for strong internal validity is the random assignment of sample groups into experimental and control groups. For instance, if participants in the experimental group were more motivated than those in the control group, then the motivation of the participants, rather than the independent variable, could explain any observed differences between the groups. Therefore, researchers must carefully control all aspects of their experiment to ensure high internal validity.
2. External validity: The use of randomly selected samples in experiments is intended to achieve external validity, which refers to the ability to generalize the results obtained from the sample to the entire population. This generalizability depends on

whether the methods of the experiment support the application of the results to the specified population, setting, or area. For instance, if an experiment is conducted in a laboratory with college students, the results might not be applicable to older adults in the real world. Therefore, researchers must carefully consider the external validity of their experiment and, if necessary, conduct additional studies to test the generalizability of their findings. The main objective of external validity is to attain generalization of the results obtained from a sample group in a laboratory setting to the entire population. Experiments tend to have strong external validity when participants in a controlled situation are similar to the population they are intended to represent. For example, if you are studying the shopping patterns of Hispanic female college students at Ulta and Sephora stores and how the shoppers are influenced by luxury beauty brands or popular drugstore brands, your experimental research would have high external validity if you observed this specific sample in these particular stores every week for several months. If you observed these students purchasing more luxury beauty brands in Sephora stores and more drugstore brands in Ulta stores, you could confidently generalize their shopping patterns in these two beauty stores to those of the entire population of Hispanic female college students in the United States.

However, some experiments conducted outside the laboratory, also known as field experiments, tend to have lower internal validity due to a reduced level of control. This is something researchers need to take into account when designing their studies and interpreting their results.

Field Experiments

Whereas most experimental research is administered in labs, field experiments are designed to manipulate situations in a natural setting or outside of laboratories. Field experiments aim to closely mimic the situations under which a causal relationship occurs in society. Researchers observe whether the manipulation or treatment of one independent variable impacts a dependent variable within the context of a natural setting. Natural settings can include open places such as sports events, shopping malls, college campuses, airports, beaches, and hospitals. Despite the challenges of administering treatment in an open setting, field experiments must include some form of manipulation of the independent variable to measure changes in the dependent variable.

Researchers often conduct field experiments in real-world settings where participants are unaware they are being observed. This approach allows for the randomization of individuals in natural contexts, aiding researchers in identifying causal effects. In field experiments, data are collected after administering a treatment in a real-life setting. This method capitalizes on the advantage of studying real human behavior in a natural environment, assuming that people are unlikely to alter their behavior when they believe no one is watching. An example of a field experiment is the popular TV show *What Would You Do?* on ABC, which explores how people react to strangers in controversial situations. The show's host, John Quiñones, uses hidden cameras to observe and comment on how people behave when faced with provocative scenarios that require them to make a decision quickly. The show creates and manipulates these scenarios as a treatment, such as an episode in August 2020 that staged an event about the U.S.–Mexico border wall. The scenario in an ABC press release includes the following:

> A couple of Latino men are in a restaurant speaking Spanish as they wait to order their food. A customer nearby overhears them and questions their immigration status. He tells the men that until there is a border wall, there is no way of knowing who is in the United States legally. How will others who witness the conversation react in New York? What will the reaction be in El Paso, Texas, just a few miles from the U.S.–Mexico border?[7]

The TV staff conducted a social experiment by installing hidden cameras in restaurants located in New York and Texas. The experiment involved observing customers as they debated their views on the border wall. It was interesting to see how people expressed their opinions on national security, humanity, and the immigration system. One customer suggested a neutral approach by proposing the construction of a border wall with a door. The experiment showed that conducting field experiments can provide researchers with valuable insights into social contexts and people's daily lives. However, some researchers have raised ethical concerns about not informing the participants who are unknowingly being observed in such experiments.

Leveraging AI Tools for Seamless Experimental Research in College

The world of experimental research can be daunting for any student, demanding meticulous planning, rigorous execution, and insightful analysis. Fortunately, the landscape is shifting, and emerging AI tools are poised to empower college students on their research journey. These cutting-edge technologies play a pivotal role in enhancing various facets of the research process, encompassing organization, experimental design, data analysis, writing assistance, collaboration, and peer review. We will explore how college students can benefit from utilizing AI technology when organizing, designing, and analyzing their experimental research projects for class as follows:

- Experimental design assistance: AI tools can assist students in designing their experiments by suggesting appropriate methodologies, sample sizes, and variables to consider. These tools can help students optimize their experimental design based on the objectives and constraints of the research, ensuring a more robust and well-structured study.

- Data collection and management: AI technology can streamline the process of data collection by automating data entry, organization, and storage. By utilizing AI-powered tools, students can efficiently gather and manage experimental data, reducing errors and saving time in the research process.
- Statistical analysis support: AI tools can aid students in conducting statistical analyses by recommending suitable tests and interpreting results. These tools can help students identify patterns, trends, and relationships within their data, guiding them in drawing meaningful conclusions from their experiments.
- Error detection and correction: AI tools can help students identify errors or inconsistencies in their experimental data analysis. By flagging potential issues and offering suggestions for improvement, AI can enhance the accuracy and reliability of research findings, ensuring the validity of the study.[8]

By incorporating AI technology into experimental research projects, college students can benefit from improved efficiency, accuracy, and guidance throughout the research process. These AI tools can support students in organizing their experiments, designing robust studies, collecting and managing data effectively, conducting statistical analyses, testing hypotheses, and detecting errors.[9] As AI continues to advance, its role in experimental research is likely to grow, offering even more benefits to student researchers. Ultimately, leveraging AI technology in experimental research can empower students to conduct high-quality research projects and enhance their learning experience in the classroom.

Application of an AI-Powered Tool

Box 12.1
Using Google Gemini to Develop an Experimental Design

Using an AI-Powered Tool (Google Gemini) for an Experimental Design

Command syntax: Design an experiment to see if AI-powered software like Gemini can affect college students' writing literacy.

Answer: Sure, here is an experiment designed to see if AI-powered software like Gemini can affect college students' writing literacy:

Hypothesis: AI-powered software like Gemini can improve college students' writing literacy.

Independent variable: AI-powered software like Gemini

Dependent variable: College students' writing literacy

Control group: A group of college students who do not use AI-powered software like Gemini.

Experimental group: A group of college students who use AI-powered software like Gemini.

Procedure:

1. The experiment will be conducted over a period of one semester.
2. All participants will be randomly assigned to either the control group or the experimental group.
3. The control group will not use AI-powered software like Gemini.
4. The experimental group will use AI-powered software like Gemini to help them with their writing assignments.
5. At the end of the semester, all participants will take a writing test.
6. The scores on the writing test will be compared between the control group and the experimental group.

Expected Results:

The experimental group is expected to have higher scores on the writing test than the control group. This is because AI-powered software like Gemini can provide students with immediate feedback on their writing, help them identify and correct errors, and suggest ways to improve their writing.

Limitations:

One limitation of this experiment is that it is only conducted over a short period of time. It is possible that the effects of AI-powered software on writing literacy may not be seen until after a longer period of use. Another limitation is that the experiment is conducted in a controlled setting. It is possible that the results may not be generalizable to real-world settings.

Conclusion:

This experiment design can be used to test the hypothesis that AI-powered software like Gemini can improve college students' writing literacy. The results of this experiment will provide valuable information about the potential benefits of using AI-powered software in education.

SUMMARY

- ✓ Experimental research examines a causal relationship between two variables, the independent variable and the dependent variable.
- ✓ Experiments occur in a controlled environment where researchers can measure precisely the impact of the independent variable on the dependent variable.
- ✓ Generally, experimental research occurs in lab settings in strategic communication, especially for media and advertising effects.
- ✓ As the unique feature of experimental research, the treatment belongs to the independent variable, manipulated by the researcher.
- ✓ A manipulation check is a measure administered to participants who demonstrate their recognition of the manipulation of the independent variable.
- ✓ The participants in the experimental group receive the treatment whose impact the researcher is interested in.
- ✓ The participants in the control group do not receive the experimental treatment.
- ✓ While extraneous variables affect only the dependent variable, confounding variables affect both independent and dependent variables.
- ✓ In a laboratory experiment, researchers are able to identify the precise effects of the independent variable on the dependent variable.
- ✓ Before implementing experiments, researchers focus on creating an optimal environment guided by the experimental research checklist.
- ✓ Experimental design is a way to carefully plan an experiment scientifically, aiming to fulfill the academic expectation of causal (internal) validity.
- ✓ There are three primary types of experimental design: preexperimental, quasi-experimental, and true experimental.
- ✓ The four different types of true experimental design include the posttest-only control group design, the pretest-posttest control group design, the Solomon four-group design, and the factorial design.
- ✓ Reliability in experimental research refers to how close repeated experiments are to each other in their results.
- ✓ Validity is more important than reliability in experimental research because it represents the entire experimental concept.
- ✓ Internal validity is a crucial measure in experimental research that deals with the true cause of results.
- ✓ The main goal of external validity is to achieve generalization of research results.

✓ Field experiments are designed to manipulate situations in a natural setting or outside of laboratories.

✓ AI tools can support students in organizing their experiments, designing robust studies, and collecting and managing data effectively.

Key Terms

1. Treatment
2. Causal relationship
3. Manipulation
4. Extraneous variables
5. Validity
6. Experimental/control group
7. Quasi-experimental design
8. True experimental research design
9. Reliability
10. Field experiments

Chapter 13
Content Analysis

Chapter Learning Outcomes

- Recognize the main purpose of content analysis.
- Explain how data are obtained for content analysis.
- Identify texts used for content analysis.
- Describe detailed steps of conducting content analysis.
- Discuss advantages of content analysis.
- Apply statistical tests to quantitative content analysis.
- Differentiate between semiotic analysis and rhetoric analysis.
- Discuss how qualitative content analysis is applied.
- Explain coding, categorization, and intercoder reliability.
- Perform a coding process with social media campaigns.
- Become familiar with the unique design of content analysis research.
- Identify coding schemes.
- Revolutionize content analysis with artificial intelligence.

Strategic communication research encompasses a wide array of topics, including communication systems, platforms, channels, technologies, and their impacts. The field involves the analysis of human behavior to understand how individuals, organizations, and governments communicate within society. Ethical practices are paramount in both qualitative and quantitative research methods involving human participants, such as interviews, focus groups, ethnography, surveys, and laboratory and field experiments. While the majority of strategic communication research centers on human-involved communication activities, content analysis stands out as a unique research method that scrutinizes nonhuman behavior in communication.

Content analysis is primarily used to examine media content, including newspaper and magazine articles, TV show characters, and social media posts. This research method entails a systematic investigation and analysis of recorded information in texts, images, and symbolic material, distinguishing it from other communication research methods that rely on data from human participants. Researchers can employ this method to gather data on traditional and social media content and analyze them for valuable insights beneficial to the media, the entertainment industries, and the academic community. It is crucial to note that the term *content* covers a variety of communication artifacts or messages, such as words, videos, news articles, social media posts, and website images. Researchers categorize content analysis into two types based on the analytical techniques used: quantitative content analysis and qualitative content analysis.

Quantitative Content Analysis

Quantitative content analysis is employed in quantitative research to scrutinize communication content using various techniques. The goal is to identify specific traits or messages conveyed through media data, which can encompass both textual content and media images. Researchers using the quantitative content analysis technique presume that texts and images in traditional and social media reflect significant social issues pertinent to public life. To reveal notable characteristics or messages, these texts and images are gathered and analyzed through systematic coding, assessment of keyword frequency, time and space measurements. A fundamental concept of quantitative content analysis is *measuring the manifest*, which refers to the counting of observable and tangible properties exhibited in printed or aired media, as well as those presented through visual or spoken communication.

According to Bernard Berelson's book *Content Analysis in Communication Research*, employing quantitative content analysis assists strategic communication researchers in achieving the following objectives:

- Uncover global differences in communication content.
- Detect the presence of messages in the media.
- Identify the intentions, focus, or communication trends of an individual, group, or institution in communicating with target audiences.
- Describe attitudinal and behavioral responses to messages intended for target audiences.
- Identify patterns of specific messages in context.[1]

How to Conduct a Quantitative Content Analysis

Conducting a quantitative content analysis involves eight key steps:

1. Identify content analysis topics: Remember, content analysis does not require human participants for your research. Any media content that piques your interest can lead to the discovery of a research topic from an academic perspective.
2. Formulate a hypothesis or research question: With the topic you are interested in, develop your own hypothesis or research question that guides you in determining what data to collect.
3. Decide the unit of content to be analyzed: Determine the specific segment of content that you seek to analyze (e.g., texts, images, signs, television shows, videos).
4. Sample the content: Choose a sample from your units of content and see if the sample contains specific patterns, concepts, characteristics, messages, or themes that can be representative of the population.
5. Construct a coding scheme: Set categories to classify the content into meaningful and relevant groups.
6. Check intercoder reliability: Share the process of classifying content into categories with another coder to check if their classification agrees with your own.
7. Analyze the results: Find patterns or characteristics in the content and analyze them using the appropriate analysis method.
8. Make interpretations: If possible, generalize your conclusions and discuss social trends or reflections of the real world in the content you analyzed.

Fundamental Elements of Quantitative Content Analysis

From these eight steps, we recognize three fundamental elements of quantitative content analysis: coding, categorization, and intercoder reliability.

- Coding: A code is a label or name unit, and coding is the process of labeling or naming your data, dividing it into different segments or classifications to discover any patterns in the content. Coding in content analysis is similar to identifying categories of answers to a survey that summarize the responses and place them into different groups for comparison. For example, if you were to code corporate slogans such as Nike's "Just Do It," you would analyze the slogans into words or phrases that represent the product's or company's identity and place them in categories such as inspiration, emotion, persuasion, command, or description. If you had to place the Nike slogan into one of these categories, you would decide which category it belongs to, perhaps command or inspiration. This is an example of coding in content analysis.
- Categorization: A category is formed by researchers who place coded units together into different groups. Hence, codes are organized into a category of

similar content that shows a particular pattern. Researchers need to decide how many and what units are to be coded for the categorization process. For example, if you as a researcher wanted to conduct research on the tendency for fashion magazines to feature pictures of femininity, the photos obtained for your content analysis could be categorized into several body types, such as triangle, rectangle, diamond, oval, and hourglass.[2]

- Intercoder reliability: When you conduct quantitative content analysis, you go through the categorization and coding process after data collection. You decide how to divide the coded data into each category, but you need to ensure that the coded data were placed into the correct category. Intercoder reliability ensures that your categorization process was performed reasonably in comparison with another coder. In other words, intercoder reliability demonstrates that independent coders participate in the coding process and agree or disagree with the categorization created by you. For example, suppose you and your classmate, as an independent coder, try to code and categorize dozens of news articles about the billionaire divorce between Amazon founder Jeff Bezos and his wife MacKenzie Scott. Your categorization of the articles includes the interpretation of article tone, such as positive for Bezos, positive for MacKenzie, negative for Bezos, negative for Mackenzie, and neither. You and the coder chose one article, and you coded the article as negative for Bezos, but the coder coded it as neither. This is an example of coder disagreement, and in this case, intercoder reliability is low. Simply put, intercoder reliability measures the extent to which the different coders tend to assign the same coded unit into the same category. One simple formula among many to measure intercoder reliability is given in Table 13.1.

Coding Scheme and Design of Quantitative Content Analysis

While quantitative content analysis is considered one of the quantitative research methods, it has some distinctive features, including the coding scheme and the research design,

Table 13.1

One of many formulas for intercoder reliability	Exercise
$PA = A / n \times 100$	Suppose you and your coder coded 50 news articles about the billionaire divorce, and you and your coder agree on the categories for 45 of the news articles. The intercoder reliability is:
PA = percentage agreement	$PA = 45 / 50 \times 100 = 90\%$
A = number of agreements n = number of units coded	It should be noted that although there is no fixed agreement on the absolute level of intercoder reliability, researchers generally take 70% or higher as an acceptable level.

especially for data obtained from texts, images, symbols, and so on, as opposed to directly from human participants. Since the research design and coding scheme of quantitative content analysis are unique features, we should understand how to begin and end the research design in quantitative content analysis through a step-by-step process, and we will do so with an example of social media campaigns.

1. Find What Interests You

Imagine having a research interest in social media campaigns. You understand the impact of social media campaigns organized by influential organizations and politicians. Mainstream news media outlets use social media posts generated by these figures for their news stories, which ultimately inform the public of their messages. For example, even if you don't follow Kim Kardashian on Instagram, you may learn about her divorce from Kanye West from news articles written by entertainment journalists who use Instagram posts as news sources. Another example is Elon Musk tweeting about new Tesla models, including the Cybertruck. You don't need to follow him on X, as the media will alert you if Musk tweets anything new about Tesla vehicles. You can observe how powerful and famous people use social media to enhance their interests and recognize the theoretical and practical importance of social media from both critical theory and marketing perspectives.

2. Decide the Topic

Based on your theoretical and conceptual framework of the relationship between social media and powerful people's promotion of their interests, you explore the relationship between social media and powerful people's promotion of their interests. Specifically, you conduct research on President Donald Trump's use of Twitter (now X) and his strategic communication tactics for his political agenda. Your research title is "The Art of Donald Trump's Tweets in a Narrative Fantasy Paradigm," and you analyze how Trump created an alternative reality through his Twitter messages. With approximately 24,000 tweets during his presidency, Trump was known as the king of Twitter.[3] Therefore, you are using his tweets as your research data because they demonstrate his unfiltered opinions about controversial social issues and how he thought about other people. Journalists often reproduced and commented on his tweets as news sources, and the public was exposed to his daily posts through TV news, newspaper websites, and talk shows.

3. See If the Content Analysis Is Applicable

To gather information on Trump's thoughts and feelings during his presidency, you decided to analyze his personal Twitter account, which exclusively featured text-based tweets. As you sift through his tweets from January 20, 2017, to January 20, 2021, it becomes clear that Twitter was Trump's outlet for unfiltered and controversial expression. Each tweet garnered significant media attention due to its often insulting content, making it a newsworthy source. You opt for content analysis as your research method, as it allows for the analysis of media texts without involving human participants, making it ideal for examining social media content in all its forms. Additionally, the majority of the raw material is readily available online, making it easily accessible for research purposes. You collect your data for the content analysis from the Trump Tweet Archive at https://www.thetrumparchive.com.

4. Explore Data Availability

The next step is to define the content you want to explore. Since Trump's tweets were aimed to spread his messages to the public, you assume that his tweets may or may not reflect his views on reality in the real world. You investigate whether his tweets demonstrate issues or agendas that are relevant to the way he creates a reality for himself as a private citizen or for others as president of the United States. As an avid news consumer during the Trump presidency, you used to read news articles and watch television news every day, wondering which tweets by Trump grabbed the media's attention. In addition, you were curious about what Trump tweeted about as part of his daily activity with what messages he intended for the public. It is noteworthy that you are pleased with the fact that you have more than enough data available for your research, but it also feels overwhelming because of the massive amount of data. Since you will not go through all tweets, you plan to sample 10 percent of his entire tweets.

5. Choose a Sample and Sampling Method

In your sampling process, the population is all Trump's tweets ($N = 24{,}000$), and the sample is 10 percent of the population ($n = 2{,}400$). The sample size of 2,400 seems reasonable and doable for your research if the tweets are randomly selected. You decide to use systematic sampling, a probability sampling method in which sample units from a larger population are selected beginning at a random starting point and proceeding at a fixed, periodic interval. In other words, you use the *n*th technique for the random sampling process. As the archive website offers all records of Trump's tweets in chronological order, you choose your lucky number 7, and every seventh tweet is obtained and examined. You go over all the 2,400 tweets as the units for coding, trying to discover some patterns or unique characteristics based on the content of his tweets.

6. Develop Categories as a Coding Scheme

After selecting the units for coding, you set up a coding scheme that consists of a set of codes defined by the words or phrases that you determine for classifying the data by topic or theme. In the coding scheme, you first create categories into which the units will be placed. In other words, based on the category definitions you have decided upon, each tweet unit is assigned a code corresponding to its category. In your Trump tweet case, it is impossible to develop a coding scheme in advance because you cannot predict what Trump has tweeted about until you examine the tweets. Hence, you go over each tweet of the sample and identify specific and common topics or themes he tweeted about. You may establish a list of seven categories from the sample of his tweets:

- Media bias/fake news
- National security/Russia
- Economy/jobs
- Foreign policy/America first
- Immigration/border wall
- Health care/Obamacare
- The opponent's problems/Democrats

From the 2,400 sample tweets, you identify this list of seven categories on which Trump's tweets were focused. For quantitative content analysis, you need to code the tweets, place each coded tweet (unit) into one of the categories, and then count the number for each category. When coding and categorizing the tweets, you maintain the standards of the coding scheme. For example, your coding scheme should have clear standards as shown in Table 13.2.

7. Ensure That the Categories Are Mutually Exclusive and Collectively Exhaustive

While coding and placing the units into categories in the coding scheme process, you pay attention to two important principles of coding schemes: that codes are mutually exclusive and collectively exhaustive. The units being placed into categories must be mutually

Table 13.2 Coding Scheme Examples

Category	An example of Trump's tweets
Media bias/fake news	It is just more Fake News. Actually, I find it very sad to watch!
National security/ Russia	No, Russia did not help me get elected. You know who got me elected? I got me elected. Russia did not help me at all.
Economy/jobs	GDP number just announced. Biggest and Best in the History of our Country.
Foreign policy/ America first	AMERICA FIRST, and MAKE AMERICA GREAT AGAIN, will have a GIANT VOICE long into the future.
Immigration/border walls	I will be signing an Executive Order to temporarily suspend immigration into the United States.
Health care/ Obamacare	ObamaCare must be fully repealed or it will destroy America's small businesses.
The opponent's problems/Democrats	Biden can only enter the White House as President if he can prove that his ridiculous "80,000,000 votes" were not fraudulently or illegally obtained.

exclusive, meaning that each tweet can be assigned to one and only one category. For example, suppose one of Trump's tweets says, "Why does the Fake News Media continuously assume Sleepy and Crazy Joe Biden is going to win?" You code and place the tweet into one of the categories, and you see a problem since the tweet could be placed into either the "The opponent's problems/Democrats" category or the "Media bias/fake news" category. You must put it into one category, not both. As a result, the coding scheme in content analysis requires mutual exclusivity. Being collectively exhaustive refers to the requirement that categories cannot overlap. If you add one more category to the coding scheme, the new category should be distinct from the other categories. For example, if a new category, "COVID vaccine," is added, it could overlap with the category "Health care/Obamacare," and the new category violates the collectively exhaustive principle. Thus, it is recommended that you add an extra category for a minimal number of units that belong to none of the other categories.

8. Code and Count Frequency

Your coding scheme examples should provide clear coding principles for both you and another coder to use as a set of instructions for coding each tweet. By going over each tweet together and sorting them into categories, the coding scheme will demonstrate how many tweets belong in each category. For instance, you and your coder may agree on a frequency table like that in Table 13.3.

Once you and your coder have completed your respective coding tables and adjusted the difference, the frequency table will be finalized. This requires you and your coder to fill out the frequency table and compare the results. If any discrepancies are found, an intercoder reliability test should be conducted with a minimum threshold of 70% or, better, over 80%.[4] Once both parties agree on the final coding scheme, the results can be placed into the appropriate categories on the frequency table.

Table 13.3 Data Frequency of Trump's Tweets

Category	Number of tweets	Percentage
Media bias/fake news	630	26.25
National security/Russia	201	8.34
Economy/jobs	385	16.07
Foreign policy/America first	278	11.58
Immigration/border walls	456	19.1
Health care/Obamacare	130	5.52
The opponent's problems/Democrats	247	10.04
Other	73	3.1
Total	2,400	100

Inferential Statistics of Quantitative Content Analysis

The content analysis of Trump's tweets provides a percentage categorization of the topics or themes the former president tweeted about. This simple description of the tweet content frequency can be interesting and useful, as it demonstrates his love-hate relationship with the media. Trump was known for his friendly relationship with conservative media outlets and his troubled relationship with liberal media outlets. The example of Trump's tweets in a content analysis demonstrates the fundamental basics of what content analysis is and how content analysis is conducted from the viewpoint of descriptive statistics. Researchers who specialize in quantitative content analysis include the aspect of descriptive statistics as an important part of their research results, but their scholarly research goes further with the use of inferential statistics with hypothesis testing.

Given that the fictional frequency table for our example reveals Trump's biggest Twitter interest—the media—you, as a researcher, formulate a hypothesis to figure out what triggered his tweeting habit about the media. Based on the knowledge about his too obvious love-hate relationship with conservative and liberal media outlets, you further seek whether the way the media framed their news stories about the Trump administration provoked his polarized relationship with conservative and liberal media outlets. News framing has to do with how news outlets select an agenda based on a perception of reality and how they support that agenda by the perspectives from which news stories are told. You assume that journalists reporting particular issues or agendas tend to use biased sources for their personal news angles as an aspect of news framing. You argue that journalists select, emphasize, and present news stories in a way that fulfills the expectation of their media companies from a framing perspective.

Based on the news framing concept and Trump's tweets about the media, your research question and hypothesis are as follows:

> RQ_1: Is the news coverage of President Trump predominantly framed in a way that meets the media angles derived from their conservative or liberal bias?
>
> H_a: Conservative and liberal media outlets will differ in their news coverage of President Trump in terms of tone, or the way a media outlet speaks to its audience.

Now you need to decide what media outlets you use and what framing categories you identify for the content analysis. To make the process simple, you select Fox News and CNN as the most representative sample for conservative and liberal media outlets during the Trump presidency. You collect all news articles about Trump published by Fox News and CNN. You may find too many articles from each site, so you decide to sample 100 articles from each site by using systematic sampling. After obtaining 100 articles each as the units of data, you and your coder go through the coding process. For the way Fox News and CNN frame news stories about Trump, you categorize the units as (1) positive tone or (2) negative tone. Your coding sheet could appear as shown in Box 13.1.

Box 13.1
CODING DIRECTIONS FOR A STUDY COMPARING NEWS OUTLETS FRAMING FOR OR AGAINST TRUMP

A. Identity the news outlet for each article (Fox News 1; CNN 2).

B. Tone of the news article (positive 1; negative 2).

The reason for the numbers 1 and 2 is to identify the tone of each article on a nominal scale for when you place the data into statistical software such as SPSS or Excel. After you and your coder separately examine 200 articles, 100 each from both Fox News and CNN, all coded news articles will be compared for intercoder reliability. Suppose that you and the coder have agreed on the coding and placed the articles into a frequency table as shown in Table 13.4.

For researchers to conduct hypothesis testing of a quantitative content analysis, the chi-square test is commonly performed to determine whether there is a statistically significant difference between the levels of the variables. There are multiple ways of calculating chi-square for hypothesis testing: (1) by hand, (2) using statistical software, or (3) using an online chi-square calculator (https://www.socscistatistics.com/tests/chisquare/default2.aspx).

After filling in the category information in the boxes on the website, you will obtain the results from the calculator. You conclude that there is a statistical difference between news outlets for the coverage tone of Trump: χ^2 (1, $n = 200$) = 124.97, $p < .05$. (APA-style reporting of chi-square: χ^2 (df, n = sample size) = chi-square statistic value, $p = p$ value.) You observe that Fox News published the greatest number of positive news articles about

Table 13.4 Data Frequency of News Outlets and Tone

		Media outlets	
		Fox News	**CNN**
Tone	Positive	91	42
	Negative	9	88

Table 13.5 An Example of a Multiple Frequency Table

		Media outlets			
		Fox News	***Wall Street Journal***	**CNN**	***New York Times***
Tone	Positive				
	Negative				
	Neutral				

Trump, as opposed to CNN, which published the greatest number of negative news articles about Trump. The difference is statistically significant based on the quantitative content analysis. The table you used is called a 2×2 contingency table, with two columns and two rows. The method of quantitative content analysis allows you to add more categories to a frequency table for a more detailed analysis. If you want to add the websites of newspaper companies in the columns and neutral tone in the rows, a new table (4×3) of frequency categories is formed, as shown in Table 13.5.

Traditionally, quantitative content analysis in strategic communication has been used to analyze types of violence in newspapers, portrayals of race on television shows, and objectification of bodies in movies and advertising. For example, female characters of the James Bond movies, aka the Bond girls, are often analyzed in content analyses. In a 2007 journal article, the researchers analyzed 20 James Bond movies from 1962 (*Dr. No*) to 2002 (*Die Another Day*), aiming to discover how female characters were portrayed over time in the moves.[5] They created a coding sheet for the sexual objectification of Bond girls, as shown in Box 13.2.[6]

Box 13.2
Coding Sheet for the Portrayal of Bond Girls

Coding and Coder Instruction Sheet for Female Body Objectification of Bond Girls

A. Hair color: Indicate what color hair the female character has

1. Blond (all shades from the palest blond to dark blond) 2. Red (all shades from the lightest red to deep red) 3. Light Brown (mostly brown with some blond highlights) 4. Medium Brown (brown with no blond highlights) 5. Dark Brown (brown and almost appearing black) 6. Black 7. Gray (all or predominantly gray)

B. Hair Style: Indicate the style of the female character's hair according to the following categories:

   1. Straight (hair appears to be straight) 2. Wavy (hair appears to have some waves and is not completely straight but not totally curly) 3. Curly (hair appears to have mostly curls) 4. Afro (hair appears to have very tight curls)

C. Height: Indicate whether the female character is tall (5′8″ or more), medium (5′4″–5′7″), or short (5′3″ or less). Assess this with the assumption that Bond is approximately 6 feet tall.

   1. Tall 2. Medium 3. Short

D. Physical Appearance: Indicate whether the female character is extremely attractive (professional model status), attractive (very pleasant looking, above average), average (pleasant looking but average in looks), below average (not pleasant looking, below average in looks), extremely unattractive (extremely unpleasant looking, or considered ugly).

   1. Extremely Attractive 2. Attractive 3. Average 4. Below Average 5. Extremely Unattractive

E. Body Size: (from Thompson & Gray, 1995). Using the female figures below, indicate the number that best matches the shape of the female character's body.

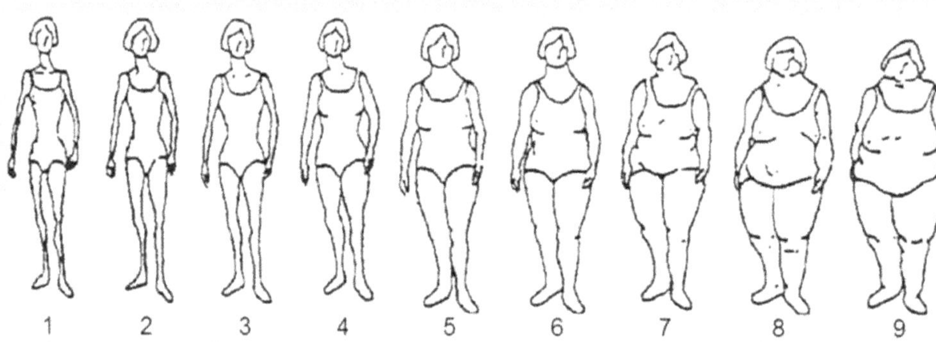

QUALITATIVE CONTENT ANALYSIS

While quantitative and qualitative content analyses share the common goal of categorizing data to identify patterns or themes in recorded or written communication, they differ in their approach to creating categories and analyzing data. Quantitative content analysis focuses on the frequency of specific texts for statistical testing, while qualitative content analysis interprets the content of textual data subjectively to find meaning. Researchers who specialize in qualitative research are more interested in constructing meaning from messages in texts, rather than counting the frequency of occurrences for hypothesis testing. Therefore, qualitative content analysis typically concentrates on discussing the implications of textual meaning as researchers aim to discover socially constructed meaning within data sets, often obtained from media texts. In summary, researchers use qualitative content analysis to analyze textual data, commonly obtained from online or offline media content, rather than data gathered from human participants.

Textual Analysis

The research method of qualitative content analysis has its roots in textual analysis. This approach involves describing and interpreting various types of texts, including those found in traditional media, social media, and advertising. By analyzing the content of the texts, researchers can connect them with social or cultural issues and explain underlying phenomena from a social or cultural context. In strategic communication research, textual analysis is used to describe and interpret the characteristics of texts that contain specific types of messages. Before applying the two major approaches of rhetorical analysis and semiotic analysis in qualitative content analysis, it is important to understand the methodological principles of these approaches.

- Rhetorical analysis: The word *rhetoric* is associated with Aristotle's definition, the art of persuasion. Rhetorical analysis guides researchers in breaking down a whole text into pieces for the purpose of examination in pursuit of an explanation of what arguments or messages are implied to persuade the audience.[7] Looking at texts, researchers analyze what is happening in the text, why the author might have chosen to use a particular move or set of rhetorical moves, and how those choices might affect the audience. Since Aristotle divided rhetoric into two fields—public speech and discussion—rhetorical analysis has advanced into explaining how writers or speakers relate their written or spoken messages to specific social situations in hopes of attempting to influence others through discourse. A core concept of rhetorical analysis is the rhetorical situation, in which the communicative context of a text is comprehensively understood in the situation where the message was created. Using rhetorical analysis, researchers apply the big three rhetorical elements to analyze how well the messages reach out to the audience:

    1. Ethos/credibility: How does the writer or speaker convey the validity and importance of the message based on reliable sources and trustworthiness?
    2. Pathos/emotion: How do messages influence the audience's emotions of happiness, sympathy, anger, courage, resentment, sadness, etc., through written or spoken communication?

3. Logos/logic: What proof does the writer or speaker provide to gain the trust of the audience, and with what persuasive techniques such as repetition, inductive logic, or deductive logic?

- Semiotic analysis: Semiotics is a field of study that explores the creation and transmission of meaning through the use of signs and symbols within society. It involves analyzing written, spoken, and visual communication to understand their functions. Experts in strategic communication use semiotic analysis to examine the language of signs and symbols present in media texts. For example, an advertisement is semiotically analyzed for its signs, symbols, and meanings transmitted to the target audience. Semiotic analysis identifies two key components of communication transmission regarding the expression of meaning via signs: (1) the signifier, which refers to the physical sign, including images or letters conveying meaning, and (2) the signified, which refers to the personal interpretation of a signifier. When each signifier has a signified, an act of semiotic communication is constructed, meaning that together they create a sign or symbol in society. A good example is the word *dope*. If we take the spoken word *dope* as the signifier, the signified might refer to illicit drugs in one context or situation. But in another, it might refer to something as excellent or great, so the relationship between signifier and signified can change over time and in different contexts.[8] Semiotics from a strategic communication perspective can be viewed as the study of marketing signs and symbols. Semiotic analysis is designed to take a deeper look into the purchasing patterns that shape consumer behavior in association with their responses to advertising messages in visual images transmitted through traditional and social media.

Design and Scenario of Qualitative Content Analysis

Suppose you conduct qualitative content analysis about alcohol advertising after the COVID-19 pandemic. You are interested in the relationship between alcohol commercials and alcohol consumption patterns as affected by the virus. Your research question is formulated as follows:

> *RQ*: How are alcohol brands reinventing their marketing campaigns after the COVID-19 pandemic in the United States and the world?

The coronavirus crisis caused people to stay indoors and limited their outside activities, leading to an increase in alcohol consumption. News articles reported that parents, in particular, were drinking more alcohol to cope with stress and frustration. This piqued your interest in how alcohol companies were adapting their advertising strategies during these challenging times. To investigate this further, you plan to collect data on alcohol product advertising on both traditional and social media platforms. Additionally, you are interested in understanding the cultural values associated with alcohol consumption in different countries. Using qualitative content analysis, you aim to examine how alcohol companies are using the pandemic as an opportunity to promote global marketing campaigns for increased alcohol consumption. Specifically, you will analyze their campaign signs, symbols, images, and words to interpret the social and marketing implications of their messaging.

You justify the reason you use qualitative content analysis as your research method by arguing that the method leads you to systematically code and categorize the textual data. As a result, you will discover any patterns in the campaign texts and the themes of their messages. The collected data draw on the period between March 2020 and January 2023 when the pandemic influenced human lives around the world. You do keyword searches on Google and social media platforms to explore data about marketing and advertising campaigns by alcohol brands during the research period, and you gather all alcohol advertisements promoted both in traditional media such as television, newspapers, and magazines and on social media platforms, especially with the hashtag (#) campaigns all around the world.

After examining each unit of alcohol product advertisement—for example, a television commercial, newspaper ad, or hashtagged promotion on X—you qualitatively code and categorize all units and classify them with specific themes. You may point out that four key themes emerge:

1. Alcohol brands send the message of becoming a part of combating the crisis.
2. Alcohol brands send the message of contributing to the community hit by the virus.
3. Alcohol brands reemphasize the party spirit during quarantine.
4. Alcohol brands utilize the visual images of face masks and social distancing in their promotional campaigns.

In qualitative content analysis, you need to demonstrate textual evidence for each theme as shown in Table 13.6.

Qualitative content analysis in the digital age is commonly used to analyze online texts and images. Researchers select hashtag campaigns in the social media world, exploring and analyzing particular social issues. They choose one specific hashtag campaign nationally known in social media (e.g., #IceBucketChallenge, #MeToo, #Coronavirus, #Swifties, #Bitcoin, #UkraineWar, #ActOnClimate, #StopAI) and then collect textual data relevant to the campaign from social media platforms. For example, a research team collected X (Twitter) data on the #ToiletPaperEmergency in the early stage of the coronavirus when consumers were overhoarding toilet paper. The researchers used a qualitative

Table 13.6 Themes and Evidence of Unit in Qualitative Content Analysis

Themes	**Unit of each theme**
Combating COVID	Vodka brand Grey Goose provides the essential alcohol needed for hand sanitizer, partnering with @Loreal.  Source: Grey Goose Vodka (fair use).
Contributing to the community	Rum brand Bacardi commits $3 million to provide financial aid to the bar and restaurant industry impacted by the COVID-19 crisis through #RaiseYourSpirits. #RAISEYOURSPIRITS Source: Bacardi (fair use).
Reemphasizing the party spirit	Tequila brand Jose Cuervo launches a social media campaign "Who's Making Margs?" featuring a series of parties hosted by celebrity influencers.  Source: Jose Cuervo (fair use).
Utilizing COVID prevention visual images	Beer brand Dos Equis offers beer drinkers a unique way to measure social distancing: a 6-foot cooler.  Source: Dos Equis (fair use).

content analysis on the data to identify sentimental themes that fell into five categories: (1) humor or sarcasm, (2) marketing or profiteering, (3) opinion and emotions, (4) personal experience, and (5) support or information.[9] Based on the X content analysis, they found that "the spontaneous contagion of fear and panic through social media could fuel psychological reactions in the midst of crises," and negative social media posts regarding toilet paper purchasing behavior could trigger "public anxiety and panic."[10]

Revolutionizing Content Analysis With Artificial Intelligence

Content analysis, the meticulous dissection of communication content, transcends mere counting and categorization. It empowers researchers to delve into the heart of strategic communication, unlocking its nuances and revealing its impact on individuals and societies. Whether conducted quantitatively, measuring frequencies and distributions, or qualitatively, exploring deeper meanings and emotions, it illuminates the how and why behind powerful messages. In our contemporary era of digital communication, the significance of content analysis has soared. The profusion of online content, ranging from social media posts to digital news articles, presents a vast repository for research. Content analysis serves as the key to unraveling trends, patterns, and the profound impacts of digital communication.

Imagine AI-powered text analysis tools seamlessly scanning thousands of social media posts, instantly capturing sentiment shifts and identifying emerging topics. Picture machine learning algorithms meticulously categorizing news articles, uncovering hidden biases and framing techniques. These are just a few examples of how AI supercharges content analysis for college students:

- Faster data processing: Imagine a research project on social media reactions to a political campaign. Instead of manually coding of thousands of tweets on X, AI tools can automate the process, identifying positive, negative, and neutral sentiment, freeing up time for deeper analysis.
- Enhanced accuracy: AI algorithms trained on vast data sets can achieve remarkable accuracy in categorizing text, minimizing human error, and ensuring reliable results.
- Unveiling hidden patterns: Complex statistical techniques like topic modeling, powered by AI, can reveal hidden thematic structures within large data sets, offering insights into complex social phenomena.[11]
- Deeper qualitative analysis: Qualitative coding software assisted by AI can help researchers manage and organize interview transcripts and other qualitative data, allowing them to focus on interpreting meaning and identifying key themes.[12]

By embracing the potential of AI in content analysis, college students can not only delve deeper into their research questions but also develop valuable skills coveted in today's data-driven world. AI can uncover the hidden meanings in communication content, reveal the strategies used by communicators, and gain insights into the effects of these strategies on audiences. In the digital age, the combination of content analysis and AI offers a powerful tool for navigating the complex landscape of strategic communication.

Application of an AI-Powered Tool

Box 13.3
Example of Using Microsoft Copilot for Content Analysis

Using an AI-Powered Tool (Microsoft Copilot) for Content Analysis
Command syntax: Act as a content analysis expert and explain how to apply content analysis to TikTok tutorial videos about how to use Microsoft Copilot for college assignments.

Answer: Sure, content analysis is a research method used to identify patterns and themes in communication data. To apply content analysis to TikTok tutorial videos about how to use Microsoft Copilot for college assignments, you could follow these steps:

1. Define your research question: What do you want to learn from analyzing these videos?
2. Select a sample of videos: Choose a representative sample of TikTok tutorial videos about how to use Bing AI Chat for college assignments.
3. Develop a coding scheme: Create a set of categories and rules for coding the data in the videos.
4. Code the data: Apply the coding scheme to the videos and record the results.
5. Analyze the data: Use statistical methods to analyze the coded data and draw conclusions.

When developing a coding scheme for TikTok tutorial videos about how to use Microsoft Copilot for college assignments, you could consider categories such as:

- Video content: What topics are covered in the video? Are there any specific tips or tricks mentioned?
- Video style: Is the video informative or entertaining? Is it fast paced or slow paced?

- Video creator: Who created the video? Are they a student, teacher, or influencer?
- Video engagement: How many views, likes, and comments does the video have?

When selecting a sample of videos to analyze, you could consider factors such as:

- Relevance: Are the videos relevant to your research question?
- Popularity: Are the videos popular among TikTok users?
- Recency: Are the videos recent and up to date?

Summary

✓ Content analysis is the most popular research method for analyzing media content such as newspaper and magazine articles, characters in television shows, and social media posts.

✓ Content analysis is defined as the systematic investigation of a body of texts, images, and symbolic material.

✓ The "content" refers to various groups of communication messages printed or recorded in all forms of traditional and social media.

✓ The data of quantitative content analysis include both traditional textual content and media images.

✓ In quantitative content analysis, texts and images need to be collected and analyzed by systematic coding, keyword frequency, and time and space measurements.

✓ A code is understood as the unit of a label or name, and coding is the process of labeling or naming your data into different categories.

✓ Codes are associated with a category that contains similar content that shares a particular pattern.

✓ Intercoder reliability ensures that the coding and categorization process by the author was performed reasonably with another coder or coders.

✓ The units placed into the categories must be mutually exclusive, meaning that no unit of data fits into more than one category.

✓ Collectively exhaustive refers to the requirement that all possible outcomes or events are covered by the categories.

✓ Quantitative content analysis in strategic communication has been used to analyze types of violence in newspapers, portrayals of race on television shows, and objectification of bodies in movies and advertising.

✓ Rhetorical analysis guides researchers to break down a whole text into pieces for the purpose of examination in pursuit of an explanation of what arguments or messages are implied to persuade the audience.

✓ Whereas quantitative content analysis focuses on the frequency of specific texts for statistical tests, qualitative content analysis applies subjective interpretations of the content of textual data to find meaning.

✓ Semiotic analysis focuses on analyzing the functions of written, spoken, and visual signs that we use to communicate.

✓ Semiotics in a strategic communication perspective can be viewed as the study of marketing signs and symbols, and semiotic analysis is designed to take a deeper look into the purchasing patterns that shape consumer behavior.

✓ Content analysis is a useful research method in traditional and social media research thanks to the availability of online data.

✓ The symbiosis of content analysis and AI emerges as an indispensable tool for navigating the intricate landscape of strategic communication.

KEY TERMS

1. Texts
2. Quantitative content analysis
3. Qualitative content analysis
4. Code
5. Coding
6. Intercoder reliability
7. Mutual exclusivity
8. Themes
9. Semiotic analysis
10. Rhetoric analysis

Chapter 14

Reporting and Presentation of Research Findings

Chapter Learning Outcomes

- Recognize different types of academic writing styles.
- Explain the academic writing fundamentals based on the APA style.
- Identify the final paper structure.
- Discuss the importance of the discussion section.
- Apply the APA style to in-text citations and the reference section.
- Differentiate between student papers and conference papers.
- Discuss how title pages are organized.
- Explain the functions of an abstract.
- Acknowledge the existence of limitations in the research paper.
- Identify new trends in academic research papers in APA format.
- Leverage AI for scholarly research.

Having mastered the process of conducting academic research, we now turn our attention to the art of writing an academic research paper. Understanding qualitative and quantitative research methods equips researchers with the knowledge of key concepts and practices such as sampling, data analysis, the literature review, and research ethics. With social media emerging as the primary platform for most organizations and the public, the field of strategic communication provides a plethora of research areas to delve into. While traditional media outlets like television, newspapers, radio, and magazines have been overshadowed by social media, some researchers still explore topics within traditional media. Nevertheless, the predominant trend in strategic communication research has shifted toward social media, resulting in a notable increase in research papers over the past decade. This trend is expected to continue, especially with the integration of AI, as college students, who represent the future of research, are proficient in utilizing various social media platforms.

Numerous colleges mandate that students enroll in research courses prior to graduation. If your major is in advertising, public relations, journalism, or communication/

media studies, you will likely need to take at least one communication research course. These courses facilitate the identification of research interests and topics related to human communication between organizations and their target audiences, business-to-business communication, or interpersonal communication. A specific research course, strategic communication, zeroes in on research topics pertinent to media campaign strategies and tactics. In this course, students learn how strategic communicators utilize traditional and social media to disseminate corporate or organizational messages to target audiences with the intent of persuasion. If you are enrolled in this course, you will likely discover intriguing research topics related to social media marketing, media effects, advertising, public relations campaigns, and media strategies for local or national elections.

HOW TO WRITE THE FINAL RESEARCH PAPER

In the research course, students are urged to develop their own research topic and conduct research. To formulate research questions and/or hypotheses, students examine and read scholarly articles. As part of the data collection process, students select a sample of participants and observe, administer, or interview them based on the chosen research method. Upon completion of data collection, students employ analytical techniques to derive their findings. While these steps adhere to academic research standards, the final research paper often poses the most formidable and overwhelming challenge for students.

Despite the successful execution of research and data analysis, completion of the final research paper is necessary to meet course requirements. Although it may be challenging, it is a feasible task for most students. To college students, writing papers for class can often seem like a daunting task. It can be exhausting, time consuming, and stressful, particularly with the added pressure of grades. Professors anticipate that students will submit papers that are meticulously crafted, original, and scholarly, with absolutely no signs of plagiarism. Those majoring in strategic communication are subject to even more stringent writing standards. Nonetheless, it is worth noting that the process of writing a research paper presents a valuable opportunity for students to refine their academic writing abilities, including the cultivation of distinct styles and structures.

RESEARCH PAPER STYLES AND FORMATS

The three most popular research paper styles among researchers are the APA (American Psychological Association), the *Chicago Manual of Style* (*CMOS*), and the Modern Language Association (MLA). The APA is predominantly used in the academic fields of social science, business, and communication. The *CMOS* is favored in the field of history, including journalism history, while the MLA is typically reserved for writers in English studies.

For research in strategic communication, we adhere to the APA style. In late 2019, the 7th edition of the style was introduced, and researchers in strategic communication strive to incorporate the main guidelines of writing format into their research papers. These guidelines serve as a foundation for effective scholarly communication, outlining the paper preparation with regard to font, font size, margins, and spacing. They are easy to follow, and no mistakes can be made, as follows:

- Use a standard font: 12-point Times New Roman.
- Use 1-inch margins on every side of the page.
- Double-space all parts of the paper, including the abstract, text, and block quotations.
- Include a page number on every page.
- If submitting for publication, insert a running head on every page.
- Indent the first line of each paragraph of text 0.5 inch.[1]

It gets more complicated when we deal with the guidelines for in-text citations and the mechanics of APA style. Here are the 10 most important matters students need to pay attention to, according to the *APA Style and Grammar Guidelines*:[2]

1. Citing a quote: When creating a citation for a quote, you provide the author's last name, the year, and the page number for both narrative and parenthetical citations. Here are two examples:
    a. According to Muskin (2024), "Students are capable of making profits in Bitcoin, but they should know the consequences of failure" (p. 91).
    b. A study found that "students are more likely to purchase products from companies that apply zero-carbon technology to their facilities" (Guerra, 2024, p. 52).
2. Citing two authors or more than two authors: When a citation has two authors, you cite both authors' last names. When a citation has three or more authors, include the last name of the first author followed by "et al." Here are two examples:
    a. Flins and Korry (1995) argued that the writing process could be compared to a walk on unpaved roads with the moon in the sky.
    b. A more traditional campaign may have been overwhelmed by the broad reactions to social and cultural beliefs of the younger generation in the digital age (Whittle et al., 2025).

If the author and date are unknown (this usually happens for online sources), use the first word or two of the title in the parentheses and use the abbreviation "n.d." for no date, for example: The document illustrates the history of global wars against starvation ("World drought," n.d.).

3. Paraphrasing: When presenting someone's sentence or idea in your paper, you either quote or paraphrase it. A paraphrase is a restatement of a text in your own

words, used to deliver and synthesize information more concisely. When paraphrasing, you cite the original work using either the narrative or parenthetical citation format. Since there exists a fine line between plagiarism and paraphrasing, you need to cite all original sources at the end of every paraphrased sentence or paragraph, including the attribution of credit to the original author for ideas. Here is an example: According to *New York Times* columnist Thomas L. Friedman, the world is flat from a globalization perspective (1999).

4. Using the right punctuation: When placing punctuation, be sure you use the right one. To pause, a comma (,), semicolon (;), or colon (:) is used.
   - A semicolon is used either to separate two independent clauses that are not joined by a conjunction or to combine sentences that are very closely related, for example: Researchers in communication tend to stay current with the media; they read newspapers and watch news programs even on Sundays.
   - A colon is used to list items, for example: There are mainly three things to do in life: maintain your body health, go to work, and celebrate living.
   - A comma is used between elements in a series of three or more items, for example: Humans are socially weird creatures according to a study by Smith, Greer, and Carey (2001).
5. Recognizing the difference between hyphens, en dashes, and em dashes:
   a. Hyphens (-) are used to join words/into a single concept, for example: A government-driven economy causes drastic inflation around 9%.
   b. En dashes are used to indicate ranges in numbers and dates as well as in forming complex compound adjectives: In the post–Civil War period, Andrew Johnson's administration (1865–1869) pushed for quick restoration of the seceded states to the Union.
   c. Em dashes (—) can be used to indicate an interruption, for example: The new smartphones—iPhone and Galaxy—will take us to the next level of the machine learning algorithm.
6. Using the right numbers: When using numbers, you spell out numbers below 10 and use numerals for 10 and above, for example: The research selected the participants who were in the eighth and ninth grades; students in the 10th and 11th grades were not selected. You ensure that numbers beginning a sentence are spelled out, for example: Thirteen participants were chosen from the group of cancer survivors. It is also important to use numerals that represent statistics, mathematical functions, or measurements, for example: 9.7 kg; 9% of participants; 5 hr, 46 min; 9-mg dose; divided by 7; 4 A.M.; the 3rd percentile; and a ratio of 10:3.

7. Using italics correctly: Italics are used when you first mention key terms or phrases, often accompanied by a definition, for example: *FOMO* is defined as "anxiety that an exciting or interesting event may currently be happening elsewhere, often aroused by posts seen on social media" (Lillie et al., 2018, p. 11). Make sure that italics are used for titles of books, films, web pages, TV shows, and other stand-alone works, for example: In the show *Friends*, Rachel Green and Joey Tribbiani became roommates and tried to have a romantic relationship. Another example is: *The Journal of American Strategic Communication* will include a special edition for articles about the use of virtual reality in the public relations industry.

8. Using bias-free language: When sexual orientation is mentioned, avoid the use of derogatory terms, such as *homo* or *tranny*, associated with negative stereotypes. Instead, use specific descriptors such as *lesbian woman*, *gay man*, or *transgender person*. When using terms to refer to socioeconomic status, avoid using broad, pejorative, and generalizing terms such as *the homeless*, *inner-city*, *ghetto*, *poverty stricken*, and *welfare reliant*. Instead, use more specific descriptions: "people whose incomes are below the federal poverty threshold," "people experiencing homelessness," and "people who are unable to work because of a disability." When it comes to legal status, avoid using *illegal aliens* and *illegal immigrants*. Instead, use "people who are undocumented," "DACA students," or "undocumented people from [the name of the country]."

9. Using the correct identity: When identifying participants' race or ethnicity, refer to race as physical differences that groups and cultures consider socially significant. Hence, the concept of race includes Alaska Native, African American or Black, Asian, European American or White, Native American, and Native Hawaiian or Pacific Islander. Regarding ethnicity, it pertains to shared cultural characteristics such as language, ancestry, practices, and beliefs. For example, ethnicity includes Mexican American, Chicano, and Cuban American. Whenever possible, use the racial and/or ethnic terms that your participants themselves use. When referring to non-White racial and ethnic groups collectively, use terms such as "people of color" or "underrepresented groups" rather than "minorities."

10. Referring to sex and gender: Since the language related to gender identity and sexual orientation has evolved rapidly, be careful when you refer to gender or sex. The term *gender* refers to a social construct and a social identity, and you are recommended to use specific terms such as *cisgender women*, *cisgender men*, *transgender women*, *transgender men*, and *nonbinary person*. The term *sex* refers to biological sex assignment, and you use men and women, or boys and girls.

11. Referring to age: When describing the age of participants, use appropriate terms according to their age groups. For example, an individual aged 12 years and younger is described as, a child, girl, or boy; an individual aged 13–17 years is described

Title of Your Paper

Your name

Department name, Institution name

Course number, Course name

Instructor's name

Due date

Figure 14.1 Title page structure
Source: Created by author.

as an adolescent, young person, or youth; and an individual aged 18 years and older is described as an adult, woman, or man. Traditional terms that describe older people—*the elderly*, *senior citizens*, *the aged*—are replaced with *older adults*, *persons 65 years and older*, or *the older population*.

RESEARCH PAPER STRUCTURE

There are two types of APA paper structures—student papers and professional (conference) papers—and we focus on how to develop the student paper type in APA style. To complete the final research paper, begin with the title page. The title page is the first page of an APA-style paper; it includes the paper title, the course number and name, the instructor name, the due date of the assignment, and a page number in the page's top right corner. The paper title should be placed three to four lines down from the top of the title page, centered, and typed in bold font. Other components are placed below the title with one double-spaced blank line. Figure 14.1 illustrates the title page structure.

Following the title page, students adhere to the standard format of a research paper, which includes sections for the introduction, the literature review, research questions and/or hypotheses, methods, results, and discussion. The conclusion section can be added if necessary, or it can be integrated into the discussion section. Let's briefly discuss what should be considered for each section in the standard template for a student research paper presented in Box 14.1.

BOX 14.1
TEMPLATE OF A RESEARCH PAPER

Introduction

The introduction is your opportunity to grab your audience's interest by presenting your topic in the initial paragraphs. You should provide background information and detail the main issue of your research, offering an overview of the paper's structure. Be sure to answer the following questions within the first few pages of your paper:

- What is your research about? Why should your audience care?
- Why is your research topic important to your audience and specific communities?

It is important to provide only the most relevant background information in this section, as the focus is on situating your research topic within a broader research context.

Literature review

In this section, rather than merely summarizing academic sources from scholarly articles, you should critically evaluate what other researchers have done with relevance to your research topic. You demonstrate your familiarity with the topic and scholarly context by developing a conceptual framework and theoretical framework. You inform your audience that you are knowledgeable about the research topic while integrating and synthesizing topic-relevant studies that deal with the following matters:[1]

- Trends and patterns (in theory, method, or results): Do certain approaches become more or less popular over time?
- Themes: What questions or concepts recur across the literature?
- Debates, conflicts, and contradictions: Where do sources disagree?
- Pivotal publications: Are there any influential theories or studies that changed the direction of the field?
- Gaps: What is missing from the literature? Are there weaknesses that need to be addressed?

In writing your literature review, you need to make connections between scholarly sources to create unique insights or theoretical ideas about the research topic while establishing your research as filling a particular gap in the ongoing discussion of your research area. You link your literature review section to your research questions and/or hypotheses, meaning that the literature review guides you to formulate the research question and/or hypothesis.

RQ_1:

H_a:

Method

In this section, you should make a convincing case arguing why your specific research method is the most appropriate for answering your research question or testing your hypothesis. This is where you explain every step of how you conducted your research, with a focus on sampling. Keep in mind that you should justify your choices for the following components:

- The research method: Explain why you chose a focus group, a content analysis, a survey, an experiment, or in-depth interviews, etc., and why this was the best method to find answers or reach conclusions for your research.
- The sampling: Detail how you collected your data, including a description of the participants, the process of employing them, and the place you conducted your research. More importantly, you need to explain some characteristics of your sample that represent the population.
- Ethical concern: Explain how you protected the participants while conducting research with them, including how you obtained their consent.

Results or findings

The results/findings section of your research paper is where you report the results/findings of your research based on the information gathered as a result of the methodology you applied. This section clearly and objectively states the analyzed outcomes of the data without bias or subjective interpretation. You adopt a bit different writing styles in this section based on either the qualitative method or the quantitative method.

- Quantitative results: The results can only confirm or reject the hypothesis underpinning your research. You need to present tables, charts, graphs, and other figures if necessary. For example, a sentence can be written thus: As Figure 1 shows, 10 out of 50 participants (20%) in Group A responded positively to the treatment; however, Group B responded negatively on average ($M = 50$, $SD = 3$, $X^2 = 11.8$, $p < .05$, $df = 1$).
- Qualitative findings: The findings focus on data that enable you to answer your research question directly. You also present important excerpts of your transcripts to illustrate the best examples which highlight an analytic point in terms of answering the research question. For example, a sentence can be written thus: The female participant described how she had used the Walmart app, saying, "While I was using the app, I was not thinking clearly about what to buy so I just clicked on what looks cheap and placed them in the cart and checked them out" (interviewee 12).

Discussion

The discussion section is where you demonstrate your academic acumen by interpreting the significance of your results/findings in light of how your research relates to the literature review and provides new insights about your topic. This section primarily focuses on evaluating what your research found and making an argument in support of your findings by either agreeing with what was already known about the research topic, disagreeing with it, or presenting something new.

For instance, suppose previous research showed that housewives prefer Pinterest over other social media platforms when seeking parental advice for bullied children. After conducting a literature review, you find this information intriguing and develop research questions to determine if Pinterest would be better than Facebook in terms of seeking parental advice on this matter and if househusbands would use Pinterest for the same purpose.

After conducting research, you find that among mothers, the Facebook community serves better as a social media platform for parental advice about bullied children. Among the reasons that househusbands use Pinterest, a search for parental advice does not bring up the topic of bullied children. Based on your results, you explain the new understanding of the topic while describing how the results are similar to or different from your literature review in support of your overall conclusion. It is common practice to include the following content in the discussion section of your paper:[2]

- Explanation of results: Elaborate on whether the results were expected or unexpected. Present explanations for the results/findings and delve deeper if the results/findings were unexpected or especially significant or meaningful. If necessary, highlight any unusual or unanticipated patterns or trends that emerged from your results/findings and interpret their meaning.
- References to previous research: Compare your results with those from other studies or use previous studies to support a claim. This is where you use the material from the literature review section. This can include revisiting key sources already cited in your literature review section. You attempt to compare your results with what other researchers previously found on the topic.
- Deduction: Make a claim for how the results can be applied more generally, including describing lessons learned, proposing recommendations that can help improve a situation, or recommending best practices.

Researchers consider the discussion section the most important part of a research paper because it most effectively demonstrates your ability to make a critical argument and justification for your research method and results/findings. Based on the evidence, you can infuse your results/findings with meaning in the process of giving your interpretation. When writing this section, be sure to include answers to such questions as:

- Do your results/findings support or seem similar to previous studies by other researchers regarding the topic, or the opposite of what other researchers have found or argued?

- If your results/findings are so different from previous research, what do you find different, and why so different?
- Do you find existing theories relevant to what your results/findings demonstrate about the topic?
- What contribution does your research make to a specific group of people or community? Does your research offer any practical solutions or advice for them?

There is often overlap between the discussion and conclusion sections. Some researchers place both sections under the discussion while others like to separate them. Either way is acceptable in an academic paper. In your research conclusion, you need to summarize your research in one or two paragraphs.

Limitations and Further Research

The sections on limitations and future research are optional. Some researchers also integrate these two sections into the discussion section. All research has flaws, and no research is perfect. Acknowledging the limitations or shortcomings of your research is important to demonstrate your humility as a researcher, although many researchers wish to skip the limitations section in their papers out of concern about undermining their research credibility. This section is not about describing the poor quality of your research but about commenting on what could not be done due simply to limitations of resources such as time, budget, diverse participants, or laboratories. You can also mention that a different method could lead to different results. In a nutshell, pointing out the limitations of your research shows that you are aware of the impact of the weaknesses and admit the imperfection of any kind of research in the academic community.

Keep in mind that acknowledging your research limitations leads to an opportunity to make recommendations for further research. You need to connect your research limitations to these recommendations, offering ideas for how future research by others can be developed and conducted as scientific research improving on your limitations. Your research limitations could be addressed by other research methods, larger samples, or a longer research period in a way that can be implemented for any unanswered questions. Thanks to your research presentation, others may develop more research ideas.

1. Shona McCombes. (2023). How to write a literature review. Scribbr. https://www.scribbr.com/dissertation/literature-review.
2. Adapted from Sacred Heart University. (2020). Organizing academic research papers: 8. The discussion. Sacred Heart University Library webpage. https://library.sacredheart.edu/c.php?g=29803&p=185933.

How to Add the References Section

In order to properly compose an academic research paper, students must adhere to a standard format that includes a cover page, a discussion or limitations section, and a references section. The references section is a crucial component of the research paper, as it is where students must cite the scholarly journal articles that informed their research. While we previously discussed how to properly cite sources in-text, it is important to also understand the rules for citing sources in the references section using APA format. Here are some basic guidelines to follow for the reference structure:

- APA references generally include information about the author, publication date, title, and source.
- Formatting guidelines for the APA references section are (1) double-spacing (within and between references), (2) a hanging indent of 0.5 inch, and (3) 12-point Times New Roman font.
- Each source is ordered alphabetically by the first or single author's last name.

The references section also requires specific formatting of citations for different types of publication:

- Book: Author's last name, Initial(s)., & Author's last name, Initial(s). (Year of publication). *Title of book* (Edition ed.). Publisher.
    - Melonie, T., & Conna, S. T. (2025). *The principle of advertising for students: A practical guide* (5th ed.). Cognella.
- Journal article: Author's last name, Initial(s)., & Author's last name, Initial(s). (Year of publication). Title of article. *Title of Journal, Volume*(Issue), Pages. https://doi.org/DOI
    - Anderson, L. (2011). The advent of American model of economic globalization in the digital age. *Journal of Digital Economics, 3*(4), 74–98. https://doi.org/10.1177/15d250r00010w4
- Newspaper article: Author's last name, Initial(s). (Year, Month Day of publication). Title of article. *Newspaper.* https://URL
    - Callahan, A. (2024, February 17). How red wine lost its health halo. *The New York Times.* https://www.nytimes.com/2024/02/17/well/eat/red-wine-heart-health.html
- Website: Author's last name, Initial(s). (Year, Month Day of publication). *Title of work.* Website. https://URL
    - Pitt, M. (2015, April 21). *Plastic bottles likely impact the salmon population.* The Plastic Damage of Planet. https://www.theplasticplanet.com/updates/bottle-damage-ocean-planetlife

- YouTube video: Channel. (Year, Month Day of publication). *Title of video* [Video]. Website. https://URL
    - Global Fitness. (2023, May 12). *D45 minutes for Tabata and HIIT workout for entire body in 6 month plan* [Video]. YouTube. https://youtu.be/5gty9nhKL

Advice for Professional (Conference) Papers

Professors teaching strategic communication research often assign group or individual projects, with a final paper due by the end of the semester. This approach provides students with practical experience in conducting research related to strategic communication. The course culminates in a research presentation and paper submission. Some colleges also encourage students to take their research further by presenting at regional or national conferences for undergraduate and graduate research. These conferences require compliance with the conference APA-style format for research paper submission, which includes a title page with page header and author note, as well as an abstract page with keywords. Notably, there are differences between student papers and conference papers, the latter being more formal and adhering to specific formatting requirements. A sample of the conference (professional) paper is shown in Box 14.2.

Box 14.2
Conference Paper Formats

ANALYSIS OF CORPORATE MANAGEMENT[1]

Analysis of Corporate Management of Online Media Bias

John J. Sweeney[1] and Jennifer S. Cruz[2]

[1] E. W. Scripps School of Journalism, Ohio University

[2] Department of Marketing, University of Hawaii

Author Note

We have no conflicts of interest to disclose. Correspondence concerning this article should be addressed to John J. Sweeney, E. W. Scripps School of Journalism, Ohio University, Scripps Hall 200, University Drive, Athens, Ohio, 45701, United States. Email: Sweeneyj@ohio.edu.

ANALYSIS OF CORPORATE MANAGEMENT[2]

Abstract

Social media has allowed consumers to participate in reputation management as they share their experiences with corporate products and services on social media platforms in the review format. More recently, consumers expand their review-sharing horizon to the media in terms of online news reporting with their analytic comments on fake news and politically biased news. This paper tackles the issue of online reputation management in the era of social media for online news. It explores the strategies of online news managers using social media platforms as their news distribution channels, using content analysis based mainly on online news data collection and in-depth interviews with managers who monitor online news consumer reviews. The results of this paper reveal that online management for news reporting is systematically organized under the cost-benefit analysis for profits, and online media outlets feed customized news articles to their target audiences, either conservative or liberal.

Keywords: online media, strategies for reputation, social media channels, comments

A conference paper, compared with a student paper, adds the abstract section. An abstract refers to a short summary of a research paper. It commonly includes between 100 and 250 words, and you write the abstract after you complete your research paper, meaning that the abstract is the very last thing you write. Researchers suggest three common approaches to writing the abstract as a concise summary of the entire paper:

- The function of the abstract is to describe your research paper rather than evaluating or defending the excellence of the paper.
- You should begin the abstract with a brief but precise statement of your research topic or issue, followed by information on the research method and design, major findings, and conclusions.
- The abstract should include vital keywords used in the content and method. This helps readers decide whether to read your entire paper or not.[3]

The Long Journey of Research in Strategic Communication

Upon submitting their final research papers and receiving their grades, college students often breathe a sigh of relief, having completed their demanding research classes. However, for students in social science and communication, quantitative research can pose more challenges than qualitative research due to the involvement of statistics. Some students express frustration, feeling that if they were adept in numbers, they would have pursued a major in business, finance, or economics instead of strategic communication. Nevertheless, basic statistical knowledge is crucial for effective research and passing the research class.

Moreover, many employers in the field of strategic communication expect their college-educated employees to conduct internal research using both surveys and focus groups. Even though many students may not plan on pursuing further research or using statistics in their careers, some end up pursuing higher education for a master's or doctoral degree. These advanced degrees are designed to train students to become professional researchers. It is widely known that graduate programs place a significant emphasis on research, while also offering opportunities for personal fulfillment and continued research endeavors.

After completing your research class, you should feel more confident in reading scholarly journal articles. The training you received has equipped you with statistical and textual knowledge on how to discover and utilize these scholarly articles, which is essential for evaluating their academic value. With this understanding, you are capable of deriving meaning from scholarly articles and critically assessing research results from an academic perspective. You possess the skills to write a thorough literature review and formulate your own research questions and hypotheses. Ultimately, you can develop your research abilities and apply them in your final research project, as well as in work and everyday life, alongside the critical and analytical thinking skills you have acquired throughout the course.

Unlocking Academic Excellence by Leveraging AI for Scholarly Research

As we bring this chapter and the entire book to a close, let's delve into the transformative impact of AI on academic research, particularly for college students grappling with the demands of extensive research papers.

AI can play a vital role in various stages of the research paper writing process:[4]

1. Topic selection: AI empowers students to identify trending topics and gaps in current literature by analyzing vast data sets, providing valuable insights for further exploration.
   - AI-powered topic modeling tools like MeaningCloud or Cortext can analyze vast data sets, uncovering hidden connections and emerging trends within the field of strategic communication.
2. Literature review: AI navigates the literature landscape by swiftly scanning scholarly articles, identifying relevant studies, and highlighting key findings.
   - AI literature review tools like Writefull or Scilit can actively engage with relevant research, summarizing key findings and identifying methodological strengths and weaknesses.
3. Data analysis: In fields relying heavily on quantitative data, AI handles large data sets, performing complex analyses efficiently, thus saving time and effort.
   - Tools like SPSS Modeler or KNIME can handle massive data sets, performing sophisticated statistical analyses and generating visual representations that illuminate hidden patterns and relationships.

4. Crafting clarity: Real-time writing assistance from AI includes grammar, style, and coherence suggestions.
    - AI writing assistants like Grammarly or QuillBot are valuable allies in the fight against grammatical errors and stylistic inconsistencies.
5. Navigating the style guide maze: AI ensures proper citation and adherence to style guides (e.g., APA, MLA, Chicago), streamlining the often tedious formatting process.
    - AI tools like Citation Machine or Zotero ensure that your references and paper format strictly adhere to the required style guide, whether APA, MLA, or Chicago.
6. Proofreading and catching those elusive errors: AI assists in proofreading by identifying errors in spelling, grammar, and punctuation.
    - AI proofreading tools like ProWritingAid or WhiteSmoke scan your paper for spelling mistakes, grammatical errors, and even stylistic inconsistencies.
7. Plagiarism patrol: AI can compare a student's paper with a vast database to ensure originality.
    - AI plagiarism checkers like Turnitin or Unicheck compare your paper against a vast database of sources, highlighting potential plagiarism risks.

While AI can significantly enhance the research process, it is essential to remember that it serves as a tool to aid, not replace, the researcher. The critical thinking, creativity, and intellectual rigor essential in academic research are uniquely human capabilities that AI cannot replicate. Students should leverage AI to enhance their research skills, not to substitute their intellectual efforts. Therefore, AI presents promising opportunities to streamline the research process, allowing students to focus on intellectual challenges and enriching their academic journey. As we look ahead in the 21st century, the integration of AI in academic research will continue to evolve, opening up new frontiers in knowledge and understanding.

Application of an AI-Powered Tool

Box 14.3
ChatGPT's Advice for the Final Research Paper

Using an AI-Powered Tool (ChatGPT) for Some Advice for the Final Paper Preparation

Command syntax: Offer helpful suggestions for a college student who has to write a final research paper in 2 weeks.

Answer: Writing a final research paper can be a challenging task, especially when the deadline is just around the corner. Here are some helpful suggestions for a college student who has to write a final research paper in 2 weeks:

1. Understand the assignment requirements: It is crucial to read and understand the requirements of the assignment thoroughly. Make sure you know what the topic is, the format and length of the paper, the deadline, and any other specific instructions.
2. Choose a research paper topic: Select a topic that interests you and is relevant to your course. Brainstorm ideas, conduct preliminary research, and choose a topic that is neither too broad nor too narrow.
3. Conduct preliminary research: Gather relevant information on your topic from various sources such as books, academic journals, online databases, and other credible sources. Take notes and organize your findings.
4. Develop a thesis statement: Based on your research, develop a clear and concise thesis statement that summarizes the main argument of your paper.
5. Create a research paper outline: Create an outline that includes the introduction, main body, and conclusion of your paper. Organize your notes and research findings into coherent sections.
6. Write a first draft of the research paper: Use your outline to write a first draft of your paper. Don't worry about perfection at this stage; focus on getting your ideas down on paper.
7. Write the introduction: Write an introduction that hooks the reader's attention and provides background information on your topic. End with a clear thesis statement that summarizes the main argument of your paper.
8. Write a compelling body of the text: Develop the main body of your paper with clear and concise paragraphs that support your thesis statement. Use evidence from your research to support your arguments. Be sure to properly cite your sources.
9. Write the conclusion: End your paper with a conclusion that summarizes your main arguments and restates your thesis statement. Offer some final thoughts and suggestions for further research.
10. Edit and proofread: Once you have completed your first draft, revise, edit, and proofread your paper. Check for grammar, spelling, and punctuation errors. Make sure your paper is well organized and flows logically.

11. Include recommendations for future research: If applicable, suggest directions for future research and highlight ways in which other researchers can reproduce or replicate your results to draw further conclusions. Make sure your recommendations are concrete, specific, and supported by a clear rationale.

By following these steps, you can write a well-researched and well-organized final research paper in two weeks. Remember to start early, stay focused, and seek help from your instructor or peers if needed. Good luck!

Summary

- ✓ The variety of research areas in the field of strategic communication enables researchers to explore many possible topics.
- ✓ The paradigm of exploring research topics in strategic communication has shifted to the social media world from the traditional media represented by television, newspapers, radio, and magazines.
- ✓ Students in the research class on strategic communication will find something interesting in social media marketing, media effects, advertising, public relations campaigns, and election campaigns on social media platforms.
- ✓ Students who major in communication are strongly expected to write better than students in other majors, and the final research paper can offer them an opportunity to enhance their academic writing skills.
- ✓ The top three most popular research paper styles for researchers are the APA (American Psychological Association) writing format, the *Chicago Manual of Style* (*CMOS*) writing format, and the Modern Language Association (MLA) writing format.
- ✓ The APA style is the most commonly used style in the field of social science and communication.
- ✓ There are two types of APA paper structures: student papers and professional papers.
- ✓ For students to complete their final research papers, the entire piece begins with the title page.
- ✓ The introduction section allows students to present the topic in the first set of paragraphs as a chance to get the audience interested.
- ✓ The literature review section demonstrates that rather than simply summarizing academic sources from scholarly articles, the student tries to critically evaluate what other researchers have done on the research topic.

- ✓ The method section is where the student explains every step of how the research was conducted with a focus on the sampling process.
- ✓ The section on results or findings clearly and objectively states the analyzed outcomes of the data without bias or interpretation.
- ✓ Researchers consider the discussion section the most important part of a research paper because it most effectively demonstrates the researcher's ability to make critical arguments and justification of the research method and results.
- ✓ There is often overlap between the discussion and conclusion sections.
- ✓ Acknowledging research limitations provides an opportunity to make recommendations for further research.
- ✓ The reference section requires specific citation formatting for different types of publication.
- ✓ A conference (professional) paper compared with a student paper adds the abstract section.
- ✓ The abstract should include the vital keywords used in the content and method.
- ✓ Graduate programs are all about research, a little fun, and further research.
- ✓ AI navigates the literature landscape by swiftly scanning scholarly articles, identifying relevant studies, and highlighting key findings.

KEY TERMS

1. Research topics in social media
2. APA style
3. Final paper
4. In-text citations
5. References
6. Abstract
7. Bias-free language
8. Keywords
9. Title page
10. Page header

Notes

Chapter 1

1. Dictionary.com. (Accessed in 2023). *Research.* https://www.dictionary.com/browse/research?s=t.
2. Merriam-Webster.com. (Accessed in 2023). *Research.* https://www.merriam-webster.com/dictionary/research.
3. Study.com. (Accessed in 2022). *What is research? Definition, purpose & typical researcher.* https://study.com/academy/lesson/what-is-research-definition-purpose-typical-researchers.html.
4. See *Today Show* at https://www.today.com/video/study-drinking-coffee-could-lengthen-your-life-568372291748.
5. Clark E. Moustakas. (1990). *Heuristic research: Design, methodology, and applications*, pp. 6–10. Sage.
6. National Communication Association. (2021). *What is communication?* https://www.natcom.org/about-nca/what-communication.
7. John B. Watson. (1998). *Behaviorism*. Routledge.
8. Joe Heimlich & Nicole Ardoin. (2008). Understanding behavior to understand behavior change: A literature review. *Journal of Environmental Education, 39*(1), 15–33. https://doi.org/10.3200/JOEE.39.1.15-33.
9. *Stanford Encyclopedia of Philosophy*. (2003). Edmund Husserl. https://plato.stanford.edu/entries/husserl.
10. A. D. de Groot & A. A. Spiekerman. (2020). The empirical cycle in science. *Methodology*, pp. 1–32. De Gruyter Mouton, 2020. https://doi.org/10.1515/9783112313121-003.
11. Marianne Lederer. (2010). Interpretive approach. In Y. Gambier & L. van Doorslaer (Eds.), *Handbook of translation studies* (Vol. 1, pp. 173–179). John Benjamins Publishing.
12. Adapted from Michael Cuthill. (2000). An interpretive approach to developing volunteer-based coastal monitoring programmes." *Local Environment, 5*, 127–137.
13. Wendy Leeds-Hurwitz, ed. (1995). *Social approaches to communication*. Guilford Press.
14. Nadia. (2024). *How many ads do we see a day?* https://siteefy.com/how-many-ads-do-we-see-a-day.

Chapter 2

1. Melissa G. Hunt, Rachel Marx, Courtney Lipson, & Jordyn Young. (2019). No more FOMO: Limiting social media decreases loneliness and depression. *Journal of Social and Clinical Psychology, 37*(10). https://doi.org/10.1521/jscp.2018.37.10.751.
2. Holly B. Shakya & Nicholas A. Christakis. (2017, April 10). A new, more rigorous study confirms: The more you use Facebook, the worse you feel. *Harvard Business Review.* https://hbr.org/2017/04/a-new-more-rigorous-study-confirms-the-more-you-use-facebook-the-worse-you-feel.
3. Kamaron McNair. (2022, December 19). *10 real-world things people have done after watching TikTok* [Videos]. CNBC. https://www.cnbc.com/2022/12/19/how-tiktok-influences-users-to-spend-money.html.
4. Chris Gaetano. (2019, February 1). *Study: Quitting Facebook makes people happier, less informed.* New York State Society of Certified Public Accountants. https://www.nysscpa.org/article-content/study-quitting-facebook-makes-people-happier-less-informed-020119#sthash.RidpaBN3.dpbs.

5. Papers Owl. (2020). *What is APA?* https://papersowl.com/blog/research-paper-in-apa-format.
6. Leihong Wu. (2023). Development of benchmark datasets for text mining and sentiment analysis to accelerate regulatory literature review. *Regulatory Toxicology and Pharmacology, 137.* https://doi.org/10.1016/j.yrtph.2022.105287.
7. Francesco Vincenzo Giarmoleo. (2024, February 4). What ethics can say on artificial intelligence: Insights from a systematic literature review. *Business and Society Review.* https://onlinelibrary.wiley.com/doi/full/10.1111/basr.12336.

Chapter 3

1. Centers for Disease Control and Prevention. (2021). *The Tuskegee timeline.* https://www.cdc.gov/tuskegee/timeline.htm.
2. Tuskegee University. (2021). *About the USPHS syphilis study.* https://www.tuskegee.edu/about-us/centers-of-excellence/bioethics-center/about-the-usphs-syphilis-study.
3. History.com. (2023). *Tuskegee experiment: The infamous syphilis study.* https://www.history.com/news/the-infamous-40-year-tuskegee-study.
4. Ibid.
5. Stanley Milgram. (1963). Behavioral study of obedience. *Journal of Abnormal and Social Psychology, 67*(4), 371–378.
6. Cari Room. (2015, January 28). Rethinking one of psychology's most infamous experiments. *The Atlantic.* https://www.theatlantic.com/health/archive/2015/01/rethinking-one-of-psychologys-most-infamous-experiments/384913.
7. Saul McLeod. (2020). The Stanford prison experiment. *Simple Psychology.* https://www.simplypsychology.org/zimbardo.html.
8. Laura Stark. (2016). The unintended ethics of Henry K Beecher. *The Lancet, 387*(10036): 2374–2375. https://www.thelancet.com/journals/lancet/article/PIIS0140-6736(16)30743-7/fulltext#%20.
9. *Britannica.* (2024). The nature of utilitarianism. https://www.britannica.com/topic/utilitarianism-philosophy.
10. Joan Marques. (2015). Universalism and utilitarianism: An evaluation of two popular moral theories in business decision making. *Journal of Values-Based Leadership, 8*(2), Article 3.
11. Mark D. White & Robert Arp. (2008, July 25). Should Batman kill the Joker? *New York Times.* https://www.nytimes.com/2008/07/25/opinion/25iht-edwhite.1.14793506.html.
12. Ravindra B. Ghooi. (2011). The Nuremberg Code—A critique. *Perspectives in Clinical Research, 2*(2), 72–76. https://www.ncbi.nlm.nih.gov/pmc/articles/PMC3121268.
13. American Medical Association. (2013). *World Medical Association Declaration of Helsinki.* https://www.wma.net/wp-content/uploads/2016/11/DoH-Oct2013-JAMA.pdf.
14. U.S. Department of Health and Human Services. (2021). *Read the Belmont Report.* https://www.hhs.gov/ohrp/regulations-and-policy/belmont-report/index.html.
15. Association for Education in Journalism and Mass Communication. (2005). *AEJMC code of ethics research.* https://www.aejmc.com/home/2011/03/ethics-research.
16. Janice M. Morse. (1991). Subjects, respondents, informants, and participants? *Qualitative Health Research, 1*(4), 403–406. https://doi.org.10.1177/104973239100100401.
17. Keren R. Dunn. (2021). Institutional review boards and ethics committees. In S. Piantadosi & C. L. Meinert (Eds.), *Principles and Practice of Clinical Trials.* Springer. https://doi.org/10.1007/978-3-319-52677-5_65-1.
18. U.S. Department of Health and Human Services. (2024). *Engagement of institutions in human subjects research.* https://www.hhs.gov/ohrp/regulations-and-policy/guidance/guidance-on-engagement-of-institutions/index.html.
19. U.S. Department of Health and Human Services. (2021). *Informed consent checklist (1998).* https://www.hhs.gov/ohrp/regulations-and-policy/guidance/checklists/index.html.
20. Stephen Behnke. (2009). *Reading the ethics code more deeply. Monitor on Psychology, 40*(4). https://www.apa.org/monitor/2009/04/ethics.

21. Office of Research Integrity. (2023). *Definition of research misconduct.* https://ori.hhs.gov/definition-misconduct.
22. American Psychological Association. (2019). *Plagiarism.* https://apastyle.apa.org/style-grammar-guidelines/citations/plagiarism.
23. Ibid.
24. Lisa Sugiura, Rosemary Wiles, & Catherine Pope. (2017). Ethical challenges in online research: Public/private perceptions. *Research Ethics, 13*(3–4), 184–199. https://doi.org/10.1177/1747016116650720.
25. Duke University. (2024). *Artificial intelligence policies: Guidelines and considerations.* https://learninginnovation.duke.edu/ai-and-teaching-at-duke-2/artificial-intelligence-policies-in-syllabi-guidelines-and-considerations.

Chapter 4

1. *APA Dictionary of Psychology.* (2023). Sampling theory. https://dictionary.apa.org/sampling-theory.
2. PBS. (2020). *3 ways that the U.S. population will change over the next decade.* https://www.pbs.org/newshour/nation/3-ways-that-the-u-s-population-will-change-over-the-next-decade.
3. *Britannica.* (2023). United States presidential election of 1936. https://www.britannica.com/event/United-States-presidential-election-of-1936.
4. Ibid.
5. Frank Newport. (2020). *75 years ago, the first Gallup poll. Gallup Inc.* https://news.gallup.com/opinion/polling-matters/169682/years-ago-first-gallup-poll.aspx.
6. PBS. (2021). *FMC program segments 1930–1960.* https://www.pbs.org/fmc/segments/progseg7.htm.
7. Lumen Business Statistics. (2021). *Sample surveys.* https://courses.lumenlearning.com/boundless-statistics/chapter/sample-surveys.
8. Gary Langer. (2008, October 8). *Sampling error: What it means.* ABC News. https://abcnews.go.com/PollingUnit/sampling-error-means/story?id=5984818.
9. Google AI. (2024). Making AI helpful for everyone. https://ai.google.
10. Omni Calculator. (2024). *Sampling error calculator.* https://www.omnicalculator.com/statistics/sampling-error.
11. Dynatrace. (2024). *Industry's first hypermodal AI.* https://www.dynatrace.com.
12. Absorb. (2024). *Simplify learning.* https://www.absorblms.com.

Chapter 5

1. Ethan Ramsden & Catherine Talbot. (2024, January 5). The role of TikTok in students' health and wellbeing. *International Journal of Mental Health and Addiction,* 1–23. https://doi.org/10.1007/s11469-023-01224-6.
2. Indeed.com. (2022, August 8). *Guide to survey methods: Definition, types and advantages.* https://www.indeed.com/career-advice/career-development/survey-method.
3. Pro Survey. (2023). *Advantages and disadvantages of online surveys.* https://www.proprofssurvey.com/blog/advantages-disadvantages-of-online-surveys.
4. Ng Chirk Jenn. (2006). Designing a questionnaire. *Malaysian Family Physician: The Official Journal of the Academy of Family Physicians of Malaysia, 1*(1), 32–35.
5. Survey Monkey. (2021). *Survey introductions.* https://help.surveymonkey.com/articles/en_US/kb/Tip-Creating-an-effective-survey-introduction.
6. National Public Research. (2019). *Mail surveys.* https://nationalpublicresearch.com/services/mail-surveys.
7. See the Nielsen Company (U.S.), LLC. (2021). *TV ratings.* https://www.nielsen.com/us/en/solutions/measurement/television.
8. Pew Research Center. (2021). *Collecting survey data.* https://www.pewresearch.org/methods/u-s-survey-research/collecting-survey-data.

9. Call Hippo. (2017). *Infographic: The best day and time to make a business call.* https://callhippo.com/blog/seo/best-day-time-make-business-call.
10. JotForm. (2023). *Online shopping store.* https://www.jotform.com/build/210758578478170.
11. SurveyMonkey. (2022). *Ways to send your survey.* https://help.surveymonkey.com/articles/en_US/kb/How-to-collect-responses?bc=Ways_to_Send.
12. Survey Anyplace. (2019). *What's the average survey response rate?* https://surveyanyplace.com/average-survey-response-rate.
13. Nima Torabi. (2023). Comprehensive guide for product professionals. *Medium.* https://medium.com/beyond-the-build/unlocking-the-power-of-ai-in-product-management-a-comprehensive-guide-for-product-professionals-53198782153e.
14. Hanane Allioui. (2023). Exploring the full potentials of IoT for better financial growth and stability: A comprehensive survey. *Sensors (Basel), 23*(19). https://www.ncbi.nlm.nih.gov/pmc/articles/PMC10574902.
15. Rakesh Kochhar. (2023). *The American Trends Panel Survey.* Pew Research Center. https://www.pewresearch.org/social-trends/2023/07/26/survey-methodology-2023-ai-and-jobs.
16. Fengchun Miao. (2021). *AI and education: Guidance for policy-makers.* UNESCO. https://unesdoc.unesco.org/ark:/48223/pf0000376709.

Chapter 6

1. Daniel Chandler & Rod Munday. (2011). *A dictionary of media and communication.* Oxford University Press.
2. A. E. Pezalla, J. Pettigrew, & M. Miller-Day. (2012). Researching the researcher-as-instrument: An exercise in interviewer self-reflexivity. *Qualitative research: QR, 12*(2), 165–185. https://doi.org/10.1177/1487941111422107.
3. Adapted from USC Libraries. (2021). *Organizing your social sciences research paper.* https://libguides.usc.edu/writingguide/theoreticalframework.
4. Young Joon Lim. (2015). Theorizing strategic communication in parsimony from the U.S. government perspective. *KOME: An International Journal of Pure Communication Inquiry, 3*(1), 1–15.
5. Ibid.
6. Andrew Holmes. (2020). Researcher positionality: A consideration of its influence and place in qualitative research—A new researcher guide. *Shanlax International Journal of Education, 8*(4), 1–10.
7. E. Guba & Y. Lincoln. (1992). *Effective evaluation: Improving the usefulness of evaluation results through responsive and naturalistic approaches.* Jossey Bass.
8. H. Noble & R. Heale. (2019). Triangulation in research, with examples. *Evidence-Based Nursing, 22*, 67–68. https://doi.org/10.1136/ebnurs-2019-103145.
9. USC Libraries. (2023). *Organizing your social sciences research paper.* https://libguides.usc.edu/writingguide/researchdesigns.
10. IBM. (2024). *What is natural language processing (NLP)?* https://www.ibm.com/topics/natural-language-processing.
11. Abid Haleem. (2022). Artificial intelligence (AI) applications for marketing: A literature-based study. *International Journal of Intelligent Networks, 3*, 119–132. https://www.sciencedirect.com/science/article/pii/S2666603022000136?via%3Dihub.
12. D. L. Morgan. (2023). Exploring the use of artificial intelligence for qualitative data analysis: The case of ChatGPT. *International Journal of Qualitative Methods, 22.* https://doi.org/10.1177/16094069231211248.

Chapter 7

1. New York Health Foundation. (2019). *A guide for designing and conducting in-depth interviews.* https://nyhealthfoundation.org/wp-content/uploads/2019/02/m_e_tool_series_indepth_interviews-1.pdf.

2. Ibid.
3. Erika Ryuken. (2021). *Conducting effective qualitative research interviews.* eLearning. https://news.elearninginside.com/conducting-effective-qualitative-research-interviews.
4. Joseph Stromberg. (2019, January 22). Focus groups shape what we buy. *Vox.* https://www.vox.com/the-goods/2019/1/22/18187443/focus-groups-brand-market-research.
5. N. T. Ochieng, K. Wilson, C. J. Derrick, & N. Mukherjee. (2018). The use of focus group discussion methodology: Insights from two decades of application in conservation. *Methods in Ecology and Evolution, 9*, 20–32.
6. R. A. Krueger & M. A. Casey. (2008). *Focus groups: A practical guide for applied research* (4th ed.). Sage.
7. David Cristofaro. (2017). *6 expert tips for effective focus group moderation.* Actionable Research. https://www.actionable.com/blog/focus-group-moderation-tips-1.
8. Katie Abrams & Ted Gaiser. (2017). *Online focus groups.* Research Gate. https://www.researchgate.net/publication/315114356_Online_Focus_Groups.
9. Brian A. Hoey. (2021). *Research project summaries: What is ethnography?* https://brianhoey.com/research/ethnography.
10. Christophe Debout. (2016). L'étude de cas qualitative [Qualitative case study]. *Soins, 806*, 57–60. French. https://doi.org/10.1016/j.soin.2016.04.018.
11. Stephanie Schomer. (2020, January 19). How Popeyes Louisiana Kitchen uses viral marketing to create explosive growth. *Entrepreneur.* https://www.entrepreneur.com/article/363044.
12. S. Ebneyamini & M. R. Sadeghi Moghadam. (2018). Toward developing a framework for conducting case study research. *International Journal of Qualitative Methods, 17*(1). https://doi.org/10.1177/1609406918817954.
13. Jill Avery & Koen Pauwels. (2019). Brand activism: Nike and Colin Kaepernick. *Harvard Business School Case*, 519–046. https://www.hbs.edu/faculty/Pages/item.aspx?num=55349.
14. W. Leeson, A. Resnick, D. Alexander, & J. Rovers. (2019). Natural language processing (NLP) in qualitative public health research: A proof of concept study. *International Journal of Qualitative Methods, 18.* https://doi.org/10.1177/1609406919887021.
15. M. Wankhade, A. C. S. Rao, & C. Kulkarni. (2022). A survey on sentiment analysis methods, applications, and challenges. *Artificial Intelligence Review, 55*, 5731–5780. https://doi.org/10.1007/s10462-022-10144-1.
16. S. A. Rana, Z. H. Azizul, & A. A. Awan. (2023, October 26). A step toward building a unified framework for managing AI bias. *PeerJ Computer Science.* https://doi.org/10.7717/peerj-cs.1630.

Chapter 8

1. Adopted and modified from Virtual Research Library. (2023). *What is quantitative research and what are the different types?* https://lmicresearch.org/quantitative-overview-general-principles.
2. Enago Academy. (2021). *How to develop a good research hypothesis.* https://www.enago.com/academy/how-to-develop-a-good-research-hypothesis.
3. Timothy Levine. (2011). Statistical conclusions validity basics: Probability and how Type 1 and Type 2 errors obscure the interpretation of findings in communication research literatures. *Communication Research Reports, 28*(1), 115–119.
4. Hugo Keuzenkamp. (2000). *Probability, econometrics and truth: The methodology of econometrics.* Cambridge University Press, 2000.
5. QuestionPro Survey. (2023). *Interval scale: Definition, characteristics with examples.* https://www.questionpro.com/blog/interval-scale.
6. Ibid.
7. NICE Satmetrix. (2021). *What is net promoter?* https://www.netpromoter.com/know.
8. Net Promoter. (2021). *Measuring your net promoter score.* https://www.netpromotersystem.com/about/measuring-your-net-promoter-score.

9. Statistics Solutions. (2021). *Levels of measurement*. https://www.statisticssolutions.com/levels-of-measurement.
10. Daniel Muijs. (2004). Validity, reliability and generalisability. In *Doing quantitative research in education with SPSS* (pp. 64–84). Sage.
11. Africa Arino. (2003). Measures of strategic alliance performance: An analysis of construct validity. *Journal of International Business Studies, 34*(1), 66–79.

Chapter 9

1. La Trobe University. (2023, April 26). *Descriptive statistics: Measures of variability*. https://latrobe.libguides.com/maths/measures-of-variability.
2. Rick Turner. (2013). Standard normal (Z) distribution. In M. D. Gellman & J. R. Turner (Eds.), *Encyclopedia of Behavioral Medicine*. Springer. https://doi.org/10.1007/978-1-4419-1005-9_1075.
3. See presidential approval polls at the Pew Research Center. https://www.pewresearch.org/topic/politics-policy/leaders/presidential-approval.
4. Unità. (2024). *Learning unleashed: The 35 best online courses and learning websites for 2024*. https://www.unita.club/unita-blog/learning-unleashed-the-35-best-online-courses-and-learning-websites-for-2024.
5. Business Wire. (2023). *Carnegie Learning announces LiveHint AI*. https://www.businesswire.com/news/home/20231130974040/en/Carnegie-Learning-Announces-LiveHint-AI%E2%84%A2.
6. S. Friedrich, G. Antes, S. Behr, et al. (2022). Is there a role for statistics in artificial intelligence? *Advances in Data Analysis Classification, 16*, 823–846. https://doi.org/10.1007/s11634-021-00455-6.
7. Daria Diuzhakova. (2023). *5 best AI tools for data analysts*. Intech. https://intechhouse.com/blog/5-best-ai-tools-for-data-analysts.

Chapter 10

1. Gill Marshall & Leon Jonker. (2011). An introduction to inferential statistics: A review and practical guide. *Radiology, 17*(1), E1–E6. https://doi.org/10.1016/j.radi.2009.12.006.
2. Ronald L. Wasserstein, Allen L. Schirm, & Nicole A. Lazar. (2019). Moving to a world beyond “$p < 0.05$,” *American Statistician, 73*(Suppl. 1), 1–19. https://doi.org/10.1080/00031305.2019.1583913.
3. Kent State University. (2024). *SPSS tutorials: Independent samples t test*. https://libguides.library.kent.edu/spss/independentttest.
4. N. L. Leech, K. C. Barrett, & G. A. Morgan. (2005). *SPSS for intermediate statistics: Use and interpretation* (2nd ed.). Lawrence Erlbaum Associates.
5. I. H. Sarker. (2021). Machine learning: Algorithms, real-world applications and research directions. *SN Computer Science, 2*(article no. 160). https://doi.org/10.1007/s42979-021-00592-x.
6. Ibid.
7. Sajid Ali. (2023). Explainable artificial intelligence (XAI): What we know and what is left to attain trustworthy artificial intelligence. *Information Fusion, 99*. https://www.sciencedirect.com/science/article/pii/S1566253523001148.

Chapter 11

1. Modified from M. L. McHugh. (2013). The chi-square test of independence. *Biochemia Medica, 23*(2), 143–149. https://doi.org/10.11613/bm.2013.018.
2. Modified from Statistics Solutions. (2023). *Correlation (Pearson, Kendall, Spearman)*. https://www.statisticssolutions.com/correlation-pearson-kendall-spearman.
3. Ibid.
4. Stats Tutor. (2021). *Spearman's correlation*. https://www.statstutor.ac.uk/resources/uploaded/spearmans.pdf.
5. CFI Education Inc. (2021). *What is regression analysis?* https://corporatefinanceinstitute.com/resources/knowledge/finance/regression-analysis.

6. E. C. Alexopoulos. (2010). Introduction to multivariate regression analysis. *Hippokratia, 14*(Suppl. 1), 23–28.
7. Claire Chen. (2023). *AI will transform teaching and learning. Let's get it right.* Stanford University. https://hai.stanford.edu/news/ai-will-transform-teaching-and-learning-lets-get-it-right.
8. Sajid Ali. (2023). Explainable artificial intelligence (XAI): What we know and what is left to attain trustworthy artificial intelligence. *Information Fusion, 99.* https://www.sciencedirect.com/science/article/pii/S1566253523001148.

Chapter 12

1. Rutgers University Library. (2022, November 22). *Systematic reviews in the health sciences.* https://libguides.rutgers.edu/c.php?g=337288&p=2273209.
2. Trustees of the University of Pennsylvania. (2021). *Standards for experimental research.* https://www2.math.upenn.edu/~pemantle/papers/Preprints/response-standards.pdf.
3. Adapted from John W. Creswell. (2014). *Research Design* (4th ed.). Sage. https://study.sagepub.com/sites/default/files/26101_08ca.doc.
4. Ojmarrh Mitchell. (2015). Experimental research design. In W. G. Jennings (Ed.), *The Encyclopedia of Crime and Punishment.* Wiley. https://doi.org/10.1002/9781118519639.wbecpx113.
5. Bruce B. Frey. (2018). Posttest-only control group design. In Bruce B. Frey (Ed.), *The Sage Encyclopedia of Educational Research, Measurement, and Evaluation.* Sage. https://methods.sagepub.com/reference/the-sage-encyclopedia-of-educational-research-measurement-and-evaluation/i16244.xml.
6. Lumen Leaning. (2021). *The reliability and validity of research.* https://courses.lumenlearning.com/waymaker-psychology/chapter/reading-reporting-experimental-research.
7. ABC Press Release. (2020). *"What Would You Do?" features scenario inspired by the debate over the US-Mexico border wall.* https://www.dgepress.com/storage/uploads/FA/13/FA13244B-4383-5C67-5B96-8A12F654114C/press-release-11-1171468.pdf.
8. See H. Wang, T. Fu, Y. Du, et al. (2023). Scientific discovery in the age of artificial intelligence. *Nature, 620,* 47–60 (2023). https://doi.org/10.1038/s41586-023-06221-2.
9. Ibid.

Chapter 13

1. Adapted from Bernard Berelson. (1952). *Content analysis in communication research.* Free Press.
2. Simone M. Scully. (2019). *What are the most common body shapes?* Health Line. https://www.healthline.com/health/women-body-shapes#10-common-shapes.
3. Niall McCarthy. (2021). *End of the road for Trump's Twitter account.* Statista. https://www.statista.com/chart/19561/total-number-of-tweets-from-donald-trump.
4. Cliodhna O'Connor & Helene Joffe. (2020). Intercoder reliability in qualitative research: Debates and practical guidelines. *International Journal of Qualitative Methods, 19.* https://doi.org/10.1177/1609406919899220.
5. Kimberly A. Neuendorf & Thomas D. Gore. (2007). *"Bond girls," shaken and stirred: A content analysis of James Bond films* [PDF file]. https://www.academia.edu/76957296/_Bond_Girls_Shaken_and_Stirred_A_Content_Analysis_of_James_Bond_Films.
6. Adapted from Kimberly A. Neuendorf & Thomas D. Gore. (2006). *James Bond 007 analysis codebook* [PDF file]. https://oarklibrary.com/search/result/d45f3018-715b-47ec-a021-323d98113ea3?title=James%20Bond%20007%20Analysis%20Codebook.
7. Melanie Gagich & Emilie Zickel. (2018). *A guide to rhetoric, genre, and success in first-rear writing.* MSL Academic Endeavors. https://pressbooks.ulib.csuohio.edu/csu-fyw-rhetoric.
8. Media Texthack Team. (2021). *Signs and signifiers.* Media Studies 101. https://opentextbc.ca/mediastudies101/chapter/signs-and-signifiers.
9. Janni Leung, Jack Yiu Chak Chung, & Calvert Tisdale. (2021). Anxiety and panic buying behaviour during COVID-19 pandemic: A qualitative analysis of toilet paper hoarding contents on Twitter.

International Journal of Environmental Research and Public Health, 18(3). https://res.mdpi.com/ijerph/ijerph-18-01127/article_deploy/ijerph-18-01127-v2.pdf.
10. Ibid.
11. Vusumuzi Maphosa & Mfowabo Maphosa. (2023) Artificial intelligence in higher education: A bibliometric analysis and topic modeling approach. *Applied Artificial Intelligence, 37*(1). https://doi.org/10.1080/08839514.2023.2261730.
12. D. L. Morgan. (2023). Exploring the use of artificial intelligence for qualitative data analysis: The case of ChatGPT. *International Journal of Qualitative Methods, 22.* https://doi.org/10.1177/16094069231211248.

Chapter 14

1. Adapted and modified from American Psychological Association. (2019). *Style and grammar guidelines* (7th ed.). https://apastyle.apa.org/style-grammar-guidelines.
2. Ibid.
3. Sarah Conte. (2021). *Make a great first impression: 6 tips for writing a strong abstract.* AJE Scholar. https://www.aje.com/en/arc/make-great-first-impression-6-tips-writing-strong-abstract.
4. Deniz, G. (2023). The role of artificial intelligence (AI) in the academic paper writing and its prospective application as a co-author: A letter to the editor. *European Journal of Therapeutics, 30*(1), 84–86. https://doi.org/10.58600/eurjther1808; H. Baber, K. Nair, R. Gupta, & K. Gurjar. (2023, November 28). The beginning of ChatGPT: A systematic and bibliometric review of the literature. *Information and Learning Sciences.* https://doi.org/10.1108/ILS-04-2023-0035; D. Jungwirth & D. Haluza. (2023). Artificial intelligence and public health: An exploratory study. *International Journal of Environmental Research and Public Health, 20*(5).

Index

About the Author

Young Joon Lim is a professor at the University of Texas, Rio Grande Valley, where he specializes in public relations and research methodology. An expert in the intersection of technology and communication, Dr. Lim has authored *Transforming Public Relations: AI & Social Media Strategies*, a seminal work that explores the evolving landscape of public relations in the context of emerging technologies. *Transforming Public Relations: AI & Social Media Strategies*, a seminal work that explores the evolving landscape of public relations in the context of emerging technologies. Additionally, he has coauthored *SilverComm: Marketing Practices and Messages for the Age of Aging*, further showcasing his expertise and thought leadership.

Dr. Lim's unique approach to teaching integrates AI and social media, equipping his students with the skills and knowledge necessary to excel in the digital age. His commitment to academic excellence and innovative research continues to shape the future of public relations and AI communication.

www.ingramcontent.com/pod-product-compliance
Ingram Content Group UK Ltd.
Pitfield, Milton Keynes, MK11 3LW, UK
UKHW051932150926
475560UK00005B/358

9 781538 197868